Palgrave Macmillan Studies in Banking and Financial Institutions

Series Editor: **Professor Philip Molyneux**

The Palgrave Macmillan Studies in Banking and Financial Institutions are international in orientation and include studies of banking within particular countries or regions, and studies of particular themes such as Corporate Banking, Risk Management, Mergers and Acquisitions, etc. The books' focus is on research and practice, and they include up-to-date and innovative studies on contemporary topics in banking that will have global impact and influence.

Titles include:

Steffen E. Andersen
THE EVOLUTION OF NORDIC FINANCE

Seth Apati
THE NIGERIAN BANKING SECTOR REFORMS
Power and Politics

Vittorio Boscia, Alessandro Carretta and Paola Schwizer
COOPERATIVE BANKING IN EUROPE: Case Studies

Roberto Bottiglia, Elisabetta Gualandri and Gian Nereo Mazzocco (*editors*)
CONSOLIDATION IN THE EUROPEAN FINANCIAL INDUSTRY

Dimitris N. Chorafas
CAPITALISM WITHOUT CAPITAL

Dimitris N. Chorafas
SOVEREIGN DEBT CRISIS
The New Normal and the Newly Poor

Dimitris N. Chorafas
FINANCIAL BOOM AND GLOOM
The Credit and Banking Crisis of 2007–2009 and Beyond

Violaine Cousin
BANKING IN CHINA

Vincenzo D'Apice and Giovanni Ferri
FINANCIAL INSTABILITY
Toolkit for Interpreting Boom and Bust Cycles

Peter Falush and Robert L. Carter OBE
THE BRITISH INSURANCE INDUSTRY SINCE 1900
The Era of Transformation

Franco Fiordelisi
MERGERS AND ACQUISITIONS IN EUROPEAN BANKING

Franco Fiordelisi, Philip Molyneux and Daniele Previati (*editors*)
NEW ISSUES IN FINANCIAL AND CREDIT MARKETS

Franco Fiordelisi, Philip Molyneux and Daniele Previati (*editors*)
NEW ISSUES IN FINANCIAL INSTITUTIONS MANAGEMENT

Kim Hawtrey
AFFORDABLE HOUSING FINANCE

Jill M. Hendrickson
REGULATION AND INSTABILITY IN U.S. COMMERCIAL BANKING
A History of Crises

Otto Hieronymi (*editor*)
GLOBALIZATION AND THE REFORM OF THE INTERNATIONAL BANKING AND MONETARY SYSTEM

Sven Janssen
BRITISH AND GERMAN BANKING STRATEGIES

Alexandros-Andreas Kyrtsis (*editor*)
FINANCIAL MARKETS AND ORGANIZATIONAL TECHNOLOGIES
System Architectures, Practices and Risks in the Era of Deregulation

Caterina Lucarelli and Gianni Brighetti (*editors*)
RISK TOLERANCE IN FINANCIAL DECISION MAKING

Roman Matousek (*editor*)
MONEY, BANKING AND FINANCIAL MARKETS IN CENTRAL AND EASTERN EUROPE
20 Years of Transition

Philip Molyneux (*editor*)
BANK PERFORMANCE, RISK AND FIRM FINANCING

Philip Molyneux (*editor*)
BANK STRATEGY, GOVERNANCE AND RATINGS

Imad A. Moosa
THE MYTH OF TOO BIG TO FAIL

Simon Mouatt and Carl Adams (*editors*)
CORPORATE AND SOCIAL TRANSFORMATION OF MONEY AND BANKING
Breaking the Serfdom

Anders Ögren (*editor*)
THE SWEDISH FINANCIAL REVOLUTION

Özlem Olgu
EUROPEAN BANKING
Enlargement, Structural Changes and Recent Developments

Ramkishen S. Rajan
EMERGING ASIA
Essays on Crises, Capital Flows, FDI and Exchange Rate

Yasushi Suzuki
JAPAN'S FINANCIAL SLUMP
Collapse of the Monitoring System under Institutional and Transition Failures

Ruth Wandhöfer
EU PAYMENTS INTEGRATION
The Tale of SEPA, PSD and Other Milestones Along the Road

The full list of titles available is on the website:
www.palgrave.com/finance/sbfi.asp

Palgrave Macmillan Studies in Banking and Financial Institutions
Series Standing Order ISBN 978–1–4039–4872–4
(*outside North America only*)

You can receive future titles in this series as they are published by placing a standing order. Please contact your bookseller or, in case of difficulty, write to us at the address below with your name and address, the title of the series and the ISBN quoted above.

Customer Services Department, Macmillan Distribution Ltd, Houndmills, Basingstoke, Hampshire RG21 6XS, England

European Banking

Enlargement, Structural Changes and Recent Developments

Özlem Olgu
Assistant Professor in Accounting and Finance, Koç University, Turkey

palgrave
macmillan

First published 2011 by
PALGRAVE MACMILLAN

Palgrave Macmillan in the UK is an imprint of Macmillan Publishers Limited, registered in England, company number 785998, of Houndmills, Basingstoke, Hampshire RG21 6XS.

Palgrave Macmillan in the US is a division of St Martin's Press LLC, 175 Fifth Avenue, New York, NY 10010.

Palgrave Macmillan is the global academic imprint of the above companies and has companies and representatives throughout the world.

Palgrave® and Macmillan® are registered trademarks in the United States, the United Kingdom, Europe and other countries.

ISBN 978–0–230–23171–9

This book is printed on paper suitable for recycling and made from fully managed and sustained forest sources. Logging, pulping and manufacturing processes are expected to conform to the environmental regulations of the country of origin.

A catalogue record for this book is available from the British Library.

Library of Congress Cataloging-in-Publication Data
Olgu, Özlem, 1979–
European banking : enlargement, structural changes and recent developments / Özlem Olgu.
p. cm.
Includes index.
ISBN 978–0–230–23171–9 (hardback)
1. Banks and banking—European Union countries. 2. Financial services industry—European Union countries. I. Title.
HG2974.O44 2011
332.1094—dc22 2011008036

10 9 8 7 6 5 4 3 2 1
20 19 18 17 16 15 14 13 12 11

Printed and bound in Great Britain by
CPI Antony Rowe, Chippenham and Eastbourne

To my husband, Özgur Akdeniz

Contents

List of Figures

List of Tables

Preface

Even though the EU has achieved considerable progress on political and economic convergence among its 27 member countries over the last decade, financial structures of individual member countries still remain diverse. In fact, the introduction of the euro on 1 January 1999 to the euro area countries was a historic event involving years of careful planning and preparation so that more than 320 million people in 16 EU countries share the euro as their currency. However, the first ten years of the euro coincided with an unprecedented enlargement, increasing the number of EU member states from 15 to 27, which brought in further heterogeneity in terms of economic, political and cultural differences among the members.

Moreover, the recent global financial crisis has hit Europe particularly hard – perhaps harder than other regions of the world – mainly as a result of the collapse in global trade, the extent of exposure to toxic assets, reliance on securitization and dependence on world markets. It is observed that the impact of the financial crisis on the process of European financial integration has not been homogeneous. Those segments that had experienced the highest degree of integration over the last decade have been heavily hit by the crisis, and in many cases have seen a sharp reversal in the positive trend over the period 2007–2008. This is especially the case for unsecured money, government bond and equity markets. Besides, the evidence presented throughout this book supports the fact that the most important prerequisite for achieving a sound financial system is the livelihood of an economy as well as proper regulatory and supervisory strategies. It is also highlighted that there might be different indicators and causes of financial crises, including those of a political and institutional nature that may be relevant for a particular country at a particular moment, as well as bank-specific factors.

I believe that recent developments in the European economy and banking sector make it worthwhile to undertake a comprehensive overview of developments. This book, intended both for academics and practitioners, has several purposes. First, it aims to portray the historical, macroeconomic and structural changes as well as the enlargement and developments of the European banking sector, with the major emphasis on the launch of the euro, regulatory changes and the recent global financial crisis. Second, it intends to examine the financial structure and performance of the European banking industry and to look at its future by examining recent and future developments, considering the probable candidate countries. Most of the figures in this book cover the period until 2008, representing the most recent data available during the data collection process of this project. Third, the future prospects of the European banking sector are considered in the context of European financial integration, the potential effects, both from political and economic perspectives, of including Turkey in the list of EU member countries as well as the recent global financial crisis. Overall, the book contributes to the European banking sector's past, present and future.

I would like to thank several people who have significantly contributed to this book. In particular, I am indebted to my parents, Kazım and Pembe Olgu, and in-laws, Cemaziye and Fehmi Akdeniz, for their efforts to encourage me to believe in success, which has been the main source of my confidence in achieving this work. Special thanks to my husband, Özgur Akdeniz, who provided unconstrained and continuous support during the critical times of this journey, and who believed in me from the beginning to the end. I would also like to express my gratitude to my research assistants, Hüseyin Bahadır Benli, Ömer Yildiz, Şeref Dündar and Canan Karataş, for their valuable efforts and help during the data collection process. Thanks are also due to Lisa von Fircks, Renée Takken and Priya Venkat for editing the manuscript.

I have greatly benefited from the data and stability reports published by the European Central Bank (ECB) and European Commission in this book. However, the views expressed are entirely mine and do not necessarily reflect those of Koç University. Every effort has been made to contact all copyright holders, but, if any have inadvertently been omitted, the publishers will be pleased to make the necessary arrangements at the earliest opportunity.

ÖZLEM OLGU

List of Abbreviations

AIFM	Alternative Investment Fund Managers
ATM	Automated teller machine
BiH	Bosnia and Herzegovina
BIS	Bank for International Settlements
BRSA	Banking Regulation and Supervision Agency
BSC	Banking Supervision Committee
BSRP	Banking Sector Restructuring Program
CAD 3	Capital Adequacy Directive 3
CARDS	Community Assistance to Reconstruction, Development and Stability in the Balkans
CBT	Central Bank of Turkey
CDO	Collateralized debt obligation
CDS	Credit default swaps
CEBS	Committee of European Banking Supervisors
CEEC	Central and East European Countries
CEIOPS	Committee of European Insurance and Occupational Pensions
CESE	Central, Eastern and Southern Europe
CESR	Centre for Economic and Social Rights
CPI	Consumer price index
CRA	Credit rating agencies
CRD	Capital Requirements Directive
CSTF	Customer and short-term funding
CTI	Cost-to-income ratio
DM	Deutsche mark
EC	European Community
ECB	European Central Bank
ECOFIN	Economic and Financial Affairs
ECSC	European Coal and Steel Community
ECU	European currency unit
EECs	Eastern European countries
EEC	European Economic Community
EFA	European Framework for Action
EFRAG	European Financial Reporting Advisory Group
EFTPOS	Electronic Fund Transfers at Point-of-sale

EMI	European Monetary Institute
EMS	European Monetary System
EMU	Economic and Monetary Union
ERDF	European Regional Development Fund
ERM	European Restructuring Monitor
ERM	Exchange Rate Mechanism
ERP	Economic Recovery Plan
ESCB	European System of Central Banks
ESF	European Social Fund
EU	European Union
EULEX	EU Rule of Law Mission
EUR	Euro
EURATOM	European Atomic Energy Community
EUREPO	Rate for a Unified Euro GC Repo Market
EURIBOR	Euro Area Interbank Offered Rate
EUROPOL	European Police Office
FCL	Flexible credit line
FDI	Foreign Direct Investment
FESE	Federation of European Stock Exchanges
FISCO	Fiscal Compliance
FMRD	Financial Markets Regulatory Dialogue
FSA	Financial Stability Arrangements
FSAP	Financial Services Action Plan
FSB	Financial Stability Board
FSF	Financial Stability Forum
FYROM	Former Yugoslavian Republic of Macedonia
GDP	Gross domestic product
HHI	Herfindahl–Hirschman Index
HICP	Harmonized Indices of Consumer Prices
IASCF	International Accounting Standards Committee Foundation
ICTY	International Criminal Tribunal for the former Yugoslavia
IFRS	International Financial Reporting Standards
IMF	International Monetary Fund
IORP	Institutions for Occupational Retirement Provision
IPA	Instrument for Pre-accession Assistance
IPOs	Initial Public Offerings
IT	Information technology
KM	Convertible mark
M&As	Mergers and Acquisitions
MBS	Mortgage-backed securities

sMIFID	Markets in Financial Instruments Directive
MoU	Memorandum of Understanding
MU	Monetary Union
MU-13	13 members of the Monetary Union
MU-15	15 members of the Monetary Union
n/a	not available
NBG	National Bank of Greece
NCBs	National central banks
NMS	New Member States of the EU
NSSG	National Statistical Service of Greece
OECD	Organisation for Economic Co-operation and Development
OTC	Over-the-counter
PHARE	Poland and Hungary Assistance for the Restructuring of the Economy
PIOB	Public Interest Oversight Body
POS	Point-of-sale
PPP	Purchasing Power Parity
PPS	Purchasing Power Standards
R&D	Research and development
RBS	Royal Bank of Scotland
ROA	Return on assets
ROE	Return on equity
SAA	Stabilization and Association Agreement
SASP	Structural Adjustment and Stabilization Program
SDIF	Savings Deposits Insurance Fund
SEM	Single European Market
SEPA	Single Euro Payment Area
SME	Small and medium enterprises
TEB	Turkish Economy Bank
TL	Turkish lira
UCITS	Undertakings for Collective Instruments in Transferable Securities
UK	United Kingdom
UN	United Nations
UNSC	United Nations Security Council
US	United States
USD	United States dollar
VAT	Value added tax
WB	World Bank
WEU	Western European Union
WTO	World Trade Organization

1
Introduction

Since the 1990s the European banking industry has been experiencing structural and legal changes concerning factors such as deregulation, liberalization, extraordinary upgrading in information technology (IT) and feedback from individual country economies as a reflection of the introduction of the euro (EUR) and the European Union's (EU) enlargement process. In particular, changes and developments in the deregulation process have brought about a significant increase in competition, putting pressure on banks to become increasingly concerned with analysing and controlling their costs and revenues and, in return, maintaining high performance levels.

Lately, the emphasis has been on the establishment of a common currency area in the EU, strongly reinforcing the mobility of financial flows as well as cross-border banking activities. First, on 1 January 1999, the euro was introduced to EU member countries as a consequence of the Maastricht Treaty's policy framework. Secondly, the enlargement process on 1 May 2004, which incorporated ten more countries into the EU body (Cyprus, Malta, Slovenia, Slovakia, the Czech Republic, Estonia, Hungary, Latvia, Lithuania and Poland), created pressure on the level of competition and performance of European banks. Following this, two further countries, Bulgaria and Romania, joined the EU on 1 January 2007, increasing the number of countries to 27 (EU-27).

Given the fact that new EU member countries (NMS) are heterogeneous among themselves due to variations in central planning, market economy and economic reforms, as well as geographic, environmental, historical and cultural differences, it has been difficult to manage, control and maintain financial stability within the EU-27. Therefore, the current country differences among developed and still developing European countries raise questions about the future consequences of effective integration and convergence in the economic and financial framework. Moreover, the recent global financial crisis has had a strong negative impact on the European financial market and its banking sector.

Taking the reader on a journey of discovery through macroeconomic, financial and structural changes as well as the deregulation and enlargement issues that follow, this book offers a fascinating insight into the current state of the European banking industry. It offers constructive information to academics and students as well as to practitioners who wish to have a greater in-depth understanding of the legal, regulatory, institutional and organizational aspects of the European Central Bank (ECB) within the framework of the Economic and Monetary Union (EMU), the stability of the euro, the effects of the EU enlargement process and the recent profile of the European banking sector. In particular, the EU enlargement process has further broadened this audience, and it is expected that the demand for information will increase accordingly.

I would like to emphasize here that this book is an extended version of the previously published work *Efficiency in European Banking* by Molyneux and colleagues (1996). Its primary aim is to give readers an overview of the functioning of the EU and the ECB, the EU's enlargement processes since 2004 and the effects of the recent global financial crisis on the balance sheet structures of European banks. I have outlined the main sources of change in the EU-27 banking sector in Figure 1.1.

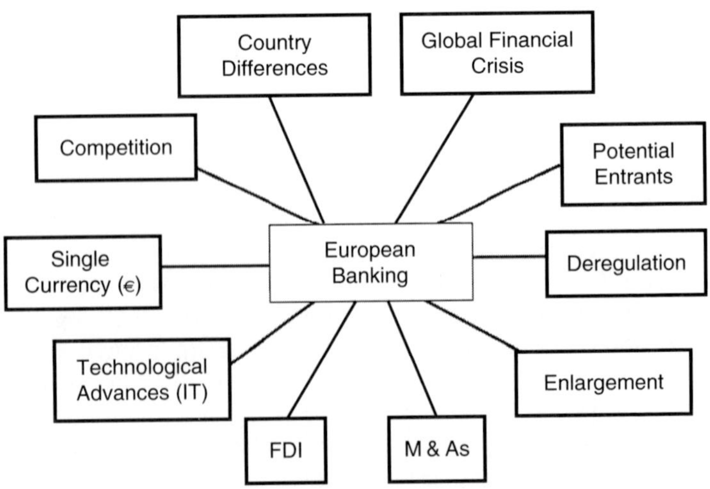

Figure 1.1 Reasons/causes of structural changes on European banks

I believe these recent developments in the EU economy and banking sector make it worthwhile to undertake a comprehensive review. This book has several objectives. First, it aims to portray the phases of banking sector developments in the EU, where the major emphasis is to examine features of augmented foreign direct investment (FDI), the wave of mergers and acquisitions (M&As) and their repercussions on the banking industry. Second, legal and structural changes, together with their impact on the financial structure and performance of the European banking sector, are explored. Third, future prospects of the European banking industry are considered in the context of enlargement and a potential new member country, Turkey, as well as the recent global financial crisis.

Starting with the EU deregulation process during the 1980s and 1990s, a concise summary of the establishment and origins of the EU, EMU and ECB is outlined in Chapter 2. Then, the reader is introduced to the functioning of the ECB and its regulatory, advisory and monetary power. It also positions ECB in the context of the objectives and arrangements of the EMU under the umbrella of the EU. Moreover, it focuses on the legal, institutional and organizational aspects of the ECB, which resulted from the realization of the EMU. Additionally, this chapter establishes an overview of the ECB's status and its role, as well as its policies and their implementation by the euro system activities.

Furthermore, Chapter 2 discusses the launch of the euro in 2002, which has subsequently replaced certain domestic currencies. In particular, Denmark, Sweden and the United Kingdom (UK) do not currently use the euro, whereas Slovenia joined the euro area in January 2007, followed by Cyprus and Malta in 2008 and Slovakia in 2009. On the other hand, eight of the NMS countries are committed to adopting the euro when they are ready. Furthermore, the price stability of the euro and basic tasks of the euro system are also revealed. In particular, this chapter assesses the financial stability of the euro area countries, both with regard to the role the euro plays in facilitating economic processes, and its ability to prevent adverse shocks from having inordinately disruptive impacts.

The enlargement process on 1 May 2004, which included ten countries (EU-10) into the EU body (Cyprus, Malta, Slovenia, Slovakia, the Czech Republic, Estonia, Hungary, Latvia, Lithuania and Poland) created pressure in terms of the competition and performance of European banks. More recently, on 1 January 2007, two more countries, Bulgaria and Romania, joined the EU, increasing the number of countries to 27. In fact, this raises questions about the future consequences of an effective integration of the European banking industry, specifically in terms of efficiency and profitability as a result of current country differences due to variations in central planning, market economy and economic reforms as well as geographical, cultural and environmental differences. In Chapter 3, the potential candidate countries are also discussed in relation to their progress in satisfying EU requirements for a member country.

Chapter 4 centres its attention on introducing recent developments in the EU, which resulted in changes in the macroeconomic structure of member countries. This chapter covers in-depth research about the macroeconomic conditions in the EU-27 over the last decades, which envelops the period of the EU's most severe regulatory and enlargement practices. It mainly focuses on the gross domestic product (GDP), GDP per capita, inflation and interest rates as well as employment/unemployment rates in individual EU countries and the EU-27 as a whole.

As a result of the deregulation process as well as the identification of numerous non-profitable banks in the European banking sector, a massive M&As wave has been acknowledged by a number of researchers. Chapter 5 examines the FDI statistics, comprehensively introducing the reader to a summary of what has changed over the last decades in the EU banking industry. In addition, banks' ongoing structural changes are discussed in relation to the number of banks, branches and employees, as well as bank concentration in individual EU countries. It is exceptionally important to identify the effects of the above mentioned factors and realize the ongoing industry changes in order to provide insight into and critical discussion of the accounting analysis introduced in the following chapter.

Chapter 6 is about the financial stability, efficiency and balance sheet structure of the European banking sector. What is important is that the efficiency and profitability of institutions has become a primary concern of investors, lenders, shareholders and, in particular, managers, in relation to planning and controlling their activities. The accounting analysis presented in this chapter provides the chance of comparing ongoing structural changes in the EU-15 and NMS banking industries. Therefore, examining the profitability and efficiency of EU-27 banks can guide financial authorities in providing advice on possible actions that can help to maintain financial stability, minimize the risk of failure and improve the performance of banks. Moreover, financial integration is considered to be one of the main factors in making Europe more efficient and competitive. The EU's financial integration has been an ongoing process since the last decade and has made substantial progress. However, it has slowed down due to the impact of the recent global financial crisis. The major objective of this chapter is to analyse recent developments and the state of financial integration in the EU; this is followed by an analysis of accounting performance indicators of commercial banks in individual EU countries.

In Chapter 7, the discussion relates to the recent macroeconomic and financial crisis in the world's leading countries and how the European financial sector has been affected. Furthermore, this chapter introduces forecasts and expectations for the near future and financial help from the EU and International Monetary Fund (IMF). In fact, the global financial crisis, which started in the US in the second half of 2007 and expanded its area of impact by subsequently spilling over to Europe and Asia, entered a new phase when Lehman Brothers, one of the leading investment banks in the US, filed for bankruptcy protection in September 2008. The situation, which emerged as a liquidity problem in the inter-bank markets during the early stages of the crisis, gradually turned into concern regarding the reliability of financial institutions. In this respect, growth expectations diminished in many economies, particularly in developed countries. In the meantime, this expected slowdown in the global economy and the downward trend in commodity prices have started to have favourable effects on the inflation rates of developed and developing countries.

The penultimate chapter focuses on current developments in the Turkish banking industry and takes a look at Turkey's prospects for EU membership. Turkey has the 16th largest economy in the world (according to 2007 figures) and is one of the oldest and more developed of the emerging markets. Even though increased competition has been monitored over the last decade, particularly due to the removal of barriers on foreign entry into the banking sector, there are still doubts about Turkey's competitive strength compared with the EU countries. The most significant factor, not only for Turkish banking but also for Turkey as a nation, is the declaration of Turkey as an EU accession country in 2005. As a result of this, Turkey should adjust its legislation and regulatory environment to that of EU by adopting the EU acquis during the convergence process. The first section of this chapter reviews the structural and institutional preparations of the Turkish banking and financial system towards adopting EU regulation and systems. Then, the focus of attention switches to the implementation process of newly reinforced capital adequacy directives (Basel II), followed by Turkey's readiness to become a member of the EU and the impact of the new Basel Accord directives on the current levels of Turkish banks' capital adequacy. Following on from this, the chapter reviews the recent M&As by foreign banks and assesses the impact of a high foreign presence on the Turkish banking industry. In the final section, Turkey's probable EU membership is discussed in terms of the macro economy and politics.

Finally, Chapter 9 summarizes the main points of each chapter and draws brief conclusions by identifying the main determinants of macroeconomic and financial disparities among the EU countries.

2
Creating a Functioning European Union

Introduction

This chapter looks at the evolution of the European Union (EU), and the establishment of the European Central Bank (ECB) and the Economic and Monetary Union (EMU) in relation to the deregulation process and legal framework. Moreover, it informs readers about the story behind the single currency, deregulation and liberalization policies applied by numerous EU countries during the 1980s and 1990s as well as procedures during to change over to the euro. Furthermore, the price stability of the euro since its introduction, as well as financial integration in the EU are discussed. The overall objective of this chapter is to explain why all these developments have been a turning point for the global financial system.

Origins of the EU, EMU and ECB

For centuries, and most recently during the period 1870–1945, Europe was the scene of devastating wars, with consequent loss of life. A number of European statesmen – Winston Churchill, Konrad Adenauer, Alcide De Gasperi, Jean Monnet and Robert Schuman – came to the conclusion that the only way to maintain a lasting peace in Europe was to integrate the countries economically and politically.[1] Following this, in 1950, the French Foreign Minister Robert Schuman proposed integrating the coal and steel communities of Western Europe, known as the European Coal and Steel Community (ECSC), as the first step towards creating the EU, which was set up in 1951. In 1967 the institutions of the three European communities (Benelux, Germany and Italy) were merged, and since then there has been a single Commission and Council of Ministers as well as a European Parliament. Accordingly, the Court of Justice, the Court of Auditors and the European Central Bank (ECB) were established. The ECB defines the roles of these institutions as:

- **The European Parliament:** The EU's institution of democratic expression, political control and legislative process.
- **The Council of the European Union:** The main decision-making institution with legislative and budgetary power, which brings together the ministers of relevant member countries.
- **The European Commission:** Follows the implementation of regulations and directives adopted by the European Council. It can appeal to the Court of Justice to ensure the application of community law.
- **The Court of Justice:** Can ascertain and give a ruling as well as control the legality of the EU's or institutions' actions.
- **The Court of Auditors:** Checks the legality and regularity of the revenue and expenditure of the Community and its good financial management.
- **The European Central Bank:** Is in charge of managing the euro and the EU's monetary policy.
- **The ECOFIN Council:** Decides whether a member country has reached the necessary degree of sustainable convergence to adopt the euro based on the Convergence Reports prepared by the ECB and the European Commission, an opinion of the European Parliament and a proposal from the European Commission.

Origins of the European Union (EU)

The origins of the EU go back to the Treaty of Paris signed in 1951, which established the ECSC.[2] At the initial stages, the ECSC consisted of six countries, namely: Belgium, Germany, France, Italy, Luxembourg and the Netherlands, which established the European Economic Community (EEC) and the European Atomic Energy Community (EURATOM) after signing the Treaties of Rome on 25 March 1957. Following this, the EURATOM developed into the European Communities (EC) and then, with the adoption of the Maastricht Treaty in 1992, the EU.[3]

The early years of the EEC were principally focused upon developing a customs union. Over the same period an economic boom created much greater prosperity in Western Europe and drove forward the liberalization of the EEC economy. In 1963, the United Kingdom (UK) made its first attempt to join the EEC, but was rejected by the French President Charles de Gaulle.

The first proposals for the EMU were created when the UK, Ireland and Denmark joined the EEC in the 1970s. It was not until the mid-1980s, at the time when Spain, Greece and Portugal joined, that the pace of European integration really picked up again with the agreement of the Single European Act (1986).[4] This laid down a timetable for the completion of the single market while looking towards creating monetary union and driving forward the agenda for political union. The fall of the Berlin Wall in 1989 and the reunification of East and West Germany in 1990 provided a huge enhancement to this process.

In 1992, the Maastricht Treaty transformed the European Community into the EU, giving it new roles in the areas of foreign and domestic policy, and setting a timetable for the creation of the euro. Subsequently, the Treaties of Amsterdam (1997)[5] and Nice (2001)[6] expanded these powers.

Over the 1957–1995 period the EU grew in size, with six successive waves of accession increasing the number of member countries to 15. This was a very slow enlargement over a long time span; the EU changed its strategy with a "big bang" enlargement in 2004. Since 2004 the number of member countries that have met the membership criteria, known as the Copenhagen criteria (details of the recent enlargement process are introduced in Chapter 3 of this book), has reached 27. The Copenhagen criteria requires prospective members to have a stable democracy, the rule of law, human rights, protection of minorities and a well-functioning market economy.

A timeline for the extension of the EU in chronological order is given in Table 2.1. Denmark, Ireland and the UK joined in 1973, followed by Greece in 1981, Portugal and Spain in 1986 and Austria, Finland and Sweden in 1995. This expansion continued with a historical enlargement programme on 1 May 2004, when the Czech Republic, Estonia, Cyprus, Latvia, Lithuania, Hungary, Malta, Poland, Slovenia and Slovakia acceded to the EU. Finally, Bulgaria and Romania are the latest members, having joined on 1 January 2007. Negotiations with Croatia and Turkey are still in progress.[7]

Origins of the European Central Bank (ECB) and its role

The ECB was established in June 1998 at Frankfurt, with its own legal characteristics.[8] Following on from this, the ECB and the European System of Central Banks (ESCB) were established, and the euro system, comprising the ECB and the national central banks (NCBs) of the EU countries, was announced as the main fulcrum of the system until all members of the EU adopt the euro. The ECB is an independent

Table 2.1 Timeline for extension of the EU

Date	Event
1957	The Netherlands, Belgium, Germany, Luxembourg, France and Italy signed the Treaty of Rome
September 1963	The Ankara Agreement signed
1973	The UK, Denmark and Ireland joined the EEC
1981	Greece joined the EEC
1986	Spain and Portugal joined the EEC
1989	The Delors Report introduced
1992	The Maastricht Treaty signed
April 1994	Hungary applied for EU membership
1995	Sweden, Finland and Austria joined the EU
October 1997	The Treaty of Amsterdam signed
March 1998	The EU set up its membership negotiations with Hungary, Poland, Estonia, the Czech Republic, Slovenia and Cyprus
December 1999	Turkey was recognized as a candidate country to the EU and negotiations were opened with Romania, Slovakia, Latvia, Lithuania, Bulgaria and Malta
February 2001	The Treaty of Nice signed
2002	The euro became the single currency in Belgium, Germany, Spain, France, Ireland, Italy, Luxembourg, the Netherlands, Austria, Portugal, Finland and Greece
February 2003	The Treaty of Nice determined the new rules concerning the size and organization of the EU to facilitate operation with 25 countries
1 May 2004	Cyprus, the Czech Republic, Estonia, Hungary, Latvia, Lithuania, Malta, Poland, Slovakia and Slovenia became members
2005	Negotiations started with Turkey and Croatia. The Former Yugoslavian Republic of Macedonia (FYROM) granted candidate status
1 January 2007	Bulgaria and Romania joined the EU

Source: Created by the author from European Commission, ECB, Eurostat Yearbook (various years).

institution with a principal objective of price stability and can be accepted as a representation of modern central banking. It is one of the key players in the creation of the EMU and the euro system. As regards accountability, the ECB has to explain to the public and their representatives in parliament how it fulfils its mandate. In particular, the ECB is required to present an annual report on its monetary policy and other activities to the European Parliament, the Council and the Commission.

The Maastricht Treaty extended the domain of the EC in many directions, creating the ESCB, with the ECB at its centre, and constructing the single currency with the objective of replacing national currencies of member countries in order to form the EMU. Unlike the ECB and the NCBs, the ESCB has no legal personality, no capacity to act and no decision-making bodies of its own. It only denotes an institutional framework that establishes an "organic link" between the ECB and the NCBs.

As the non-euro-zone countries have maintained their monetary sovereignty, their respective central banks are not involved in carrying out the ESCB's core functions. The main aim of establishing the euro system is to help the public to understand the complex structure of the ESCB more easily. The reasons behind having the euro system, instead of a single central bank, carry out central bank functions for the euro are:

I. The establishment of a single central bank for the whole euro area would not have been acceptable on political grounds;
II. The euro system approach builds on the experience of the NCBs, preserves their institutional set-up, infrastructure and operational capabilities and expertise; moreover, NCBs continue to perform some non-euro system-related tasks;
III. Given the large number of countries and the geographical spread of the euro zone, it was deemed appropriate to give domestic credit institutions an access point to central banking in each participating country.

The ECB has the right to conclude international agreements in matters relating to its field of competence and participate in the work of international organizations such as the International Monetary Fund (IMF), the Bank for International Settlements (BIS) and the Organisation for Economic Co-operation and Development (OECD). Established by the EC Treaty, the ECB is embedded in the specific legal and institutional framework of the EC. What distinguishes the euro from a national currency and the ECB from a national central bank is their supranational status within a community of independent states. Unlike comparable central banks, such as the US Federal Reserve Bank or the Bank of Japan, which are the monetary authorities of their respective national states, the ECB is a central authority that conducts monetary policy for an economic area consisting of 27 countries.

As regards monetary policy, the Treaty provisions are further specified and substantiated in the Statute of the ESCB, which is annexed to the EC Treaty as a Protocol and thereby forms an integral part of primary Community law. Under Article 9.2 of the Statute of the ESCB, the ECB ensures that tasks of the euro system are carried out either by its own activities or through the NCBs. In line with this statutory role, the ECB exercises several specific functions such as to:

- serve as the decision-making body of the ESCB and the Euro system;
- ensure consistent implementation of ECB policies;
- exercise regulatory powers and the right to impose approvals;
- initiate Community legislation and advise the Community institutions and EU members on draft legislation;
- monitor compliance with the provisions of Articles 101 and 102 of the Treaty;
- accomplish tasks of the former European Monetary Institute (EMI) that still need to be performed in Stage Three of EMU, as not all EU countries participate in EMU.

The ECB is also the embodiment of modern central banking whose overriding objective is price stability.[9] The regulatory power of the ECB enables it to fulfil its mandate autonomously without relying on legal acts by Community institutions or member countries. However, all legal measures taken by the ECB are open to review by the European Court of Justice.

Origins of the Economic and Monetary Union (EMU)

One possible starting point for the chronology of the Economic and Monetary Union (EMU) might be the Treaties of Rome, which entered into force on 1 January 1958. According to the Treaties of Rome, European countries agreed to unite, with the idea of forming a single currency. The purpose of this process was to maintain an environment for the free movement of goods, services, labour and capital without internal barriers. However, the overall region was heterogeneous prior to the 1990s due to variations in central planning, market economy, economic reforms and the level of debt, together with geographic, environmental, historical and cultural differences.

In March 1979 the process of monetary integration was relaunched with the creation of the EMU, and the participating banks agreed its operating procedures. In line with its objective to promote internal and external monetary stability, the EMU also covered the adjustment of monetary and economic policies as tools for achieving exchange-rate stability. Its participants were able to create a zone in which monetary stability increased and capital controls were gradually relaxed. The exchange-rate constraint helped the participating countries with relatively high rates of inflation to pursue disinflation policies, which fostered a downward convergence of inflation rates and brought about a high degree of exchange-rate stability.

A direct consequence of the EMU is that the EU will have a single exchange rate and a single monetary policy, and that it will be the policy mix at European level that is relevant for the rest of the world and for any international macroeconomic policy coordination. Although part of this policy mix is the result of policies set at national levels, the obligation of member countries is to closely coordinate their economic policies set out in the Maastricht Treaty (Article 3a). In order to accomplish this objective they should enable the euro area to pursue consistent policies and provide a valid reference point for international economic affairs.

The institutional setting for the EMU introduced by the Maastricht Treaty specifies a clear division of responsibilities between the Community and member states. As a consequence of the introduction of the single currency, the competence for euro-area monetary policy has been transferred to the Community. In order to fulfil its primary objective of maintaining price stability, the euro system has been given a high degree of independence from political influence. By contrast, economic policies (such as fiscal or structural policies) remain largely within the responsibility of the member countries.

In June 1988 the European Council confirmed the objective of progressive realization of the EMU and instructed a committee chaired by Jacques Delors, President of the European Commission, to propose "concrete stages" leading to the EMU. Particular concern related to the potential economic impact presented in the Delors Report (1989), which outlined three stages to solve the problems of achieving a large consensus among participant countries, and served as a background for the Maastricht Treaty (see Figure 2.1).

The first step towards achieving a Single European Market (SEM) was taken in 1992, based on the White Paper (1985) on completing the internal market. The main purposes of the White Paper were establishing guidelines for the single banking industry, creating control for home countries and establishing mutual recognition by trade liberalization

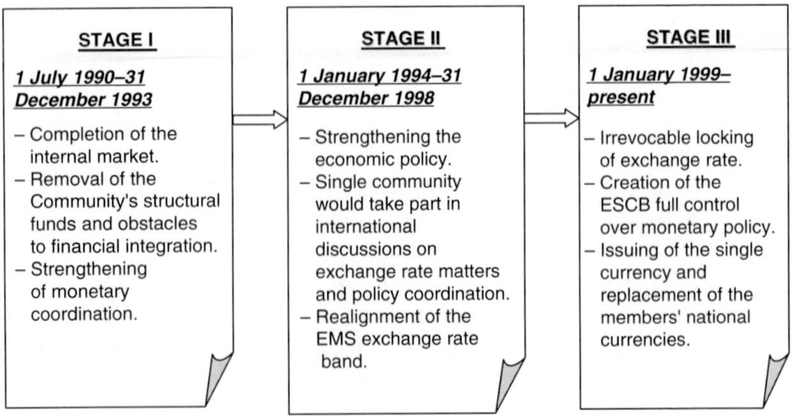

Figure 2.1 Stages outlined in the Delors Report
Source: Created by the author from the Delors Report (1989).

(Girardone, 2000). However, the basis of the White Paper was incorporated, in 1988, in the creation of the Second Banking Co-ordination Directive, which was adopted in 1989.

The principals of the Second Banking Directive were: (i) harmonizing minimum capital standards for the authorization and continuation of banking business, (ii) controlling and supervising major shareholders and banks' participation in the non-banking sector, (iii) standardizing accounting and control mechanisms, and (iv) establishing legislation on standards and own funds, solvency ratios and deposit protection schemes (Molyneux *et al.*, 1996). Overall, the Second Banking Directive implemented new procedures in the European financial system relating to regulation, standardized capital requirements and banking supervision (Schure and Wagenwoort, 2001). Finally, stage three initiated the period in which countries implement the single currency in order to create the euro zone. Following all these arrangements, the new euro banknotes and coins came into circulation on 1 January 2002.[10]

The official decision on EMU membership was taken in May 1998 with the participation of 11 member countries. The leading countries were Belgium, France, Germany, Italy, Luxembourg and the Netherlands, which were afterwards joined by the five West European countries, namely, Austria, Finland, Ireland, Portugal and Spain. Greece[11] was rejected at first due to its failure to meet the convergence criteria of the Maastricht Treaty, whereas the UK,[12] Sweden[13] and Denmark[14] preferred not to join due to domestic political reasons. Denmark and the UK both had an "opt-out clause" not to participate in the third stage of EMU. In contrast, Sweden, at the time, did not fulfil the requirements of the "convergence criteria". Following all these developments, the euro became a reality on 1 January 2002, when paper notes and coins replaced national currencies in 12 of the EU-15 countries. The timeline for the EMU is summarized in Table 2.2.

The euro-area monetary policy framework has novel features. Within the new institutional setting of the EMU, competence for the single monetary policy was transferred to the ECB, which received a

Table 2.2 Timeline for the EMU

1958	Treaties of Rome signed
1978	The European Monetary System (EMS) is launched
1989	The Delors Report maps out the road to EMU in three stages
1990	Launch of the first stage of EMU: closer economic policy coordination and the liberalization of capital movements
1992	Signature of the Maastricht Treaty, setting out the timetable for EMU and the convergence criteria
1994	Start of the second stage of EMU: creation of the European Monetary Institute (EMI). EU countries are required to work to fulfil the five convergence criteria on inflation, interest rates, government deficit and debt, and exchange-rate stability
1995	Madrid EU summit: The single currency is named "the euro", and the scenario for the third stage of EMU – the introduction of the euro – is set out
1 June 1998	The ECB starts operating
31 December 1998	The exchange rates between the euro and the currencies of the euro-area countries are irrevocably fixed as from 1 January 1999
1 January 1999	Start of the third stage of the EMU: the euro is launched and 11 of the 15 member states meet the criteria to adopt the single currency, i.e. Belgium, Germany, Spain, France, Ireland, Italy, Luxembourg, the Netherlands, Austria, Portugal and Finland

Table 2.2 (Continued)

1 January 2001	Greece joins the euro area
1 January 2002	Euro banknotes and coins are introduced
1 January 2007	Slovenia joins the euro area
1 January 2008	Cyprus and Malta joins the euro area
1 January 2009	Slovakia joins the euro area

Source: Adapted by the author from European Commission, Directorate-General for Economic and Financial Affairs (2008).

clear mandate and was granted independence from political influence. This entailed a combination of institutional independence, as well as personal, financial and functional independence. It also involved a high degree of transparency and accountability, including reporting obligations to the European Parliament.

Deregulation during the 1980s and 1990s

Even though deregulation and liberalization are generally used synonymously in this context, a slight distinction existed between them. Deregulation is defined as the act of removing controls from some sector of the economy, whereas liberalization is the act of making these controlling mechanisms less strict. The deregulation and liberalization of the European banking sector was a gradual process and the majority of EU countries had highly regulated banking markets. For instance, the Southern European countries, including Portugal, Spain and Greece, implemented significant banking reforms during 1986–1992, which were initiated in the late 1980s and maintained during 1990s. Effective progress was made with the introduction of proposals in the Single European Act of 1986, solving the existing problems and creating the single market. Over the same period, new regulation concerning customer protection and reduction of systematic risk was introduced with the purpose of providing a competitive environment for the provision of financial services (Panorama, 1994; European Commission, 1997a).

The ECB (2000b) report emphasizes that the strong deregulation and liberalization present in the euro zone provided a healthy environment. However, a high level of public ownership resulted in a low level of competition in regulated industries, which might have had a negative effect on performance levels in the industry. Therefore, privatization and regulatory reforms were proposed as mutually reinforcing measures. Gelos and Roldos (2004) presented striking reasons for changing the banking structure of the enlarged European Union (EU-25) countries, including privatization, deregulation and a liberalization process, and legal changes from a "pre-market-reform era" to an open-market economy.

From an economic perspective, literature agrees that financial liberalization strongly contributed to the development of the financial sector in the long run (Shaw, 1973; McKinnon, 1991; Bailliu, 2000; Gallego *et al.*, 2002). This issue was also confirmed by Jaffee and Levonian (2000), that is, that the removal of barriers with the EMU, deregulation and liberalization exposed countries to external financing and increased competition, which fostered financial development.[15]

In this respect, Germany and the Netherlands were the first countries to experience interest rate deregulation (1981) and liberalization (1967 and 1980, respectively).[16] Financial liberalization in France was accomplished relatively swiftly and without reversals, although it was slower in other countries, such as Spain and Italy (Gallego *et al.*, 2002). The modernization and liberalization process in Portugal was initiated in 1983, and continued with the second wave of reforms in the 1990s. The reforms basically comprised the autonomy of the Central Bank, the elimination of restrictions on interest rates and credits, and the liberalization of ownership and significant changes in the regulatory framework of the banking system (European Economy, 1997). Having identified and discussed the deregulation process in the European banking industry, the following section presents the regulatory framework with the introduction of the euro.

The new currency: the euro

Introduction of the euro

Europe's single currency, the euro, was introduced on 1 January 1999, but did not become a "real" currency until 1 January 2002. The introduction of the new currency in 12 European countries (termed as monetary unit, MU, or euro area countries in this book) was a historic event involving years of careful planning and preparation. This section enlightens readers about the story behind the single currency as well as procedures on the way in those countries that changed over to the euro.

Additionally, the price stability of the euro in the first decade since its introduction and how financial integration was achieved in the EU during this period is discussed. It can be said that the launch of the single currency went smoothly, and that the new banknotes and coins have become a fundamental component of our lives.

On 1 January 1999, the euro was introduced to member countries as a consequence of the policy framework of the Maastricht Treaty.[17] The objective was to pursue a single exchange-rate policy (Article 109 of the EC Treaty) and maintain economic growth and stability. The biggest change in moving to a single currency is that each country has relinquished control over monetary policy to the ECB. However, such a change has the shortcoming that an economic accident in one country might affect all others (Bartzokas, 2001).

In the long term, the euro was believed to be a strong and stable currency where the trend of its exchange rate depends on both domestic and foreign economic developments and policies. Its achievement mainly depends on effective information and communication systems for quick recognition and awareness by member countries and other countries trading with their euro-area partners. These issues were addressed in the Green Paper on the introduction of the euro by the European Commission in May 1995.

Thereafter, the actual euro notes and coins were put into circulation on 1 January 2002. It was emphasized in the European Commission Green Paper (1995b) that a great number of information systems were required to maintain a smooth introduction of the new currency. Moreover, many computer systems experienced an inability to function correctly with dates from 1 January 2000 onwards. Therefore, due to a heavy dependence on computer systems, it has been a dual challenge to allow the successful introduction of the euro and solve the date problem, known as the year 2000 problem (European Commission, 2001a).

Moving into more detail about the legal framework, the ECB was defined as the legal body that would implement monetary policy in the euro zone (Article 105 of the Maastricht Treaty), while exchange-rate policy was determined by the European Council (Article 109 of the Maastricht Treaty).[18] As a result of these changes and the strict control of the ECB, it was expected that the exchange risks between participating countries would disappear. This would then lead to a reduction of transaction costs, stimulate cross-border sales and purchases within the euro area, and affect the level of competition in financial and capital markets (European Commission, 2002a).

In fact, exchange rates are affected by many factors in the short term and long term. The intervention of central banks was expected to affect exchange rates in the short term, whereas fundamental economic factors such as economic growth, inflation performance, current balances, level of competition and the relative supply of domestic and foreign assets were expected to affect economic factors in the long term. It was anticipated that this would create greater labour flexibility, and tax and social security reforms, which were some of the most important factors providing information in creating the most efficient system that would help the European economy to adapt to global changes (European Commission, 2001a).

Furthermore, upon accession, the exchange-rate policies of the candidate countries became a common concern of the EU. The new EU countries would participate in the EMU with derogation of adoption of the euro. Nevertheless, they had to treat their exchange-rate policies as a matter of common concern and are expected to join the Exchange Rate Mechanism (ERM-II) for at least two years after accession (European Commission, 2001a).

Origins of the euro system

In December 1995, the Madrid European Council confirmed that stage three of EMU would start on 1 January 1999. It also named the single currency to be introduced at the start of stage three as the "euro" and announced the sequence of events leading up to its introduction. This scenario was based on detailed proposals developed by the EMI, which had also used the term "changeover to the euro" instead of "introduction of the euro" to reflect the nature of the transition to the single currency. The EMI's changeover scenario recommended a transitional period of three years starting from 1 January 1999 to accommodate differences in the pace with which the various groups of economic agents, that is, the financial sector, the non-financial corporate sector, the public sector and the general public, would be able to adapt to the single currency.

Also in December 1995, the EMI was given the task of carrying out preparatory work on the future monetary and exchange-rate relationships between the euro and the currencies of the non-euro-area EU countries. One year later, in December 1996, the EMI presented a report to the European Council, which subsequently formed the basis of a European Council Resolution on the principles and fundamental elements of the ERM-II, which was adopted in June 1997. Furthermore, in June 1997, the European Council adopted the Stability and Growth Pact, which complemented the Treaty provisions and aimed to ensure budgetary discipline within the EMU. The Pact consisted of three instruments: a European Council Resolution and two Council Regulations. It was supplemented, and the respective commitments enhanced, by a Declaration of the Council in May 1998.

Following these developments, the euro was introduced on 1 January 1999 and the conversion rates between the euro and the participating national currencies were permanently fixed. Subsequently, on 1 January 2002, new euro banknotes and coins were put into circulation in substitution for banknotes and coins in the old national currency units. The introduction of the euro as the single currency had a profound effect on operations of enterprises as well as financial institutions and has been one of the most important changes in the economic landscape of Europe. The transition to the single currency took place in three phases.

Phase A – Launch of the third stage of the EMU: In 1998, as soon as the group of countries taking part in EMU was known, the ECB was put in place. The conditions for conducting the single monetary and exchange-rate policy were finalized, and the production of euro banknotes began. Preparations in the participating countries were stepped up throughout this phase, particularly in administrations, banks and financial institutions. The economy as a whole continued to function as before, in other words on the basis of national currencies;

Phase B – Effective start of EMU: This phase began on 1 January 1999 when rates of conversion between the euro and the participating national currencies were irrevocably fixed. The currencies of the participating countries were replaced by the euro, which was denominated in its own unit (1 euro) and sub-units (100 cents) and in national currency units.

Phase C – Definitive changeover to the euro: After 31 December 2001, amounts that were still expressed in national currency units of the participating countries were expressed in euros. On 1 January 2002, and over a short subsequent period, the new euro banknotes and coins were in circulation replacing banknotes and coins in the old national currency units. This phase was completed by 1 July 2002, when euro banknotes and coins were the only banknotes and coins having legal tender status in the euro-area countries.

Price stability of the euro

The Maastricht Treaty establishes a clear hierarchy of objectives for the euro system by assigning overriding importance to price stability. This choice is based on both unambiguous historical evidence and economic theory. It supports higher living standards through various channels. It protects the real value of income and wealth, while unexpected inflation inevitably leads to unintended and arbitrary redistribution. Price stability benefits, in particular, the most vulnerable groups in society. These groups have a relatively higher share of their savings invested in cash and savings accounts, the real value of which is easily eroded by inflation. Typically, their access to financial markets is rather limited, leaving them with little room to evade the "inflation tax". In this respect, pensioners, who have to live on their pension entitlements and the savings accumulated during their working life, constitute a group that is particularly vulnerable to inflation. Price stability thus contributes to social cohesion.

Price stability also contributes to lower levels of both nominal and real interest rates. For instance, inflation erodes the real value of nominal assets and, in an inflationary environment, lenders typically require an inflation risk premium to compensate them for inflation risks associated with their investment. By contrast, lenders do not require such a risk premium in an environment of price stability. By reducing inflation risk, price stability results in lower levels of real interest rates, thereby making more investment projects profitable. In this respect, lower interest rates contribute to higher levels of employment and economic growth.

Since its introduction, the euro system has actively contributed to promoting financial integration in several ways, for example, by enhancing knowledge, raising awareness and monitoring progress in this area, based on a set of financial integration indicators developed by the ECB. It acts as a catalyst for market-based initiatives to foster financial integration. Moreover, the euro system has directly promoted financial integration by offering central banking services that are available throughout the euro area.

The euro system has also been very active since its inception in strengthening the arrangements that contribute to financial stability. This has become ever more necessary owing to increasingly integrated and rapidly evolving financial markets in Europe. The euro system therefore monitors and assesses the stability of the financial system on an ongoing basis and the ECB publishes both a semiannual Financial Stability Review on the financial system as whole and annual macro prudential and structural assessments of the EU banking sector.

Conclusion

A new institutional setting and a single monetary policy framework designed to achieve price stability were established with the creation of the EMU. At the centre of this framework is the ECB, whose primary objective is price stability. The launch of the euro required the development of an appropriate institutional setting for EMU. The combination of a centralized monetary policy with decentralized fiscal and structural policies has been broadly satisfactory. The coordination procedures reflect the increased interdependence among euro-area countries. European institutions and bodies (such as the European Parliament, the European Commission, the ECOFIN Council and others) increasingly exchange information and analyses. However, as the euro area's integration makes further progress, policies defined at the national level must give greater consideration to the requirements of the Community.

The euro system has provided regular advice and input to the development of the legal, regulatory and supervisory framework for financial services, especially at EU level. As regards the oversight of market infrastructure, the euro system has successfully contributed to ensuring the safe and efficient flow of money, securities and other financial instruments through payment and settlement systems. Moreover, Europe's single currency, the euro, was introduced on 1 January 1999, although it did not become a "real" currency until 1 January 2002. The introduction of euro in euro-area countries was a historic event involving years of careful planning and preparation. Today, more than 320 million people in 16 European countries share the euro as their currency.

3
Enlargement of the European Union

Introduction

The enlargement of the EU and the EMU were the next most important steps towards deepening European financial, political and economic integration. Conflicting arguments for earlier or later EMU enlargement can be attributed to divergent perspectives, perceptions and interests of different actors within old (EU-15) and new members (NMS) of the EU. The focus of this chapter is on the historical enlargement process since 2004, which saw the number of countries increase from 15 to 27, and on the progress of potential EU member countries.

History of the European Union enlargement

The road to European enlargement started in 1989, with the fall of the Berlin Wall and the Iron Curtain. The EU coordinated the "PHARE" programme of financial assistance, designed to help the newly established democratic governments in the Central and East European Countries (CEEC) to rebuild their economies and to encourage political reform.[1] The first step towards membership of these countries was initiated on 22 June 1993 in Copenhagen. At the same time, the European Council laid down three major criteria, known as the Copenhagen criteria, which candidate countries must meet before they can join the EU. The Copenhagen criteria can be summarized as: (i) *a political criterion*: candidate countries must have stable institutions guaranteeing democracy, the rule of law, human rights and respect for and protection of minorities, (ii) *an economic criterion*: candidate countries must have a functioning market economy and be able to cope with competitive pressure and market forces within the Union, and (iii) *a membership criterion*: candidate countries should take on the obligations of EU membership as the last criterion.

As discussed in Chapter 2, the EU has gone through eight enlargements in its history. The number of member countries increased from six to 15 over the 1957–1995 period via six enlargements, whilst the most recent two, since 2004, have been extensive. The starting point of the biggest wave of enlargement in the EU history began in March 1998 when the EU formally launched accession negotiations with six applicant countries: the Czech Republic, Estonia, Cyprus, Hungary, Poland and Slovenia. Furthermore, on 12 December 1999 the Commission recommended that EU member countries should open negotiations with Romania, Slovakia, Latvia, Lithuania, Bulgaria and Malta and recognize Turkey as an official candidate country at the Helsinki European Council (European Commission, 2003a).

As a result, the European Council took one of the most momentous steps in its entire history of European unification and welcomed into the Union Cyprus, the Czech Republic, Estonia, Hungary, Latvia, Lithuania, Malta, Poland, Slovakia and Slovenia on 1 May 2004 (these countries are described as new member states, NMS, in this book). Thus, the number of EU member countries increased to 25 (EU-25). In taking this decision, the EU was not simply increasing its surface area and population but also terminating the split between the free world and the communist world in Europe. Additionally, in 2004 the European Council decided to move forward with the procedures related to possible membership of Croatia and Turkey. The EU-25, with a population of 454 million, expanded even further when Bulgaria and Romania joined in 2007.

There are three key differences between the most recent and previous enlargements: (i) the level of income in many of the accession countries was different from those of existing members, (ii) the accession countries were in the process of transition from a centrally planned to a market economy, and (iii) the volume of EU legislation that the new members were adopting was more extensive than in previous enlargements, primarily because of the creation and enhancement of the single market (Allen *et al.*, 2005).

On the other hand, the NMS countries were quite heterogeneous among themselves. For instance, Cyprus and Malta were market-oriented, while the other eight countries transformed from former socialist-planned economies to open-market economies during the 1990s. Prior to joining the EU, the GDP per capita of Cyprus and Slovenia in 2003 was 80 per cent and 70 per cent respectively of the EU-15 average in terms of Purchasing Power Parity (PPP). At the other extreme, Latvia's was only 37 per cent of the EU-15 average. As a result of the recent enlargements, the EU's population became the largest after China (see Figure 3.1).

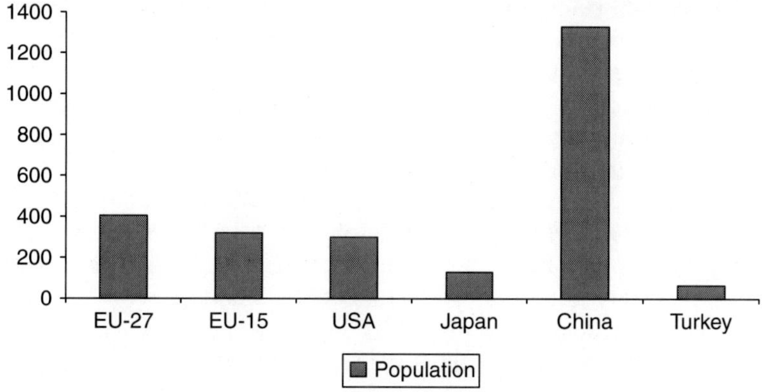

Figure 3.1 Population of selected countries, 2007 (millions)
Source: Eurostat (2008).

According to the Eurostat (2008) figures, the total population for the 12 NMS was 86 million people, while the EU-15 had 320 million people. This indicated an expansion of approximately 27 per cent in terms of population. Even though there was financial funding available from the European Commission, taking on so many new countries was a major undertaking, not just from an institutional and legal perspective, but also from a political, cultural and organizational perspective. As part of the "catching up" process, the NMS were also given high targets, which were based on convergence reports by the European Commission and the ECB.

The enlargement not only changed the population and political situation but the structure of the EU financial system. Upon accession, NMS countries were required to fulfil the same convergence criteria that were required from the EU-15 countries. There was no pre-defined timetable for the adoption of the euro by NMS, despite the fact that convergence required for membership was assessed by the Council of the EU.

In fact, the 2004 enlargement was a prominent political, rather than an economic, event. Due to its historic dimension, it virtually ended the political separation of Europe whilst the economic impact took a backseat. In population terms, with the exception of Poland (38.6 million inhabitants), all NMS countries are composed of either around 10 million inhabitants (the Czech Republic and Hungary) or much less, with the smallest countries, Malta, Cyprus, Estonia and Slovenia at 400,000, 700,000, 1.4 million and 2 million inhabitants, respectively. The recent EU enlargements not only have political importance, but amplify the cultural diversity of the EU. Apart from the cultural and national enrichment, the number of official languages jumped from 11 in EU-15 to 22 in EU-27.

Moreover, enlargement is expected to continue gradually in the near future with the accession of three more countries that have been granted candidate status, that is, Turkey in 1999, Croatia in 2004 and the Former Yugoslav Republic of Macedonia (FYROM) in 2005. Under the United Nations Security Council (UNSC) Resolution, all other Western Balkan countries, such as Albania, Bosnia and Herzegovina, Montenegro, Serbia and Kosovo, are potential candidate countries and therefore have the prospect of eventual EU membership.

One of the most interesting cases among the EU members is that of a divided country. The whole island of the Republic of Cyprus joined the EU on 1 May 2004. However, in the northern part of the island, in the areas in which the Government of Cyprus does not exercise effective control, EU legislation is suspended in line with Protocol 10 of the 2003 Accession Treaty Turkish Cypriots and Greek Cypriots living on the island have been experiencing conflict for more than 40 years, and the EU fully supports the renewed negotiations between the leaders of the two communities to reach a comprehensive settlement that will lead to the reunification of the island.

The two parts of the island still remain divided by the "Green Line" that separates the government-controlled areas from the rest of the island. The Council approved the Green Line Regulation (Council Regulation No 866/2004) on 29 April 2004, which deals with the movement of persons and goods across the line. While many people move across the Green Line every day, trade across the line remains limited, amounting to approximately 600,000 EUR per month. The situation will change once a Cyprus settlement enters into force, and it will then be possible for EU rules to be applied across the whole island. However, it is important to emphasize the fact that suspension does not affect the personal rights of Turkish Cypriots as EU citizens.

Euro-area enlargement

Even though the euro started out as the single currency of 11 countries, it is now the official currency of 16. There have been four enlargements of the euro area since its introduction, Greece joining in 2001, Slovenia in 2007, Cyprus and Malta in 2008 and Slovakia in 2009. Table 3.1 introduces the timeline of the EU countries, categorized as "year of EU entry" and "year of euro-area entry".

Table 3.1 Timeline for countries joining the EU and the EMU

EU member countries	Year of EU entry	Year of euro area entry
Austria	1995	1999
Belgium	1957	1999
Cyprus	2004	2008
Finland	1995	1999
France	1957	1999
Germany	1957	1999
Greece	1981	2001
Ireland	1973	1999
Italy	1957	1999
Luxembourg	1957	1999
Malta	2004	2008
Netherlands	1957	1999
Portugal	1986	1999
Slovakia	2004	2009
Slovenia	2004	2007
Spain	1986	1999
Estonia	2004	2011 (expected)
Latvia	2004	not yet
Lithuania	2004	not yet
Denmark	1973	opt-out
Sweden	1995	de facto opt-out
UK	1973	opt-out
Bulgaria	2007	not yet
Czech Republic	2004	not yet
Hungary	2004	not yet
Poland	2004	not yet
Romania	2007	not yet

Source: Adapted by the author from ECB and Eurostat, various years.

Currently, there are 11 EU countries that have not yet introduced the euro, with notable differences in their legal status and stage of convergence. In particular, Denmark and the UK have a special status based on an "opt-out clause", whereby the degree of convergence achieved for entering the euro area will only be assessed if they so request it. All of the nine remaining countries (Bulgaria, the Czech Republic, Estonia, Latvia, Lithuania, Hungary, Poland, Romania and Sweden) are EU countries with derogation, meaning that they are committed to eventually adopting the euro, whilst the actual timing will have to be looked at on a country-by-country basis.

Further waves of euro area enlargement are moving forward in accordance with a well-defined procedure consisting of the three phases discussed in Chapter 2. Five countries currently outside the euro area participate in ERM II, whilst two of them joined the mechanism on different dates. For instance, Denmark entered ERM II on 1 January 1999 with a fluctuation band of ±2.25 per cent around its currency's central exchange rate Estonia, Lithuania and Slovenia joined on 28 June 2004. Both Estonia and Lithuania joined with a ±15 per cent fluctuation band. These countries additionally decided to continue with their currency board arrangements as a unilateral commitment. On 2 May 2005, Latvia joined the ERM II, also with a ±15 per cent fluctuation band, but has continued to keep a fluctuation band of ±1 per cent as a unilateral commitment. Currently, Bulgaria, the Czech Republic, Hungary, Poland, Romania and Sweden are the only EU countries with derogation, and thus have not yet entered ERM II (see Table 3.2).

Table 3.2 Monetary integration plans of the non-euro-area EU countries

Countries	Intentions for ERM II	Intentions for euro adoption
Bulgaria	As soon as possible	Aims to adopt the euro as soon as possible
Czech Republic	ERM II participation for only the minimum period of two years ahead of EMU entry. Inflation targeting will be retained until monetary integration completed. The readiness to join ERM II and the euro area is assessed on a yearly basis jointly by the government and the national central bank	The latest update of the "Czech Republic's euro area accession strategy", approved by the Czech authorities in August 2007, states that some of the preconditions needed for benefiting from the adoption of the euro have yet to achieve satisfactory parameters. The main obstacles relate to the need to enhance the flexibility of the economy and fiscal policy consolidation
Denmark	Participating	No current plans. Referandum on euro adoption in September 2000 resulted in a 53% "no" vote
Estonia	Participating	Aims to adopt the euro as soon as possible
Latvia	Participating	Aims to adopt the euro as soon as possible
Lithuania	Participating	Aims to adopt the euro as soon as possible
Hungary	The Convergence Programme update does not contain any desired ERM	The Convergence Programme does not contain any desired euro-area entry date

	II entry date. It only states that participation in ERM II should be made conditional upon the restoration of fiscal credibility	
Poland	ERM II participation for only the minimum period of two years. No explicit target date for ERM II entry	The Convergence Programme does not contain any desired euro-area entry date
Romania	According to the 2007 Convergence Programme there are no intentions to join ERM II before 2012. Aims to stay in the ERM II for the minimum required period before adopting the euro	Not before 2014
Slovakia	Participating	Joined the euro area in 2009
Sweden	No current plans	No current plans. Referendum in September 2003 on euro adoption resulted in a 56% "no" vote
United Kingdom	No current plans	As soon as the government's five tests are fulfilled

Source: ESCB, 2010.

Recent progress in countries undergoing accession negotiations: Croatia, Turkey and the FYROM

Croatia

Croatia has been a candidate country for EU membership since June 2004. It was the second country to sign a Stabilization and Association Agreement (SAA) with the EU on 29 October 2001, which entered into force on 1 February 2005. On 3 October 2005 the Council decided to open accession negotiations with Croatia and on 12 February 2008 the Council adopted the new Accession Partnership for the country. The status in the accession negotiations is that there are 22 provisionally closed chapters and negotiations have been opened in 33 chapters.

In economic terms, EU–Croatia trade has substantially increased since the opening of the EU market under the Autonomous Trade Measures in 2000 and the trade provisions of the SAA in 2002. Since 2007,

Croatia has been receiving EU financial aid under the Instrument for Pre-accession Assistance (IPA). In 2008, EU–Croatia trade was at EUR 19.244 billion, which constitutes 65.5 per cent of the total trade. EU imports from Croatia totalled EUR 5.840 billion while EU exports to Croatia reached EUR 13.403 billion. In 2007 FDI from the EU was about EUR 3.57 billion (9.5 per cent of Croatia's GDP) with almost 99 per cent inflow coming from the EU-27.

Croatia has improved its ability to take on the obligations of EU membership. Progress on meeting the requirements and alignment with EU rules in most sectors has continued. However, reinforcement of the administrative structures and measures to ensure the proper implementation of the acquis in judiciary and fundamental rights, competition policy, and agriculture and rural development require further efforts.

Turkey

EU accession negotiations with Turkey began on 3 October 2005 and have moved forward since then. Eleven out of 33 negotiation chapters have been opened and Turkey continues to sufficiently fulfil the political criteria, and has made further progress over recent years, particularly in the reform of the judiciary, civil–military relations and cultural rights. As concerns the latter, the ECB stated that the opening of a public 24-hour TV channel, broadcasting in Kurdish nationwide, was a very positive step forward. Furthermore, the government has begun a process of broad consultation with political parties and civil society with a view to comprehensively addressing the Kurdish issue. The investigation of the alleged criminal network, Ergenekon, which has led to serious criminal charges against military officers and nationalist circles, is an opportunity for Turkey to strengthen the rule of law, provided that the due process of law is respected.

Concerning EU reforms and Turkey–EU relations overall, the Turkish government prioritized preparations for accession, as indicated by the appointment of a full-time Chief Negotiator and the approval of the National Programme for the Adoption of the Acquis. However, significant efforts are still required in most areas related to the political criteria, including, for example, freedom of expression and of the press, freedom of religion and the fight against torture.

In economic terms, Turkey is a functioning market economy. It should be able to cope with competitive pressure and market forces within the EU in the medium term, provided it implements its comprehensive reform programme in order to address structural weaknesses. The economy, including the financial sector, has shown flexibility despite the difficult international economic environment. The current account deficit has become less of a concern and access to external finance has remained open for both the public and private sectors.

Turkey has in fact further improved its ability to take on the obligations of membership. It has made progress in aligning with the EU's legal requirements in a number of areas, in particular in Trans-European networks, energy, and science and research. The overall level of alignment is advanced in areas such as the free movement of goods, intellectual property rights, enterprise and industrial policy, anti-trust policy, consumer and health protection, science and research, and energy. Moreover, Turkey has continued to develop a positive role, contributing to stabilization in regions such as the South Caucasus and the Middle East. In this context, diplomatic efforts to normalize relations with Armenia have moved forward significantly. Nevertheless, much alignment needs to be done, in particular on agriculture, fisheries, veterinary, policies, state aid, justice and home affairs and social policies.

The Former Yugoslav Republic of Macedonia (FYROM)

The FYROM obtained the status of candidate country in December 2005. The presidential and local elections of 2009 met most international standards. Political dialogue has improved in the sense that the governing coalition is stable, the political climate is more cooperative and the national parliament more effective. The key Accession Partnership priorities regarding the reform of the police, the judiciary, public administration and corruption have been substantially addressed.

The implementation of the Ohrid Framework Agreement remains an essential element of democracy and rule of law in the country. There has been progress in implementing the law on languages, in decentralization and in equitable representation. However, further efforts in a constructive spirit are needed to fulfil the objectives of the Agreement. While the legal and institutional framework for human rights and the protection of minorities is broadly in place, more work is needed to improve implementation in a number of fields. Regarding regional issues and international obligations, the FYROM has generally good relations with countries in the region. However, relations with Greece continue to be affected by the country's unresolved name issue. The country is engaged in talks, under the auspices of the UN, on resolving this issue.

In economic terms, the country continues to move closer towards becoming a functioning market economy. It should be able to cope with competitive pressures and market forces within the EU in the medium term, provided that it vigorously implements its reform programme in order to reduce significant structural weaknesses. Growth decelerated and became negative in 2009 following the deterioration in the international environment. Yet the financial sector remained reasonably stable, while inflation declined markedly. Some progress has been achieved in addressing structural unemployment and in reducing impediments to employment. However, unemployment remains high, in particular among the young and poorly educated, and is a major cause of concern. Further progress has been made in improving the business environment, but improvements in the administration and the rule of law are necessary to allow for smooth functioning of the market economy.

The FYROM has made good progress in improving its ability to assume the obligations of membership, in particular as concerns transport, customs and taxation, justice, freedom and security. Less progress has been achieved in certain other areas such as energy, the environment, and employment and social policy. Sustained efforts are needed to strengthen administrative capacity for the implementation and enforcement of legislation. In line with the relevant key priority of the Accession Partnership, commitments undertaken in the Stabilization and Association Agreement (SAA) have been implemented.

Recent progress in future candidate countries

Albania

Albania is a potential candidate country for EU accession, following the Thessaloniki European Council of June 2003. On 18 February 2008 the Council adopted a new European partnership with Albania and on 28 April 2009 the country submitted its application for EU membership. The EU–Albania Visa Facilitation Agreement entered into force in January 2008, while the Readmission Agreement entered into force in 2006.

Albania signed a SAA with the EU on 12 June 2006 and continued to make progress in addressing the political criteria in line with the European Partnership. The parliamentary elections in June 2009 met most international standards but further efforts are required to address the shortcomings identified regarding the rule of law and the fight against corruption and organized crime as well as the independence of state institutions. However, Albania does play a constructive role in maintaining regional stability and fostering good relations with other Western Balkan and neighbouring EU countries.

In economic terms, Albania has made further progress towards becoming a functioning market economy. However, it is required to reform and strengthen its legal system and address weaknesses in infrastructure and human capital in order to enable it to cope over the medium term with competitive pressure and market forces within the EU. Throughout 2008, Albania's economic growth continued to accelerate, but it slowed down in 2009 due to the impact of the global economic crisis, resulting in reduced exports, remittances and credit. Monetary policy remained sound and price stability was maintained, while the budget deficit grew, mainly due to the large amount of money spent on public roadworks.

Albania has made progress in aligning its legislation and policies with European standards. It now needs to enhance its efforts in the implementation of these laws and policies. In areas such as the free movement of goods, energy and small and medium-sized enterprise (SME) policy, progress achieved in previous years has been sustained. In contrast, progress has remained limited in intellectual property rights, agriculture and veterinary controls, as well as in controlling organized crime, drug trafficking and money laundering.

Bosnia and Herzegovina (BiH)

Bosnia and Herzegovina is a potential candidate country for EU accession, following the Thessaloniki European Council of June 2003. On 16 June 2008, the EU and BiH signed the SAA, which will enter into force once its ratification process has been completed. The European Commission launched a visa liberalization dialogue with BiH on 26 May 2008. A new European partnership with BiH was adopted by the Council on 18 February 2008. On 27 May 2010, the European Commission adopted a proposal enabling citizens of Albania and BiH to travel to Schengen countries without a short-term visa.[2]

BiH has made little progress in its domestic political climate and challenges to the functioning of institutions. Reform implementation has been slow, mainly due to a lack of consensus and political will, as well as the complex institutional organization of the country. In addition, a very limited number of European integration-related laws have been adopted. The authorities have not yet demonstrated sufficient capacity to take the necessary political ownership and responsibility. The role played by ethnic identity in politics has continued to hamper the functioning of the executive, the legislative and the judiciary as well as the country's overall governance. Corruption remains prevalent in many areas and is a serious problem. On the positive side, cooperation with the International Criminal Tribunal for the former Yugoslavia (ICTY) has remained satisfactory.

In economic terms, BiH has made little progress towards a functioning market economy. Further considerable reform efforts must be pursued with determination to enable the country to cope over the long term with competitive pressure and market forces within the EU. BiH has been severely affected by the recent global economic crisis, although financial and monetary stability has been preserved as a result of the timely reaction from the Central Bank when the financial crisis erupted in autumn 2008. The currency board arrangement has continued to enjoy a very high degree of credibility and the banking sector managed the impact of the crisis well. However, the quality and sustainability of public finances have further deteriorated. The restructuring and liquidation of state-owned enterprises have advanced slowly and the privatization process has not proceeded further.

The weak productive capacity and structural rigidities have slowed down job creation. Unemployment continues to be very high and the large informal employment sector remains an important challenge. The business environment is still affected by administrative inefficiencies and, unfortunately, progress towards the creation of a real single economic space within the country has been very limited.

As far as European standards are concerned, some progress has been made in the fields of customs, taxation, education and transport as well as in a number of justice, freedom and security-related areas, which has brought BiH closer to the fulfilment of the visa roadmap requirements. However, the country still needs to intensify its efforts in many areas, such as the free movement of goods, persons and services, employment and social policies, state aid, energy and the environment, and the fight against organized crime.

Montenegro

Montenegro applied for EU membership on 15 December 2008 and the Council invited the Commission to submit its opinion on Montenegro's application in April 2009. The opinion was released in the autumn of 2010. The SAA with the EU, signed on 15 October 2007, has been so far ratified by 22 member states. The Interim Agreement on Trade and Trade-related Matters, which entered into force on 1 January 2008, is being smoothly implemented, while the country's track record in implementing its obligations under the SAA is being built.

Montenegro has continued to make progress in addressing the political criteria. The parliamentary elections in March 2009 met almost all international criteria. In line with the European Partnership, Montenegro further pursued the completion of its legal framework and strengthened administrative and institutional capacity. It needs to intensify its efforts to consolidate the rule of law and, in particular, the fight against corruption and organized crime, which remain serious problems. Montenegro also has to make further efforts in the effective implementation and enforcement of legislation and in strengthening its administrative capacity, which remains a major challenge and affects all efforts to efficiently pursue reforms.

In economic terms, the country has made progress towards establishing a functioning market economy. In order to enable it to cope in the medium term with competitive pressure and market forces within the EU, it should continue with reforms to reduce structural weaknesses. The global economic crisis has had a serious impact on Montenegro's previously well-performing economy (8 per cent GDP growth in 2008), with its main industries such as aluminum and the banking sector being mostly affected. However, the economy did not slip into recession. The tourist industry seems to have performed better than expected and labour market indicators continued to improve. A series of structural reforms were pushed forward to preserve the stability of the banking sector and to limit the public deficit and debt.

All in all, Montenegro has made good progress in aligning with European standards in areas such as consumer protection and research as well as in some areas of its internal market and justice, freedom and security. Moreover, progress was achieved in the free movement of capital, customs and taxation, employment and statistics and in remaining areas under justice, freedom and security, which, however, still need further sustained efforts, especially to improve implementation capacity.

Serbia

Serbia is a potential candidate country for EU accession, following the Thessaloniki European Council of June 2003. On 29 April 2008, the EU and Serbia signed the SAA. The Serbian government has demonstrated its commitment to bringing the country closer to the EU by undertaking a number of initiatives including the implementation of provisions of the Interim Agreement. Cooperation with the ICTY has improved and the government has been relatively stable and active in preparing legislation across a range of areas and implementing a national programme on European integration. The work of the national parliament has improved through the revision of the rules of procedure and the adoption of a new law on financing political parties. Election legislation, however, has not yet been revised.

Serbia stands out due to its good capacity in public administration and the fact that the Serbian European Integration Office functions well. Nevertheless, its capacity for adopting EU integration issues needs to be improved and public administration reform accelerated. Serbia has made progress in the fight against corruption. The law enforcement authorities have shown commitment to fighting corruption, leading to the arrests of a number of suspects. However, final convictions in corruption cases are rare. Sustained efforts are needed in the fight against organized crime and to ensure the independence, accountability and efficiency of the judicial system.

In addition, there have been improvements in legal and institutional frameworks for human rights and the protection of minorities. Civil and political rights in Serbia are generally protected. However, there have been incidents involving hate speeches, threats and physical attacks against journalists, human rights defenders and the lesbian, gay, bisexual and transgender population, for which the perpetrators have not been brought to justice. Additionally, Serbia does not recognize the Kosovo declaration of independence. The government maintained parallel structures in Kosovo and held local by-elections while, at the same time, discouraging Kosovo Serbs from participating in municipal elections organized by the Kosovo authorities. The Serbian government has taken initial steps to cooperate with the EU rule of law mission (EULEX), but these efforts need to be further strengthened. There is a need for Serbia and Kosovo to reach pragmatic solutions enabling them to continue fulfilling their role in advancing regional cooperation and development.

In economic terms, Serbia was severely hit by the global economic crisis of 2007–8, such that growth slowed down by the end of 2008 and the economy entered into recession in 2009. As a result, macroeconomic stability has deteriorated and previously expansionary policies led to a significant fiscal deterioration. In this context, the IMF and the EU have provided financial assistance to Serbia, but Serbia made only limited further progress towards establishing a functioning market economy. Further efforts are required to enable Serbia to cope in the medium term with the competitive pressures and market forces within the EU.

More optimistically, Serbia has made progress in aligning its legislation and policies with European Standards and has started to implement the Interim Agreement according to the provisions and schedules established in the Agreement. Customs duties were lowered with effect from 30 January 2009, and measures were taken in the areas of competition, state aid and transit traffic. Furthermore, Serbia has adopted important SAA relevant legislation in a number of areas including agriculture, environment, employment, competition and justice, freedom and security. Administrative capacity has been improved in key areas for the implementation of the SAA, although effective implementation and enforcement of EU-related legislation needs to be improved.

Kosovo

The EU reiterated in 2008 that Kosovo (under UN Resolution 1244) has a clear European perspective in line with the rest of the Western Balkans region. The EU rule of law mission (EULEX) was deployed throughout the territory of Kosovo, assuming responsibilities in the areas of police, customs and the judiciary. The mission reached full operational capacity in April. In February, the Council renewed for 12 months the mandate of the EU Special Representative. The process of downsizing the United Nations (UN) mission in Kosovo was completed. Overall, Kosovo has made some progress in meeting the political criteria, in particular by strengthening the legal framework. The main institutions of governance are in place and fulfil their responsibilities in cooperation with relevant international organizations. However, the capacity of the public administration and of the assembly is in need of strengthening. Sustained efforts are needed on judiciary reform and to step up the fight against corruption and organized crime. Ensuring the participation of Kosovo Serbs in public life, including local elections, remains a major challenge.

In economic terms, Kosovo has made very little progress towards establishing a functioning market economy. Substantial reforms and major investments are needed to enable Kosovo's economy to cope over the long term with competitive pressure and market forces within the Union. The economy of Kosovo marked a growth of 5.5 per cent in 2009 (from 4.4 per cent in 2007), mostly based on consumption and public investment. A broad consensus on free-market policies has been maintained. The banking sector has remained sound. However, the already large trade deficit has continued to widen. Exports fell sharply in 2009, from an already very low base and the cost of finance remained high, as banks continued to attract high risk premium loans The weak rule of law, widespread corruption, high unemployment rates and uncertainty over property rights continued to be major impediments to economic development.

Progress in aligning Kosovo's legislation and policies with European standards is mixed. The legal framework has been developed further in the areas of customs, taxation, education and policing, whereas implementation of European standards in environment, energy, competition, intellectual property and free movement of goods, persons, services and capital are still at early stages. Structural reforms have advanced at a slow pace and there have been only limited improvements in the business environment. Moreover, little progress has been achieved in increasing the efficiency of public sector spending. A high level of external indebtedness and large short-term repayment obligations are key vulnerabilities of the Kosovo economy.

Conclusion

The first ten years of the euro coincided with an unprecedented expansion of the EU. Ten new countries joined the EU on 1 May 2004 and a further two followed on 1 January 2007. These enlargements were, in many respects, the largest and most comprehensive in the history of the EU. The total number of EU member countries increased from 15 to 27 and the total population went up by around 100 million to reach almost 500 million.

During the last decades, the EU-10 countries – excepting Cyprus and Malta – have been engaged in a transition process involving fundamental institutional and structural changes that have dramatically transformed former planned economies into market economies. Even though the accession countries have been members of the EU since 2004, the ongoing nature of these changes means that it will take more time before these countries fully complete the restructuring process. Recently, three countries, Croatia, Turkey and the FYROM, have been going through accession negotiations with the EU while Albania, Kosovo, Serbia, Bosnia and Herzegovina, and Montenegro have candidate country status for potential EU membership.

4
Macroeconomic Structure of the European Union

Introduction

This chapter is designed to explore the macroeconomic structural changes in the EU-27 countries over the last decade. It is exceptionally important to realize the divergence among the EU developed (EU-15) and developing countries (EU-12 or NMS) in order to provide critical investigation on the state of the European banking industry. Despite the general political and economic convergence in the EU, the macroeconomic and financial structure of various countries has remained diverse. In an attempt to investigate the prevailing substantial differences, this chapter examines the macroeconomic situation of individual EU countries through a comparison with the EU-27 average. Looking at main indicators, for instance, GDP growth, GDP per capita, interest, inflation and unemployment rates as well as important regional implications, the distinction between the EU-15 and NMS reveals a better understanding of the differences between the two groups of countries, as well as of the homogeneity and development in each group of countries over time.

Population and immigration in the EU

Starting with a comparison of population structure in the EU and the rest of the world, this section introduces a detailed description of the picture within the EU itself. In comparison with other regions, the EU's population is growing at a relatively slow pace. For instance, the world's population more than doubled, rising from 3032 million inhabitants to 6515 million over the 1960–2005 period, while the corresponding rate of change in the EU-27 was an increase of 21.9 per cent, reaching

491 million inhabitants. In terms of weights, the EU-27's population fell from 13.3 per cent of the world total in 1960 to 7.5 per cent by 2005. This trend is expected to continue, such that by 2050 the EU-27 will account for just 5.4 per cent of the world's population.

According to Eurostat figures, the world's population growth peaked during the 1985–1990 period, when the average number of global inhabitants per annum increased by 87.9 million people. By 2050, the global rate of population growth is expected to decelerate to an additional 33.1 million inhabitants each year (see Figure 4.1). Detailed annual figures are presented in Table 4A.1, in the appendix.

Moving on to Europe, the population of the EU-27 grew from 403 million in 1960 to over 495 million in 2007. Population growth in the EU-27 was strongest at the beginning of this period in the 1960s, when average annual increases were generally over 3 million persons per year, peaking at 4.2 million in 1965; this decelerated significantly in the 1970s, and by the 1980s the average increase in population was around 1.25 million persons each year. This slower level of population growth continued during much of the following 20 years, although there appears to have been a reversal in the trend observed from 2003 to 2007, as the number of EU-27 inhabitants rose by approximately 2 million a year.

In more detail, Germany had the largest population in 2007, accounting for almost 17 per cent of the EU-27 total and, together with France, the UK and Italy comprised almost 54 per cent of the total population of the EU-27. The NMS had a combined population of 103.3 million

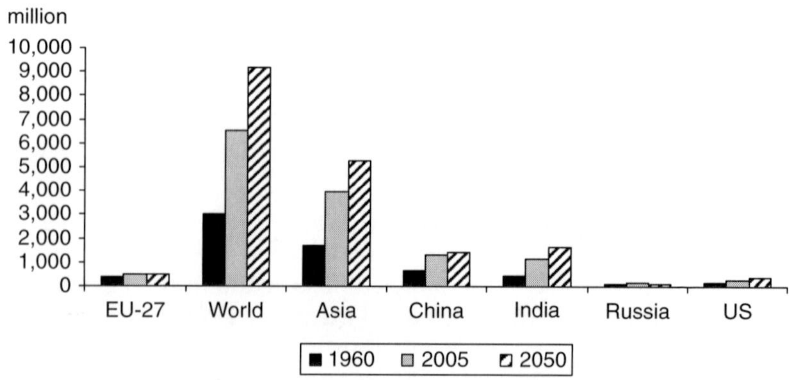

Figure 4.1 World population and population projections
Source: Eurostat, United Nations, Population Division of the Department of Economics and Social Affairs (2008).

persons in 2007, representing approximately 21 per cent of the EU-27's total population. In fact, population growth in the EU-27 in the last decade may be largely attributed to countries' increased number of inhabitants, of which Ireland, Spain and Cyprus recorded the highest population growth rates (see Table 4.1).

According to the latest Eurostat (2008) figures, the EU-27's population is forecasted as 504 million persons in 2035, which will fall to 494 million inhabitants by 2050. On one hand, the populations of Cyprus, Ireland and Luxembourg are projected to grow by over 50 per cent between 2008 and 2060, while those of Belgium, Spain, France, Sweden and the UK are expected to grow at a range of 15–25 per cent by 2060. In contrast, the populations of Poland, Estonia, Hungary, Slovakia and Germany are estimated to decrease by approximately 10–20 per cent by 2060, with even stronger declines of 20–30 per cent in Bulgaria, Latvia, Lithuania and Romania.

Population by age: is Europe becoming a continent for older people?

The EU-27's population age structure is the result of many years of high birth rates, followed by low birth rates, and is accompanied by a gradual increase in life expectancy and migration flows. Over the last 40 years, much of the European labour force has been made up of the young generation. This demographic characteristic is projected to end during the coming decades as the young generation enters retirement. Moreover, Europe's fertility rates have been declining since the 1970s, and the number of young people entering the labour market has become smaller. As a result, the proportion of people of working age in the EU-27 is shrinking, at the same time as the proportion of those who are taking retirement expand. In short, Europe is getting older, which is expected to create problems in the future.

Such problems are due to the fact that old age dependency is likely to result in increased burdens of social expenditure for the working population in the form of pensions and healthcare. Increasing labour force participation is one factor that helps to reconcile demographic developments and the social expenditure burden, while pension reforms have already been started in several EU countries. In addition, policymakers have also considered ways of creating more flexible working opportunities that may be of interest to the elderly, or have considered delaying the average age of retirement.

Table 4.1 Total populations of selected countries, 1997–2007 (millions)

	1997	1998	1999	2000	2001	2002	2003	2004	2005	2006	2007	% change 1997–2007
EU-27	478.1	480.4	481.1	482.2	483	484.5	486.5	488.6	490.9	493	495.1	3.56
Euro area	302.2	304.5	305.2	306.2	307.5	309	310.9	312.9	314.9	316.7	318.4	5.36
Austria	8	8	8	8	8	8.1	8.1	8.1	8.2	8.3	8.3	3.75
Belgium	10.2	10.2	10.2	10.2	10.3	10.3	10.4	10.4	10.4	10.5	10.6	3.92
Bulgaria	8.3	8.3	8.2	8.2	7.9	7.9	7.8	7.8	7.8	7.7	7.7	−7.23
Croatia	4.6	4.5	4.6	4.4	4.4	4.4	4.4	4.4	4.4	4.4	4.4	−4.35
Cyprus	0.7	0.7	0.7	0.7	0.7	0.7	0.7	0.7	0.7	0.8	0.8	14.29
C. Republic	10.3	10.3	10.3	10.3	10.3	10.2	10.2	10.2	10.2	10.3	10.3	0.00
Denmark	5.3	5.3	5.3	5.3	5.3	5.4	5.4	5.4	5.4	5.4	5.4	1.89
Estonia	1.4	1.4	1.4	1.4	1.4	1.4	1.4	1.4	1.3	1.3	1.3	−7.14
Finland	5.1	5.1	5.2	5.2	5.2	5.2	5.2	5.2	5.2	5.3	5.3	3.92
France	59.7	59.9	60.2	60.5	60.9	61.3	61.7	62.1	62.5	63	63.4	6.20
Germany	82	82.1	82	82.2	82.3	82.4	82.5	82.5	82.5	82.4	82.3	0.37
Greece	10.7	10.8	10.9	10.9	10.9	11	11	11	11.1	11.1	11.2	4.67
Hungary	10.3	10.3	10.3	10.2	10.2	10.2	10.1	10.1	10.1	10.1	10.1	−1.94
Ireland	3.7	3.7	3.7	3.8	3.8	3.9	4	4	4.1	4.2	4.3	16.22
Italy	56.9	56.9	56.9	56.9	57	57	57.3	57.9	58.5	58.8	59.1	3.87
Latvia	2.4	2.4	2.4	2.4	2.4	2.3	2.3	2.3	2.3	2.3	2.3	−4.17
Lithuania	3.6	3.6	3.5	3.5	3.5	3.5	3.5	3.4	3.4	3.4	3.4	−5.56
Luxembourg	0.4	0.4	0.4	0.4	0.4	0.4	0.4	0.5	0.5	0.5	0.5	25.00
Malta	0.4	0.4	0.4	0.4	0.4	0.4	0.4	0.4	0.4	0.4	0.4	0.00

Netherlands	15.6	15.7	15.8	15.9	16	16.1	16.2	16.3	16.3	16.3	16.4	5.13
Poland	38.6	38.7	38.7	38.7	38.3	38.2	38.2	38.2	38.2	38.2	38.1	−1.30
Portugal	10.1	10.1	10.1	10.2	10.3	10.3	10.4	10.5	10.5	10.6	10.6	4.95
Romania	22.1	22	21.9	21.9	21.9	21.8	21.8	21.7	21.7	21.6	21.6	−2.26
Slovakia	5.4	5.4	5.4	5.4	5.4	5.4	5.4	5.4	5.4	5.4	5.4	0.00
Slovenia	2	2	2	2	2	2	2	2	2	2	2	0.00
Spain	39.5	39.6	39.8	40	40.5	41	41.7	42.3	43	43.8	44.5	12.66
Sweden	8.8	8.8	8.9	8.9	8.9	8.9	8.9	9	9	9	9.1	3.41
UK	58.2	58.4	58.6	58.8	59	59.2	59.4	59.7	60.1	60.4	60.8	4.47

Source: Adapted by the author from Europe in Figures, Eurostat Yearbook (2008).

The ability of the EU as a whole to increase productivity and to make full use of its human resources will play an important role in determining its ability to cope with the socio-economic transformations that are linked to demographic ageing. In fact, the fastest growing age group in the EU will be those aged over 80. According to Eurostat (2007) figures, the group of very old (80 years or more) persons accounted for 4.1 per cent of the EU-27 population in 2006. On the other hand, only 67.2 per cent of EU-27 population was of working age (15–64 years old), whereas the group of people younger than 15 years old accounted for 16 per cent of the EU-27's population (of which 17.1 per cent are in Bulgaria, 14.1 per cent in Germany and 20.5 per cent in Ireland). In contrast, the group of people older than 64 years grew to 16.7 per cent in 2006, with a total of almost 20 per cent in Italy and Germany (see Table 4.2).

Immigration

Over the 1997–2007 period, net migration was the main driver of population change in the EU-27. Population growth across the EU-27 of 2.4 million persons in 2007 comprised a positive net migration of 1.9 million persons and a natural population increase of 0.5 million persons. As expected, the patterns of population change vary considerably across individual countries, such as in Germany, which experienced a decline of almost 1.2 million persons, and in Bulgaria, Latvia and Romania, whose decline was closer to 0.5 million. In contrast, there were relatively high natural population increases in Ireland, Spain, France, the Netherlands and the UK.

Negative net migration is relatively rare among the EU-27, where only six countries (Bulgaria, Latvia, Lithuania, the Netherlands, Poland and Romania) reported negative net migration over the 2000–2005 period. High negative values of net migration in Romania, Poland and Bulgaria, as well as in the Czech Republic and Slovakia at the beginning of the decade reflect differences compared with previous estimates. The highest positive values of net migration over the same period were recorded in Spain and Italy, followed by the UK, France and Germany. However, it should be emphasized that, as many European countries are currently at a point in the demographic cycle where natural population change is close to being balanced or negative, the relative importance of migration increases. This said, as Europe's population ages, natural population change might become the principal component of population change.

Table 4.2 Population by age group, 2006 (per cent of total population)

	0–14	15–24	25–49	50–64	65–79	>80
EU-27	16	12.7	36.4	18.1	12.6	4.1
Euro area	15.6	11.9	36.8	18	13.2	4.5
Austria	15.9	12.3	37.7	17.6	12.1	4.4
Belgium	17.1	12.1	35.6	18.1	12.8	4.4
Bulgaria	13.6	13.6	35.5	20.1	13.9	3.3
Croatia	15.8	13.1	35.3	18.9	14	3
Cyprus	18.4	15.8	37.1	16.6	9.4	2.6
C. Republic	14.6	13.2	36.9	21	11.1	3.1
Denmark	18.7	11.2	35.1	19.9	11.1	4.1
Estonia	15.1	15.6	34.7	17.9	13.5	3.3
Finland	17.3	12.5	33.2	21.1	12	4
France	18.6	12.9	34.4	17.9	11.6	4.6
FYRM	19.4	16.1	36.8	16.6	9.6	1.5
Germany	14.1	11.8	36.5	18.4	14.8	4.5
Greece	14.3	12	37.6	17.6	14.9	3.6
Hungary	15.4	12.9	35.8	20.1	12.3	3.5
Iceland	21.8	14.6	36	15.9	8.6	3.1
Ireland	20.5	15.2	37.8	15.5	8.4	2.7
Italy	14.1	10.3	37.5	18.3	14.6	5.1
Latvia	14.3	15.7	35.5	17.6	13.6	3.2
Liechtenstein	17.4	12.3	39.4	19.4	8.7	2.9
Lithuania	16.5	15.6	36.1	16.5	12.4	2.9
Luxembourg	18.6	11.6	38.3	17.1	11	3.3
Malta	17.1	14.4	34.9	20	10.5	3
Netherlands	18.3	12	36.5	19	10.7	3.6
Norway	19.5	12.4	35.2	18.2	10.1	4.7
Poland	16.2	16.2	36	18.2	10.6	2.7
Portugal	15.6	12.2	37.3	17.7	13.2	3.9
Romania	15.5	15.2	37	17.4	12.3	2.5
Slovakia	16.6	15.9	38	17.8	9.3	2.4
Slovenia	14.1	13.1	38	19.2	12.4	3.2
Spain	14.5	11.9	40.4	16.6	12.3	4.4
Sweden	17.3	12.4	33.3	19.7	11.9	5.4
UK	17.8	13.2	35.2	17.8	11.6	4.4

Source: Adapted by the author from Eurostat Statistical Books, European Economic Statistics, 2007.

Macroeconomic structure of the EU member countries

Size of the EU economies

As emphasized in the previous sections of this chapter, the EU-27 countries are heterogeneous in terms of size, income levels,

Table 4.3 Relative economic size of the EU countries

Groups	Country	Share in EU-27 GDP (2001)	Share in EU-27 GDP (2008)
Large countries	Germany	22.1	19.9
	France	15.6	15.6
	UK	17.2	14.5
	Italy	13	12.6
	Spain	7.1	8.8
	Subtotal	75	71.3
Medium countries	Netherlands	4.7	4.8
	Poland	2.2	2.9
	Belgium	2.7	2.8
	Sweden	2.6	2.6
	Austria	2.2	2.3
	Greece	1.5	1.9
	Denmark	1.9	1.9
	Finland	1.5	1.5
	Ireland	1.2	1.5
	Portugal	1.3	1.3
	Czech Republic	0.7	1.2
	Romania	0.5	1.1
	Subtotal	23.1	25.7
Small countries	Hungary	0.62	0.84
	Slovakia	0.25	0.52
	Slovenia	0.24	0.30
	Luxembourg	0.24	0.29
	Bulgaria	0.16	0.27
	Lithuania	0.14	0.26
	Latvia	0.10	0.18
	Cyprus	0.11	0.14
	Estonia	0.07	0.13
	Malta	0.04	0.05
	Subtotal	2	3

Source: Adapted by the author from Eurostat Statistical Books, European Economic Statistics, 2009.

economic structure and recent economic performance. Table 4.3 provides a comparison of the relative size of their economies in 2001 and 2008 based on the GDP figures measured at current prices. The EU-27 countries are classified into three groups as large, medium-sized and small countries. The first group of five large countries accounted for almost three-quarters of the EU-27 economy in 2008 (71.3 per cent), whilst the second group of 12 medium-sized countries accounted for about one-quarter (25.7 per cent) and, finally, the group of ten small countries represented only 3 per cent of the EU economy as a share in average EU-27 GDP amount.

Comparing the 2008 with the 2001 figures, it is clear that all large EU countries, with the exception of Spain and France, have lost relative weight, and that all medium-sized and small countries have maintained, and in most cases increased, their weights. Germany has the largest economy in the EU-27, which is around the same size as the combined economies of the 20 smaller EU countries. Therefore, it can be stated that the main features of the EU-27 economy will chiefly result from developments in Germany.

Trends in real GDP growth

The most frequently used measure for the overall size of an economy is gross domestic product (GDP), which corresponds to the total monetary value of all production activity in a certain geographic area. GDP at market prices is the final result of the production activity of all producer units within a certain area, and is one of the main indicators used for economic analysis, as well as comparison of living standards.

The synchronized global economic slowdown since 2008 affected major regions of the world with financial shocks and was also reflected in the EU-27 countries experiencing 0.8 per cent real GDP growth rate in 2008, considerably lower than 2007 (2.9 per cent).[1] A similar trend is observed in the EU-15 countries with 2.6 and 0.5 per cent in 2007 and 2008, respectively. Among the NMS, Estonia, Latvia, Lithuania and Slovakia are those who experienced more than 15 per cent recession, while the euro area (EA-15) experienced around 7 per cent recession over the 2007–2008 period. The GDP of the EU-27 was EUR 12,354,973 million in 2007, with the countries of the euro area accounting for a little less than three quarters (72.5 per cent) of this total. The sum of the four largest EU economies (Germany, the UK, France and Italy) accounted for almost two-thirds (64.0 per cent) of the EU-27's GDP in 2007. In an attempt to present a detailed investigation, Figure 4.2 shows the average annual GDP growth broken down into GDP per capita and average population changes for the 2001–2008 period.

The EU-27 experienced an average annual GDP growth rate of 2.0 per cent during the 2001–2008 period, but the average annual GDP per capita growth was only 1.6 per cent. This was due to a 0.4 per cent average annual increase in population. Most of the NMS were at the top of this ranking, whilst most of the EU-15 – except Germany – were at the lower end of the ranking, that is, their growth in GDP per capita was lower than GDP growth as a result of the population increase. Among

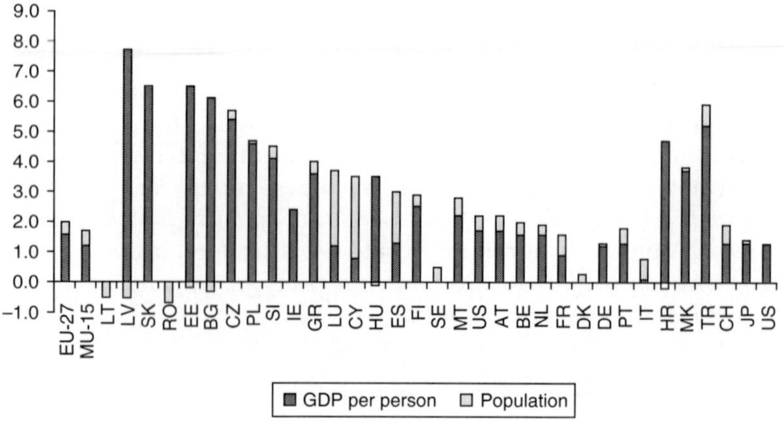

Figure 4.2 Average annual GDP growth, 2001–2008
Source: Eurostat Statistical Books, European Economic Statistics, 2009.

the non-EU countries, GDP growth mostly exceeded GDP per capita growth due to growing populations.

Table 4.4 introduces annual GDP at current prices expressed in million EUR over the 2001–2008 period. The best economic performance in Germany, following the reunification of the East and West, was accomplished by a 3 per cent GDP growth in 2001. The favourable external environment and improved external competitiveness, together with the low exchange rate of the euro, were suggested as the most striking factors in this progress.[2] Germany was observed to grow more slowly than most of the EU countries, especially since 2001, whereas France achieved 30 per cent GDP growth during the 2001–2008 period, which was much above the EU-27 average. In contrast, from the group of medium-sized countries, the Dutch economy was the only one to experience average GDP growth of approximately 33 per cent during 2001–2008. Interestingly, Greece has experienced a GDP growth above the EU average since 2001, and an average growth of 66 per cent was observed during 2001–2008. Moreover, due to increased competition in the European banking sector, Italy experienced a strong economic upswing from 2001, with 2.6 per cent average GDP growth over the period under investigation. The main factors for the economic growth were dynamic export growth and strong private consumption expenditure that were relatively higher than expectations. The EU-27 countries recorded a continuous annual GDP growth, whereas the US average has been lower than that of EU-27

Table 4.4 GDP at current prices (EUR million)

	2001	2002	2003	2004	2005	2006	2007	2008	% change 2001–2008
EU-27	9,580,243	9,941,732	10,108,220	10,602,765	11,063,072	11,676,765	12,354,973	12,506,964	30.55
Euro area	7,051,702	7,298,184	7,514,864	7,820,248	8,110,910	8,509,755	8,936,902	9,208,703	30.59
Austria	212,499	218,848	223,302	232,782	244,453	257,295	270,837	282,202	32.80
Belgium	258,883	267,652	274,726	289,629	302,112	318,223	334,917	344,206	32.96
Bulgaria	15,250	16,623	17,767	19,875	21,882	25,238	28,899	34,118	123.72
Cyprus	10,801	11,170	11,785	12,728	13,659	14,673	15,667	16,949	56.92
C. Republic	69,045	80,004	80,924	88,262	100,190	113,459	127,143	148,556	115.16
Denmark	179,226	184,744	188,500	197,070	207,367	218,341	226,544	233,331	30.19
Estonia	6,916	7,757	8,693	9,651	11,091	13,104	15,270	15,860	129.32
Finland	139,789	143,808	145,795	152,151	157,070	167,009	179,659	186,164	33.17
France	1,497,174	1,548,555	1,594,814	1,660,189	1,726,068	1,806,430	1,894,646	1,950,085	30.25
Germany	2,113,160	2,143,180	2,163,800	2,210,900	2,243,200	2,321,500	2,422,900	2,492,000	17.93
Greece	146,428	156,615	171,410	185,851	197,645	213,207	228,180	242,946	65.91
Hungary	59,388	70,581	74,580	82,236	88,664	89,969	101,370	105,244	77.21
Ireland	116,990	130,190	139,442	148,975	162,168	177,286	190,603	185,721	58.75
Italy	1,248,648	1,295,226	1,335,354	1,391,530	1,429,479	1,485,377	1,544,915	1,572,243	25.92
Latvia	9,320	9,911	9,978	11,176	13,012	16,047	21,111	23,115	148.02
Lithuania	13,577	15,052	16,497	18,158	20,870	23,979	28,423	32,292	137.84
Luxembourg	22,572	23,992	25,834	27,520	30,237	33,921	36,411	36,662	62.42
Malta	4,301	4,489	4,421	4,515	4,799	5,114	5,464	5,750	33.69
Netherlands	447,731	465,214	476,945	491,184	513,407	539,929	567,066	594,608	32.80

Table 4.4 (Continued)

	2001	2002	2003	2004	2005	2006	2007	2008	% change 2001–2008
Poland	212,294	209,617	191,644	204,237	244,420	272,089	310,613	362,095	70.56
Portugal	129,308	135,434	138,582	144,128	149,123	155,446	163,190	166,197	28.53
Romania	45,357	48,615	52,577	61,064	79,802	97,751	123,847	137,035	202.13
Slovakia	23,542	25,980	29,486	34,032	38,490	44,567	54,857	64,884	175.61
Slovenia	22,707	24,527	25,736	27,136	28,712	31,014	34,471	37,126	63.50
Spain	680,678	729,206	782,929	841,042	908,792	982,303	1,050,595	1,095,163	60.89
Sweden	251,340	264,244	275,657	287,689	294,674	313,450	331,226	328,421	30.67
UK	1,643,154	1,710,421	1,647,056	1,769,067	1,831,683	1,938,979	2,046,535	1,812,077	10.28

Source: Adapted by the author from Eurostat Statistical Books, European Economic Statistics, 2009.

since 2003. On the other hand, Japan presented a significantly lower trend compared with its counterparts.

Trends in GDP per capita

In order to look at standards of living, one of the most frequently cited statistics is that of GDP per capita. Across the EU-27 as a whole, GDP per capita was EUR 24,800 in 2007, and the highest level was recorded for Luxembourg (EUR 75,200). Even after accounting for the relatively high cost of living in Luxembourg, GDP per capita in Purchasing Power Standards (PPS) terms remained almost twice as high as in any other EU country, which can partly be explained by the importance of cross-border workers from Belgium, France and Germany. On the other hand, the lowest levels of GDP per capita were recorded in Bulgaria and Romania, where living standards were approximately 40 per cent of the EU-27 average in 2007. In fact, labour productivity among the NMS, in particular the Czech Republic, Poland, Slovenia and Slovakia, has been converging quickly towards the EU-27 average.

All the NMS countries had GDP per capita in PPP levels lower than the EU-15 countries and the euro-area average (MU-16). Among the EU-15, Greece, France, Italy, Portugal and Spain performed worse than the MU-16 average in 2007. Almost all the other countries followed a similar pattern to the MU-16 average except the Netherlands, Austria, Sweden, Luxembourg and Ireland, who recorded the highest GDP per capita figures. It is worth emphasizing that Ireland achieved remarkable progress over the decade, changing from being one of the poorest countries among the EU-15 economies in 1997 to one of the richest in terms of GDP per capita in 2007 (see Table 4.5).

Figure 4.3 shows that the GDP per capita figures expressed in PPS indexed to EU-27 equalled 100 for 2000, 2005 and 2008. In 2008, six countries had an index of 20 per cent or more above the EU-27 average and ten countries were more than 20 per cent below the EU-27 average. It is observed that a majority of EU-15 countries (12 out of 15) that were below the EU-27 average in 2000 improved their position in 2008. Consequently, the opposite is true for NMS: eight out of the 12 that were above 100 in 2001 experienced a worsening in their positions. This can be suggested as evidence of a convergence process within the enlarged EU during the period 2001–2008. The GDP per capita of countries that were relatively poorer has grown faster than that of the relatively richer since 2001.

Looking at the contributions by average growth of population and labour productivity (growth of persons employed divided by the

Table 4.5 GDP per capita in PPP, 2001–2007 (EU-27 = 100)

Countries	2001	2002	2003	2004	2005	2006	2007	% change 2001–2007
Euro area	113	112	112	110	111	110	110	−2.65
EU-27	100	100	100	100	100	100	100	0.00
Austria	125	126	127	127	125	124	124	−0.80
Belgium	124	125	123	121	119	118	118	−4.84
Bulgaria	29	31	33	34	35	37	37	27.59
Cyprus	91	89	89	90	91	90	91	0.00
C. Republic	70	70	73	75	76	77	80	14.29
Denmark	128	128	124	126	124	123	120	−6.25
Estonia	46	50	54	57	61	65	68	47.83
Finland	116	115	113	116	114	115	116	0.00
France	116	116	112	110	111	109	109	−6.03
Germany	117	115	117	116	117	116	115	−1.71
Greece	87	90	92	94	93	94	95	9.20
Hungary	59	61	63	63	63	64	63	6.78
Ireland	133	138	141	142	144	147	150	12.78
Italy	118	112	111	107	105	104	102	−13.56
Japan	114	112	112	113	113	113	112	−1.75
Latvia	39	41	43	46	49	53	58	48.72
Lithuania	42	44	49	51	53	56	60	42.86
Luxembourg	234	240	248	253	254	267	267	14.10
Malta	78	80	78	77	78	77	78	0.00
Netherlands	134	133	129	129	131	131	131	−2.24
Norway	161	155	156	164	176	184	178	10.56
Poland	48	48	49	51	51	52	54	12.50
Portugal	77	77	77	75	77	76	76	−1.30
Romania	28	29	31	34	35	38	42	50.00
Slovakia	52	54	56	57	60	64	67	28.85
Slovenia	80	82	83	86	87	88	89	11.25
Spain	98	101	101	101	102	104	105	7.14
Sweden	121	121	123	125	120	121	122	0.83
UK	120	121	122	124	122	120	119	−0.83

Source: Adapted by the author from Eurostat Statistical Books, European Economic Statistics, 2008.

population) on GDP per capita growth over the period 2001–2008, it is clear that two-thirds of EU-27 and euro-area GDP per capita growth stemmed from higher labour productivity.

The most impressive gains in labour productivity were displayed by Romania (+6.9 per cent), Lithuania (+5.5 per cent), Slovakia (+5.2 per cent), Latvia (+4.8 per cent) and Estonia (+4.7 per cent). Other NMS also experienced substantial gains, ranging from 4.1 per cent in

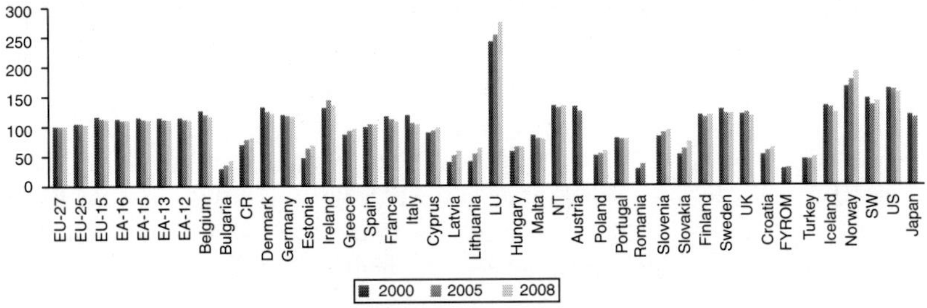

Figure 4.3 GDP per capita in PPS of selected countries, 2000–2008 (EU-27 = 100)
Source: Adapted by the author from Eurostat Statistical Books, European Economic Statistics, 2009.

Poland to 3.2 per cent in Bulgaria. Gains in other EU countries were more modest, but substantial increases were observed in the number of employed persons in Ireland (+2.6 per cent), Hungary (+3.3 per cent), Bulgaria (+3.2 per cent) and Greece (+2.4 per cent). The only country that experienced negative growth was Italy (–0.4 per cent).

The highest increase in population was observed in Bulgaria (+2.9 per cent), Latvia (+2.7 per cent), Lithuania (+2.3 per cent), Estonia (+1.8 per cent) and Luxembourg (+1.8 per cent). The respective EU-27 and MU-15 average growth rates were 0.4 per cent and 0.6 per cent per year, respectively. On the other hand, Portugal (–0.4 per cent), Romania (–0.1 per cent) and France (–0.1 per cent) experienced decreasing population figures.

Trends in inflation rates

The Harmonized Indices of Consumer Prices (HICP) provide the best measure for international comparisons of consumer price inflation and assessing price convergence and stability in the EU. The HICP are a set of EU consumer price indices calculated according to a harmonized approach and a single set of definitions. The ECB's main focus of interest has been assessing price stability in the euro area, for which a boundary of close to but below a 2 per cent annual increase in the HICP has been set up since the creation of the single market in 1999.

Annual average inflation for the euro area over the period 2001–2007 was relatively stable at around 2.2 per cent, increasing to its highest level of 3.3 per cent in 2008. In the EU as a whole, annual average inflation in 2008 stood at 3.7 per cent, which has been its highest level since the start of the HICP series in 1997. In euro-area countries, the highest ever annual average inflation rate was recorded as 3.3 per cent in 2008, following several years of stability at around 2.2 per cent. The inflation in 2008 can be explained by steep increases in energy and food prices between autumn 2007 and autumn 2008 as well as a reflection of the global economic slowdown (see Table 4.6).

Moreover, in spite of the significant convergence in inflation rates over the past decade, 2001 experienced inflation differences in each of the euro-area countries that were higher than the EU-12 average (2.1 per cent). This has emphasized the strong macroeconomic conditions in countries using opt-out, that is, Denmark, Sweden and the UK. An overall price increase was witnessed in the euro area during 2000 and 2001, reflected as 2.1 per cent in 2000 and 2.3 per cent in 2001. This was mainly due to oil prices being higher than expected.

In terms of the EU-15 countries, the highest average inflation rates in 2001 were observed in the Netherlands (5.1 per cent), Portugal (4.4 per cent), Ireland (4.0 per cent), Spain (2.8 per cent) and Greece (3.7 per cent). The high inflation rate in the Netherlands was mainly attributable to an increase in value added tax (VAT) and less wage moderation against a tightening labour market. On the other hand, the lowest rates were observed in France (1.8 per cent) and the UK (1.2 per cent).

Among the NMS, inflation rates were much higher compared with their EU-15 counterparts. For instance, Latvia (15.3 per cent), Lithuania (11.1 per cent), Estonia (10.6 per cent) and Bulgaria (12 per cent) recorded inflation rates of over 10 per cent in 2008. The only NMS that managed to keep inflation rates below 5 per cent were Cyprus (4.4 per cent), Malta (4.7 per cent), Poland (4.2 per cent) and Slovakia (3.9 per cent).

Trends in interest rates

From the beginning of the twenty-first century, global interest rates started to fall, with sizeable and successive reductions in 2001. This pattern continued within the euro area during 2002 and 2003, such that official lending rates of central banks reached historic lows. With signs of an economic recovery, there were several rate rises in the US during 2004, which were reconfirmed in 2005 and 2006. Subsequently, the federal funds rate remained unchanged between June 2006 and September 2007, when it fell to 4.75 per cent on the back of fears of a slowdown in economic activity, in particular within the housing market, with concerns over the sub-prime market.

European interest rates followed this trend, and during the period from December 2005 to July 2007 there were nine individual increases

Table 4.6 Annual inflation rates in selected EU countries, 1997–2008 (per cent)

	1997	2000	2001	2002	2003	2004	2005	2006	2007	2008	% change 1997–2008
EU-27	1.7	1.9	2.2	2.1	2.0	2.0	2.2	2.2	2.3	3.7	117.65
Euro area	1.6	2.1	2.3	2.2	2.1	2.1	2.2	2.2	2.1	3.3	106.25
Belgium	1.5	2.7	2.4	1.6	1.5	1.9	2.5	2.3	1.8	4.5	200.00
Bulgaria	10.3	10.3	7.4	5.8	2.3	6.1	6.0	7.4	7.6	12.0	16.50
C. Republic	8.0	3.9	4.5	1.4	–0.1	2.6	1.6	2.1	3.0	6.3	–21.25
Denmark	2.0	2.7	2.3	2.4	2.0	0.9	1.7	1.9	1.7	3.6	80.00
Germany	1.5	1.4	1.9	1.4	1.0	1.8	1.9	1.8	2.3	2.8	86.67
Estonia	9.3	3.9	5.6	3.6	1.4	3.0	4.1	4.4	6.7	10.6	13.98
Ireland	1.3	5.3	4.0	4.7	4.0	2.3	2.2	2.7	2.9	3.1	138.46
Greece	5.4	2.9	3.7	3.9	3.4	3.0	3.5	3.3	3.0	4.2	–22.22
Spain	1.9	3.5	2.8	3.6	3.1	3.1	3.4	3.6	2.8	4.1	115.79
France	1.3	1.8	1.8	1.9	2.2	2.3	1.9	1.9	1.6	3.2	146.15
Italy	1.9	2.6	2.3	2.6	2.8	2.3	2.2	2.2	2.0	3.5	84.21
Cyprus	3.3	4.9	2.0	2.8	4.0	1.9	2.0	2.2	2.2	4.4	33.33
Latvia	8.1	2.6	2.5	2.0	2.9	6.2	6.9	6.6	10.1	15.3	88.89
Lithuania	10.3	1.1	1.6	0.3	–1.1	1.2	2.7	3.8	5.8	11.1	7.77
Luxembourg	1.4	3.8	2.4	2.1	2.5	3.2	3.8	3.0	2.7	4.1	192.86

Table 4.6 (Continued)

	1997	2000	2001	2002	2003	2004	2005	2006	2007	2008	% change 1997–2008
Hungary	18.5	10.0	9.1	5.2	4.7	6.8	3.5	4.0	7.9	6.0	−67.57
Malta	3.9	3.0	2.5	2.6	1.9	2.7	2.5	2.6	0.7	4.7	20.51
Netherlands	1.9	2.3	5.1	3.9	2.2	1.4	1.5	1.7	1.6	2.2	15.79
Austria	1.2	2.0	2.3	1.7	1.3	2.0	2.1	1.7	2.2	3.2	166.67
Poland	15.0	10.1	5.3	1.9	0.7	3.6	2.2	1.3	2.6	4.2	−72.00
Portugal	1.9	2.8	4.4	3.7	3.3	2.5	2.1	3.0	2.4	2.7	42.11
Romania	154.8	45.7	34.5	22.5	15.3	11.9	9.1	6.6	4.9	7.9	−94.90
Slovenia	8.3	8.9	8.6	7.5	5.7	3.7	2.5	2.5	3.8	5.5	−33.73
Slovakia	6.0	12.2	7.2	3.5	8.4	7.5	2.8	4.3	1.9	3.9	−35.00
Finland	1.2	2.9	2.7	2.0	1.3	0.1	0.8	1.3	1.6	3.9	225.00
Sweden	1.8	1.3	2.7	1.9	2.3	1.0	0.8	1.5	1.7	3.3	83.33
UK	1.8	0.8	1.2	1.3	1.4	1.3	2.1	2.3	2.3	3.6	100.00

Source: Adapted by the author from Eurostat Statistical Books, European Economic Statistics, 2009.

in interest rates, as the ECB tightened its monetary policy. Following this, in October 2008, there was a coordinated interest rate reduction of 0.5 per cent by the ECB, the US Federal Reserve, the Bank of England and the central banks of Canada, Sweden and Switzerland, in order to encourage inter-bank lending, which had been affected by the global economic recession.

In terms of long-term interest rates, there is a convergence criterion for the EMU stated under Article 121 of the Treaty establishing the European Community. Article 4 of the Protocol on the convergence criteria annexed to the Treaty states that the EU countries must have an average nominal long-term interest rate that does not exceed by more than 2 per cent the three best performing EU countries in terms of price stability. Following the market turmoil that began in summer 2007 and the intervention of central banks to safeguard liquidity, the Maastricht criterion for interest rates in the euro area decreased from 4.60 per cent in July 2007 to 4.07 per cent in March 2008. Later, the rates increased within three months to 4.78 per cent in June 2008 before decreasing again, reaching 3.72 per cent in December 2008 (see Table 4.7).

In 2008, the gap between EU-27 countries' interest rates widened, with the lowest rates recorded for Sweden (3.89 per cent), Germany (3.98 per cent), the Netherlands (4.23 per cent) and France (4.23 per cent), while the highest rates were found in Hungary (8.24 per cent) and Romania (7.70 per cent). In 2000 and 2001, long-term interest rates were higher than in subsequent years, where the lowest rate in 2001 was recorded for Germany (4.80 per cent) and the highest for Poland (10.68 per cent). Between 2000 and 2005, long-term interest rates decreased significantly in the euro area, by 202 basis points, to 3.42 per cent. The lowest rate in 2005 was recorded for Ireland (3.33 per cent) and the highest in Hungary (6.60 per cent).

Moreover, inter-bank rates, which are interest rates used by banks for operations among themselves, decreased between 2000 and 2004. In contrast, the three-month Euro Area Interbank Offered Rate (EURIBOR) increased steadily in the euro area and in December 2007 reached 4.85 per cent. In February 2008, it first fell to 4.36 per cent before increasing to 5.11 per cent by October 2008. In the months that followed, central banks all over the world took measures to minimize the effect of the "credit crunch". As a result, the EURIBOR fell to 1.42 per cent in April 2009 – the lowest figure since the creation of this benchmark in 1999.

Table 4.7 Annual average long-term interest rates, 2000–2008 (per cent)

	2000	2001	2002	2003	2004	2005	2006	2007	2008	% change 2000–2008[a]
EU-27	5.44	5.01	4.93	4.24	4.39	3.7	4.03	4.57	4.55	−16.36
Euro area	5.44	5	4.91	4.14	4.12	3.42	3.84	4.32	4.3	−20.96
Austria	5.56	5.07	4.97	4.15	4.15	3.39	3.8	4.29	4.26	−23.38
Belgium	5.59	5.13	4.99	4.18	4.15	3.43	3.82	4.33	4.42	−20.93
Bulgaria	n/a	n/a	n/a	6.45	5.36	3.87	4.18	4.54	5.38	−16.59
Cyprus	n/a	7.63	5.7	4.74	5.8	5.16	4.13	4.48	4.6	−39.71
C. Republic	n/a	6.31	4.88	4.12	4.82	3.54	3.8	4.3	4.63	−26.62
Denmark	5.64	5.08	5.06	4.31	4.3	3.4	3.81	4.29	4.28	−24.11
Estonia	10.48	10.15	8.42	5.25	4.39	4.17	5.01	6.09	8.16	−22.14
Finland	5.48	5.04	4.98	4.13	4.11	3.35	3.78	4.29	4.29	−21.72
France	5.39	4.94	4.86	4.13	4.1	3.41	3.8	4.3	4.23	−21.52
Germany	5.26	4.8	4.78	4.07	4.04	3.35	3.76	4.22	3.98	−24.33
Greece	6.1	5.3	5.12	4.27	4.26	3.59	4.07	4.5	4.8	−21.31
Hungary	n/a	7.95	7.09	6.82	8.19	6.6	7.12	6.74	8.24	3.65
Ireland	5.51	5.01	5.01	4.13	4.08	3.33	3.77	4.31	4.53	−17.79
Italy	5.58	5.19	5.03	4.25	4.26	3.56	4.05	4.49	4.68	−16.13
Latvia	n/a	7.57	5.41	4.9	4.86	3.88	4.13	5.28	6.43	−15.06

Table 4.7 (Continued)

	2000	2001	2002	2003	2004	2005	2006	2007	2008	% change 2000–2008[a]
Lithuania	n/a	8.15	6.06	5.32	4.5	3.7	4.08	4.55	5.61	−31.17
Luxembourg	5.52	4.86	4.7	4.03	4.18	3.37	3.92	4.56	4.61	−16.49
Malta	n/a	6.19	5.82	5.04	4.69	4.56	4.32	4.72	4.81	−22.29
Netherlands	5.4	4.96	4.89	4.12	4.1	3.37	3.78	4.29	4.23	−21.67
Poland	n/a	10.68	7.36	5.78	6.9	5.22	5.23	5.48	6.07	−43.16
Portugal	5.59	5.16	5.01	4.18	4.14	3.44	3.91	4.42	4.52	−19.14
Romania	n/a	n/a	n/a	n/a	n/a	n/a	7.23	7.13	7.7	6.50
Slovakia	n/a	8.04	6.94	4.99	5.03	3.52	4.41	4.49	4.72	−41.29
Slovenia	n/a	n/a	8.72	6.4	4.68	3.81	3.85	4.53	4.61	−47.13
Spain	5.53	5.12	4.96	4.12	4.1	3.39	3.78	4.31	4.37	−20.98
Sweden	5.37	5.11	5.3	4.64	4.43	3.38	3.71	4.17	3.89	−27.56
UK	5.33	5.01	4.91	4.58	4.93	4.46	4.37	5.06	4.5	−15.57

[a]Percentage changes calculated during years for which data is available.
Source: Adapted by the author from Eurostat Statistical Books, European Economic Statistics, 2009.

Trends in euro exchange rates

The introduction of the euro eliminated exchange rates among the EU countries. As discussed in Chapter 2, the euro area covered 11 countries during its initial stages (Belgium, Germany, Ireland, Spain, France, Italy, Luxembourg, the Netherlands, Austria, Portugal and Finland). Later on, Greece (2001), Slovenia (2007), Cyprus and Malta (2008) and Slovakia (2009) joined the euro area. Over recent years, the currencies of the non-euro-area countries have remained stable against the euro, especially the Danish krone, the Estonian kroon, the Latvian lat and the Lithuanian litas. However, taking into account recent developments, the euro appreciated significantly against the pound sterling (by 18.1 per cent by the end of February 2009) and against the Swedish krona (by 21.9 per cent).

On the other hand, a small number of currencies appreciated against the euro during the period 2004–2007. The most significant gains were for the Romanian leu (17.7 per cent), the Polish zloty (16.4 per cent) and the Slovak koruna (15.6 per cent). This trend changed after the financial turmoil in October 2008, when the euro appreciated by the end of February 2009, compared to September 2008, against the Polish zloty by 37.7 per cent, the Hungarian forint by 23.9 per cent and the Romanian leu by 18.3 per cent (see Table 4.8).

Table 4.8 illustrates that in contrast to the moderate fluctuations between the majority of European currencies, the value of the euro increased against the currencies of important trading partners of the EU such as Japan and the US between 2002 and 2008.

The value of the euro increased by 29.1 and 50.5 per cent during the period 2000–2008 against the Japanese yen and the US dollar, respectively. However, since the second half of 2008 these currencies have appreciated significantly.

Annual employment growth

Employment performances are a key component of the Lisbon Strategy, which aims to make the EU the most competitive and dynamic knowledge-based economy in the world, capable of sustainable economic growth with more and better jobs and greater social cohesion. The Employment Guidelines introduced employment rate targets for 2010 that had been formulated by the Lisbon and Stockholm Councils in 2000/2001 as 70 per cent overall, with more than 60 per cent for women, and 50 per cent for older people. Detailed country figures on the unemployment rates for females and males over the 2001–2008 period are given in Tables 4A.2 and 4A.3 in the appendix.

Table 4.8 Euro exchange rates, annual averages, 2000–2008 (1 EUR = . . . national currency)

Currency	2000	2001	2002	2003	2004	2005	2006	2007	2008	% change 2000–2008
Czech koruna	35.599	34.068	30.804	31.846	31.891	29.782	28.342	27.766	24.946	−29.92
Danish krone	7.454	7.452	7.431	7.431	7.440	7.452	7.459	7.451	7.456	0.03
Estonian kroon	15.647	15.647	15.647	15.647	15.647	15.647	15.647	15.647	15.647	0.00
Latvian lats	0.559	0.560	0.581	0.641	0.665	0.696	0.696	0.700	0.703	25.76
Lithuanian litas	3.695	3.582	3.459	3.453	3.453	3.453	3.453	3.453	3.453	−6.55
Hungarian forint	260.4	256.59	242.96	253.62	251.66	248.05	264.26	251.35	251.51	−3.41
New Polish zloty	4.008	3.672	3.857	4.400	4.527	4.023	3.896	3.784	3.512	−12.38
Slovak koruna	42.602	43.3	42.694	41.489	40.022	38.599	37.234	33.775	31.262	−26.62
Swedish krona	8.445	9.255	9.161	9.124	9.124	9.282	9.254	9.250	9.615	13.85
UK pound sterling	0.609	0.622	0.629	0.692	0.679	0.684	0.682	0.684	0.796	30.71

Table 4.8 (Continued)

Currency	2000	2001	2002	2003	2004	2005	2006	2007	2008	% change 2000–2008
Iceland króna	72.58	87.42	86.18	86.65	87.14	78.23	87.76	87.63	143.83	98.17
Norwegian krone	8.113	8.048	7.509	8.003	8.370	8.009	8.047	8.017	8.224	1.37
Swiss franc	1.558	1.511	1.467	1.521	1.544	1.548	1.573	1.643	1.587	1.86
New Bulgarian lev	1.952	1.948	1.949	1.949	1.953	1.956	1.956	1.956	1.956	0.20
New Romanian leu	1.992	2.600	3.127	3.755	4.051	3.621	3.526	3.333	3.678	84.64
Japanese yen	99.47	108.68	118.06	130.97	134.44	136.85	146.02	161.25	152.45	53.26
US dollar	0.924	0.896	0.946	1.131	1.244	1.244	1.256	1.371	1.471	59.20

Source: Adapted by the author from Eurostat Statistical Books, European Economic Statistics, 2009.

Against these targets, the overall employment rate in the EU-25 stagnated at slightly below 63 per cent in 2003, whereas EU-15 average was 64.3 per cent (see Table 4.9). The marginal increase in the employment rate – only 0.1 per cent in 2003 – was much lower than the annual increases observed from the late 1990s until 2001, and was the result of continued rises in the employment rates for women, which were up 0.3 per cent on average to 55.0 per cent (EU-15 average was 56 per cent). In contrast, the rate declined slightly to 70.8 per cent for men (EU-15 average was 72.6 per cent).

Employment growth for the EU-25 was limited in 2003. The slowdown in employment growth, which began in the first half of 2001 and reached a stable level by the end of 2002, was followed by only a very moderate recovery in 2003. Luxembourg (+25.5 per cent), Cyprus (+22.0 per cent), Spain (+21.3 per cent) and Ireland (+19.9 per cent) experienced the highest average employment growth during the period 2001–2008. On average, 226.2 million men and women worked in the EU-27 during the year 2008. This represented a net increase of 14.7 million persons since 2001 (7.0 per cent growth). In the EU-15 the increase was 10 million persons (7.4 per cent growth). The big EU countries are naturally the biggest contributors to the increase in number of persons employed, especially Spain (+3.6 million persons), followed by Italy (+1.9 million persons), the UK (+1.7 million persons), France (+1.1 million persons) and Germany (+1 million persons).

Although, contrary to the experiences of the US and Japan, overall employment levels in the EU-27 did not essentially show any decline over the period 2000–2003, the EU labour markets showed signs of deterioration in certain areas, in particular in industry, for young people and for the low-skilled. In addition, long-term unemployment in the EU appeared to be on the rise again, increasing to 4.0 per cent in 2003 (EU-15 average was 3.3 per cent), a change from the trend of progressive decline observed, especially over the period 1998–2001.

Within the EU-27, almost half of the countries experienced negative annual employment growth. The employment situation deteriorated in 2003 in the Czech Republic, Finland, the Netherlands and Sweden. In Belgium, Denmark, Germany, Poland, Portugal and Slovenia the negative employment growth experienced in 2002 continued in 2003, while employment growth in France had ground to a standstill by the end of 2003. On the other hand, employment growth in Spain remained relatively strong at around the 2 per cent level and it was also above 1 per cent in Estonia, Greece, Ireland, Hungary, Latvia, Lithuania, Luxembourg and the Slovak Republic. Furthermore,

Table 4.9 Annual employment growth, 1996–2006 (annual percentage change)

	1996	1997	1998	1999	2000	2001	2002	2003	2004	2005	2006
EU-27	0.5	0.6	1.4	1	1.6	0.9	−0.3	0.4	0.7	0.9	1.6
Euro area	0.5	0.9	1.9	2	2.4	1.5	0.6	0.4	0.9	0.8	1.4
Austria	0.4	0.9	1.3	1.6	1	0.6	−0.1	0	0	0.5	1
Belgium	0.3	0.5	1.6	1.3	2	1.4	−0.1	0	0.6	1	1.1
Bulgaria	n/a	−3.9	−0.2	−2.1	4.9	−0.8	0.2	3	2.6	2.7	2.4
Croatia	n/a	3.2	−3	−3.3	4	−5.4	4.2	0.6	1.7	0.8	2
Cyprus	n/a	0.6	1.6	1.9	1.7	2.2	2.1	3.8	3.8	3.6	1.7
C. Republic	0.9	0.2	−1.5	−3.4	−0.2	0.5	0.6	−1.3	0.4	1	1.6
Denmark	1	1.2	1.5	1	0.4	0.8	−0.1	−1.3	0	0.7	2
Estonia	−2.3	0	−1.9	−4.4	−1.5	0.9	1.3	1.4	0	2	5.4
Finland	1.4	3.3	2	2.5	2.2	1.5	1	0.1	0.4	1.4	1.4
France	0.4	0.4	1.5	2	2.7	1.8	0.6	0.1	0.1	0.4	0.8
Germany	−0.3	−0.1	1.2	1.4	1.9	0.4	−0.6	−0.9	0.4	−0.1	0.7
Greece	−0.4	−0.5	2.9	0.3	0.5	0.3	0.2	1.5	3.4	0.9	1.5
Hungary	−0.5	0.2	1.8	3.4	1.3	0.3	0	1.3	−0.7	0	0.7
Ireland	3.6	5.6	8.6	6.2	4.6	3	1.8	2	3.1	4.7	4.3
Italy	0.6	0.3	1	1.1	1.9	2.2	1.6	1.5	0.4	0.3	1.7

Latvia	–1.9	4.4	–0.3	–1.8	–2.9	2.2	2.3	1	1.1	1.5	4.8
Lithuania	0.9	0.6	–0.8	–2.2	–4	–3.8	3.6	2.2	0	2.5	1.7
Luxembourg	2.6	3.1	4.5	5	5.5	5.6	2.9	1.8	2.3	3	3.6
Malta	1.5	0	0	0.7	8.4	1.8	0.6	1	–0.8	1.8	0.9
Netherlands	2.2	3.1	2.6	2.6	2.2	2.1	0.5	–0.5	–0.9	0	1.2
Norway	2	2.9	2.7	0.9	0.6	0.4	0.4	–1	0.5	1	3.1
Poland	1.2	1.4	1.2	–3.9	–1.6	–2.2	–3	–1.2	1.3	2.3	3.3
Portugal	n/a	n/a	n/a	1.9	1.7	1.6	0.5	–0.4	2.3	0	0.7
Romania	–1.2	–3.8	–2.3	–4.5	2.5	–0.8	–13.8	–0.7	–1.5	0.2	2.8
Slovakia	2.3	–1.2	–0.4	–2.7	–1.8	0.6	–0.5	1.8	–0.3	1.4	2.3
Slovenia	–2	–1.9	–0.2	1.4	0.8	0.5	1.5	–0.4	0.5	0.3	1.2
Spain	1.7	3.6	4.5	4.6	5.1	3.2	2.4	3.1	3.5	3.8	3.3
Sweden	–0.8	–1.3	1.6	2.1	2.4	1.9	0.2	–0.3	–0.6	0.4	1.8
UK	0.9	1.8	1	1.4	1.2	0.8	0.8	1	1	0.9	0.8

Source: Adapted by the author from Eurostat Statistical Books, European Economic Statistics, 2007.

employment growth in Italy remained positive at around the 1 per cent level, although it had declined from previously higher levels.

Despite the deceleration in economic growth, employment growth in the EU-27 continued to recover gradually from the low in 2003, but was still lower than the levels observed in the late 1990s and 2000s. Reflecting the moderate improvement in labour market conditions, the employment rate in the EU-27 increased to 63.8 per cent in 2005 (from 63.3 per cent in 2004), while the unemployment rate declined to 8.7 per cent (down from 9.1 per cent the year before).

Much of the weak employment performance of the EU over recent years has been due to the relatively poor labour market performance in Germany and Poland, although recent figures indicate that the situation may be finally turning around. At the same time, many of the southern EU countries remain well below the common EU employment targets, and still tend to exhibit marked gender differences in labour market outcomes, together with large disparities in the performance of labour markets at regional level. At individual country level, employment performance for 2005 as a whole was generally positive, with negative annual employment growth only in Germany and the Netherlands. For the vast majority of EU countries, employment expanded in 2005, with growth of over 1 per cent in ten countries. Particularly strong growth was experienced in Luxembourg (2.9 per cent), Spain (3.6 per cent) and Ireland (4.7 per cent).

Figure 4.4 presents the relationship between real GDP growth and total employment growth in the EU-27 countries on average. In 2005, employment growth in the EU continued to recover gradually from the low in 2003, despite the deceleration in economic growth compared with 2004, but remains well down on the levels observed in the late 1990s and 2000. Employment growth averaged 0.9 per cent in 2005, up on the previous year's level of 0.5 per cent.

For a more in-depth investigation, employment rates in the EU-15, EU-25, US and Japan over the 1975–2005 period are detailed in Figure 4.5. In the US, the labour market continued to show strong signs of recovery. Employment continued to expand at a faster rate than in the EU-15 and EU-25, with growth accelerating to 1.8 per cent, up from 1.1 per cent the year before and approaching the rates experienced at the end of the twentieth century. The unemployment rate fell to just above the 5 per cent level, down from 5.5 per cent in 2004. In Japan, the turnaround in the labour market observed in 2004 continued in 2005. Employment growth was positive for the second consecutive year, although, at 0.4 per cent, it was much lower than in the EU and the US, while the unemployment rate fell from 4.7 per cent to 4.4 per cent.

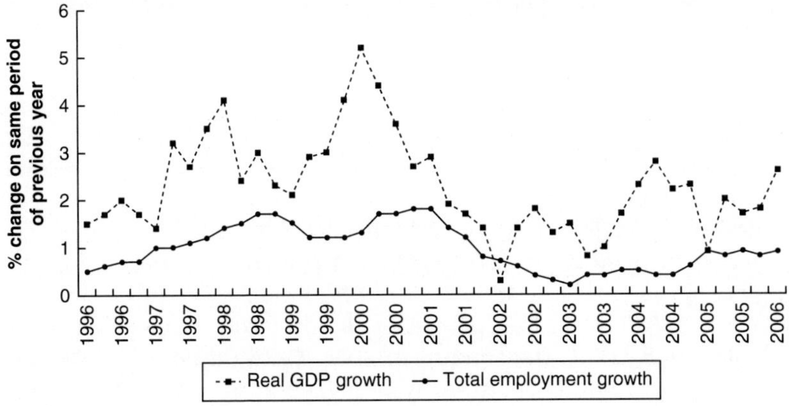

Figure 4.4 Comparison of real GDP growth and employment growth in the EU-27, 1996–2006 (annual per cent change)
Source: Eurostat, national accounts (various years).

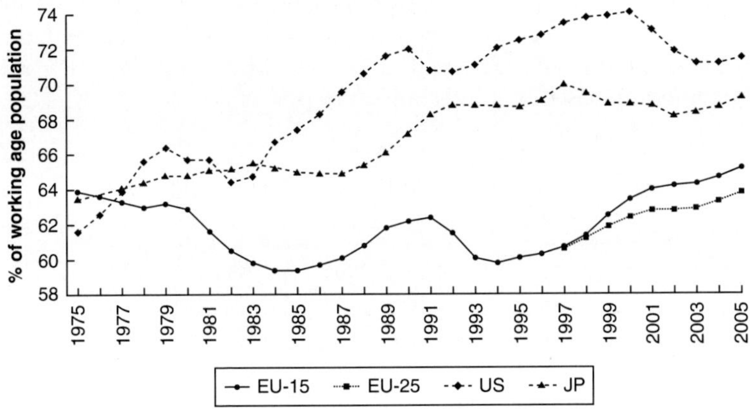

Figure 4.5 Employment rates in the EU, US and Japan, 1975–2005
Source: DG EMPL calculation based on long-term trends in employment and population, Commission Services.

Foreign direct investment (FDI)

In a world of increasing globalization, where political, economic and technological barriers are rapidly disappearing, the ability of a country to participate in global activity is an important indicator of its performance and competitiveness. In order to remain competitive in the enlarged EU, many firms experienced mergers, partnerships, joint ventures, licensing agreements and other forms of business cooperation, which can be attributable to the basics of FDI. Over the last decade, FDI in the EU has expanded more rapidly for the services sector than for goods, and as a result the European services sector has become increasingly international.

However, FDI flows fluctuate considerably from one year to the next, generally increasing during times of rapid growth, while decreasing during periods of recession. Inflows of FDI from non-EU countries into the EU-27 were valued at EUR 319,161 million in 2007, which was about double (90 per cent) the amount in 2006. Outward flows of FDI from the EU-27 to non-EU countries were valued at EUR 419,912 million. Despite the rapid increase in inward flows of FDI, the EU-27 remained a net investor abroad with net outflows of EUR 100,751 million in 2007.

Moreover, it is known that stocks of FDI show the value of all previous investments at the end of the reference period. Inward FDI stocks for the EU-27 accounted for 17.7 per cent of GDP in 2006, while outward FDI stocks were valued at 23.2 per cent of GDP. It should be noted that the relatively high importance of FDI in Luxembourg should be interpreted with caution, and results mainly from the role of Luxembourg-based holding companies (see Table 4.10).

Table 4.10 Net FDI flows with rest of the world, 2004–2007 (EUR billion)

	2004	2005	2006	2007
EU-27	84	110.3	116.2	124.1
Belgium	−7.7	−1.4	−6.5	−12.8
Bulgaria	−2.9	−2.9	−5.9	−6.3
C. Republic	−3.2	−0.94	−3.2	−5.7
Denmark	n/a	2.7	4.6	6.3
Germany	24.8	21.6	31.5	86.3
Estonia	−0.6	−1.7	−0.5	−0.8
Ireland	23.1	37	16.6	−7.2
Greece	−0.9	0.7	−1	2.5
Spain	28.8	13.5	58.5	49.5
France	19.5	24.2	34.4	48.7
Italy	2	17.6	2.3	37
Cyprus	−0.3	−0.5	−0.8	−0.7
Latvia	−0.4	−0.5	−1.2	−1.4
Lithuania	−0.4	−0.5	−1.2	−1

Luxembourg	4	6.8	−11.5	44.9
Hungary	−2.7	−4.4	−0.9	−3.3
Malta	−0.3	−0.6	−1.5	0.7
Netherlands	19.8	67.6	46	−65.6
Austria	3.6	0.4	4.6	3.1
Poland	−9.7	−5.5	−8.5	−13.2
Portugal	4.4	−1.5	−3.5	0.4
Romania	n/a	−5.2	−8.7	−7.1
Slovenia	−0.2	−0.1	0.2	0.2
Slovakia	−2.5	−1.8	6.96	6.97
Finland	−3.1	−0.4	−2	−3.1
Sweden	7.3	13	−2	12.1
UK	28.2	−76.6	−55.7	67.3

– Net = outward minus inward investment flows.
– Negative values denote disinvestment.
Source: Adapted by the author from ECB (2008c).

Macroeconomic structure of the EU candidate countries

Strong trade links exist between the Western Balkan countries, the EU and the euro area, which has facilitated the use of the euro as an invoicing currency in these countries. Western Balkan foreign trade with the EU-27, as a percentage of total trade, ranged in 2007 from around 46 per cent in Montenegro to 65 per cent in Albania. Although the share of EU-27 trade has been declining since 2003, the average level stood at around 55 per cent in the Western Balkan economies (see Figure 4.6).

The share of euro-denominated foreign exchange reserves in total reserves has been rising significantly in the whole of the Western Balkans region since 2002, and reached 86 per cent in Croatia, 82 per cent in the FYROM and 55 per cent in Albania in 2007. An additional factor contributing to the growing role of the euro as a reserve currency might be the growing share of euro-denominated debt in total foreign debt: in 2006 this reached 45 per cent in Croatia, 61 per cent in the FYROM and 75 per cent for Serbia. In addition, the strong inflow of FDI from the EU into the region during recent years has probably contributed to the growing role of the euro as a reserve currency.

In addition, the countries with EU membership prospects have increased their attention to the EMU's objectives. The candidate and potential candidate countries from the Western Balkans are becoming increasingly aware of the need for a rapid real convergence towards EU members' income levels, while targeting in parallel a medium-term

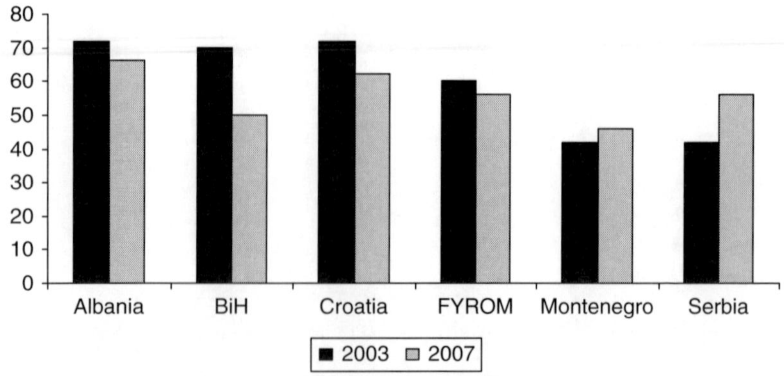

Figure 4.6 Trade with the EU, 2003–2007 (per cent of total trade)
Source: European Commission (October, 2008).

nominal convergence towards the Maastricht criteria. As discussed earlier in this book, the successful candidates need to fulfil the Copenhagen economic criteria, which require the existence of a functioning market economy and the capacity to cope with competitive pressure and market forces in the EU.

Therefore, the Western Balkan countries are pursuing a wide range of reforms in order to achieve macroeconomic stability, liberalize markets, restructure and privatize the state-owned industries, improve their business environment, and build human and physical capital. Being part of the accession process represents an additional guarantee to investors and international capital markets that the Western Balkan economies are pursuing sound public policies. This further reinforces credibility and financial stability in the region.

Economic growth in the Western Balkans

The economies of candidate countries in the Western Balkans recorded moderate to strong growth over 2003–2007, driven by both strong investment and private consumption. The most dynamic economy was that of Serbia, which has grown by 6.1 per cent on average during 2003–2007 period. It was closely followed by those of Albania, Bosnia and Herzegovina, Montenegro and Croatia. The Montenegrin economy accelerated in 2006 and 2007 against the backdrop of the FDI boom. The slowest economies were Kosovo and the FYROM, but, as in the entire region, their economies have picked up from 2006 to 2007. Growth is driven by a strong increase in private consumption in all economies but investment is also increasing steadily in most of them. The growth of

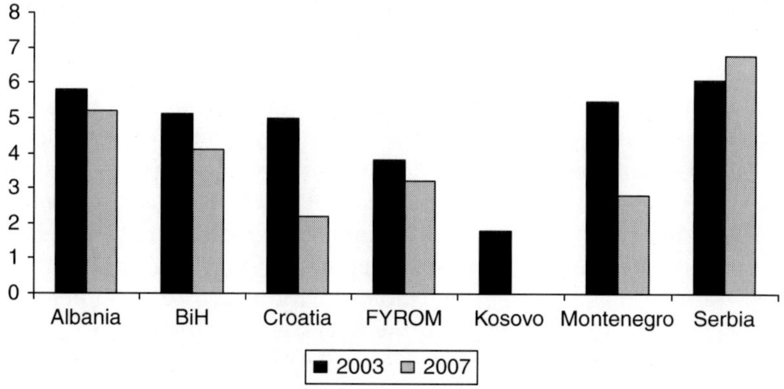

Figure 4.7 Economic growth in the Western Balkans (average per cent of 2003–2007)
Source: European Commission (October, 2008).

labour productivity in excess of real GDP growth was recorded in Serbia, Albania, the FYROM, and Bosnia and Herzegovina (see Figure 4.7).

The 1990s were years of financial and economic turmoil in the Western Balkans. The effects of three simultaneous crises, namely the breaking up of the Socialist Federal Republic of Yugoslavia, war among or within successor republics, and the dismantling of the planned economy based on social ownership led to GDP dropping sharply to pre-1990 levels in all the former Yugoslav republics. In Croatia, it came down by 60 per cent in 1993 compared with 1990. In Bosnia and Herzegovina (BiH), Serbia and Kosovo, GDP dropped to less than 45 per cent of 1990 levels.

The dismantling of the Yugoslav federation led to a fragmentation of a previously unitary economic space. National currencies were introduced into Croatia in 1991 (the Croatian dinar, replaced by the kuna in May 1994) and in the FYROM in 1992 (the denar). BiH introduced its own dinar in 1992, and, following the 1995 Dayton Peace Agreement, established a currency board arrangement and the convertible mark (KM). Moreover, Montenegro, the smaller of the two member states of the Federal Republic of Yugoslavia, unilaterally declared the deutsche mark parallel legal tender to the Yugoslav dinar in November 1999. In 2001 the deutsche mark became sole legal tender, replaced by the euro in 2002. In Kosovo, UNMIK introduced the DM in 1999, followed by the euro as of 2002.

Inflation had already reached high levels in the Socialist Federal Republic of Yugoslavia in the 1970s and 1980s. In the period 1971–1991, the average annual inflation rate had been around 70 per cent, and this further accelerated towards the end of the period, with monthly inflation numbers of more than 50 per cent in 1989. The situation was aggravated under war conditions in the early 1990s with the monetization of public deficits and wide-scale corruption. Hyperinflation in Serbia–Montenegro in 1993–1994 destroyed any possible remaining confidence in the national currency; it reached the record level of 313 million per cent in January 1994 and led to the closure and liquidation of numerous enterprises, including large banks. In Croatia, one of the wealthiest countries of the region, inflation reached 1500 per cent in 1993, prompting severe adjustment measures, which reduced it to 2 per cent in 1995.

Croatia and the FYROM de facto pegged their currencies to the euro since its inception, although officially their exchange rates are managed floats. In BiH a currency board arrangement was introduced in 1997, with the currency pegged to the deutsche mark (DM) and, as of 1 January 2002, to the euro. From 2003 to 2005, Serbia opted for a soft peg approach, pursuing a nominal depreciation of the dinar in order to stabilize the real exchange rate. More recently, it has moved towards an inflation-targeting regime. In all cases, the base money coverage by central bank currency reserves has remained above 100 per cent, meaning that even in countries who have hard peg solutions, the monetary regime still retained some of the main features of a currency board.

Initially, Albania adopted a managed float approach with the aim of stabilizing the exchange rate and it announced its intention to move towards an inflation-targeting regime. Montenegro and Kosovo represent special cases, with the use of the euro as legal tender. Under the new monetary regimes, inflation was progressively brought down close to EU levels, except for Serbia where stabilization started only at the end of 2000 and inflation has been reduced gradually to a single-digit rate (6.8 per cent at the end of 2007). Pegs were, overall, remarkably sustainable. Even in the FYROM, in spite of important foreign exchange tensions in the first half of 2001 when civil hostilities erupted in the country, the Central Bank was eventually able to hold the (informal) peg with limited fluctuations and by the end of the year the exchange rate of the denar vis-à-vis the euro had broadly come back to pre-crisis levels.

At present, Albania and Croatia are faced with domestic currency appreciation pressures owing to large capital inflows and rising productivity. The wide use of the euro within the regions might be attributable to several reasons, which include geographic proximity to the euro area, economic linkages, migration patterns and the desire to

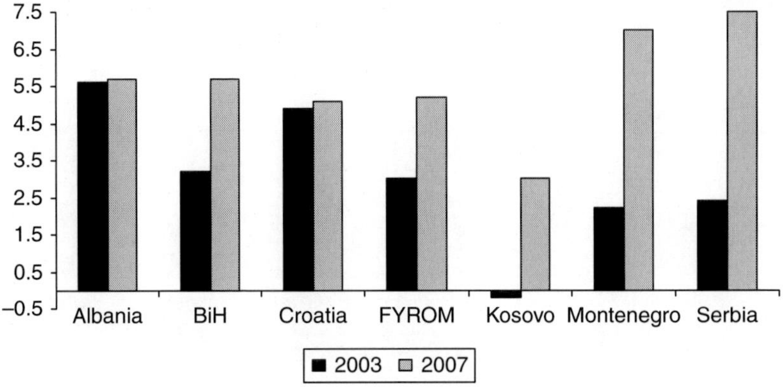

Figure 4.8 Real GDP growth in the Western Balkans (annual per cent change)
Source: European Commission (October, 2008).

minimize risk, as well as strong historical determinants, as previously mentioned.

Economic growth in the Western Balkan countries is observed as favourable, compared with the more mature economies. After initial output losses as a result of the violent conflicts of the region and initial transition steps, the economies started to quickly stabilize, and the average growth rate increased from about 3 per cent in 2003 to 6 per cent in 2007 (see Figure 4.8). The highest increases were observed in Montenegro and Serbia, while, conversely, there was not a sizeable increase in Albania and Croatia. This might be due to the fact that the last two were already performing well prior to the analysis period.

The real GDP growth in the region is particularly supported by the EU accession perspective, which promotes sound economic policies and increased amounts of FDI, thus contributing to the modernization of productive capacities in the region. However, the growth potential in the region remains lower than that in the Baltics or other NMS, which have been growing faster in recent years. Looking at Figure 4.9, if the lower starting point in terms of GDP per capita in PPP (as a share of the EU average) is taken into account (except for Croatia), the Western Balkans appear as a region that still needs to give free rein to its growth potential.

Inflation rates in the Western Balkans

The re-emergence of inflationary pressures, led by a global rise in food and oil prices in the second half of 2007, affected the Western Balkans. In the first quarter of 2008, inflation accelerated above 11 per cent in

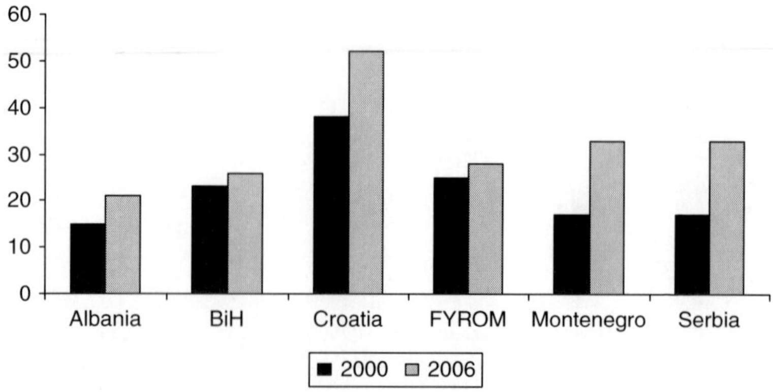

Figure 4.9 GDP in PPP terms in the Western Balkans, 2000–2006 (per cent of EU average)
Source: European Commission (October, 2008).

Serbia and Kosovo, 9.5 per cent in the FYROM, and rose above 6 per cent in BiH and 8 per cent in Montenegro. On the other hand, it remained moderate in Albania and Croatia. The inflation rise recorded in the EU-27 reflects primarily the higher share of food and energy prices in the local consumer price index (CPI) baskets. In some economies, the liberalization of administered prices will still play an important role in terms of nominal price convergence with the euro area in future years.

Public debt in the Western Balkans

Over recent years, domestic policies, supported by IMF programmes, have, overall, been tightened and provided for a fiscal consolidation. A sizeable adjustment took place in Albania, Bosnia and Herzegovina, and the FYROM, and more recently in Kosovo, Montenegro and Croatia. Kosovo remains a special case with a high volatility of budget outcomes. In fact, the pattern of fiscal consolidation has been quite different among countries. From 2000 to 2007 fiscal consolidation was mainly achieved through a mix of expenditure reduction as a share of GDP and revenue increases in candidate countries in the region, whereas potential candidate countries mainly relied on growing revenues from tax collection.

As a result, this fiscal consolidation created a reduction in public debt in the region. Figure 4.10 compares 2003 and 2007 figures in each of these countries. In Serbia and Montenegro, favourable agreements

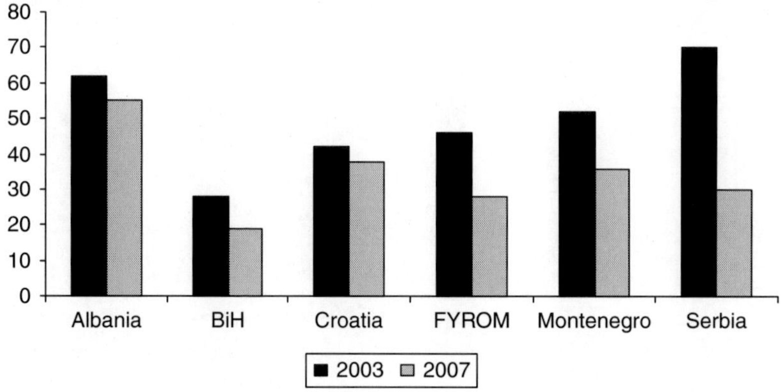

Figure 4.10 Public debt in the Western Balkans, 2003–2007 (per cent of GDP)
Source: European Commission (October, 2008).

reached with the Paris Club (66 per cent debt reduction) and the London Club further allowed for a spectacular reduction of public sovereign debt. However, some countries are still facing significant contingent liabilities, in particular Bosnia and Herzegovina, where war-related claims on the governments and other domestic liabilities could substantially add to official debt figures and call for prudent fiscal policies. Kosovo, under the UN administration, has not placed any international claims, nor issued any public borrowing.

External debt in the Western Balkans

The good coverage of deficits with non-debt financial inflows diminished public external debt and maintained robust GDP growth. The only country where external debt-to-GDP increased from 2003 to 2007 was Croatia (see Figure 4.11). Croatia stands out in the group as the country with the largest external burden. Furthermore, most of the countries displayed a comfortable level of official foreign exchange reserves. In Montenegro and Kosovo, the cushion provided by official reserves is relatively lower than in the other economies due to their special monetary arrangements with the EU.

FDI in the Western Balkans

Several Western Balkan economies, including Croatia, the FYROM, Albania and Montenegro, are relatively advanced with respect to increasing private ownership and aligning legislation with the EU acquis,

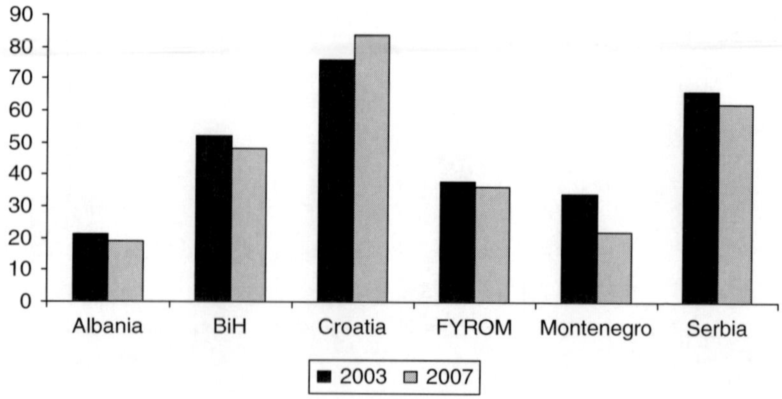

Figure 4.11 External debt in the Western Balkans, 2003–2007 (per cent of GDP)
Source: European Commission (October, 2008).

whereas Bosnia and Herzegovina, Kosovo and Serbia are less advanced. Nonetheless, the remaining challenges in ensuring an adequate functioning of markets are significant for all of them. In most of these countries, labour markets are not flexible enough, while wages in the registered economy are subject to a relatively high taxation of labour and distorted wage-setting mechanisms. Under these circumstances, competitiveness is most likely facilitated by the considerable informal sector, which results in inadequate social protection for unofficial employees and forgone revenues to the budgets.

Private ownership of companies is generally regarded as more efficient and better able to react to changing market conditions than state ownership. In the Western Balkans, the transition to a market economy started later than in Central and Eastern Europe and on average took longer. At present, the private sector's share of output has reached a relatively high level, particularly in Croatia, the FYROM, Albania and Montenegro. However, even in the more advanced economies, such as those of Croatia and Albania, privatization and restructuring have progressed slowly. In fact, the weight of the private sector is insufficient in Serbia, BiH and, to a smaller extent, in Kosovo. As a result, quasi fiscal deficits remain significant in the sector of state-owned enterprises.

FDI inflows rose in the Western Balkans between 2003 and 2007, mainly as a result of an improving business environment, accelerated privatization and ample global liquidity coupled with a buoyant investor sentiment. In all economies except for Albania and

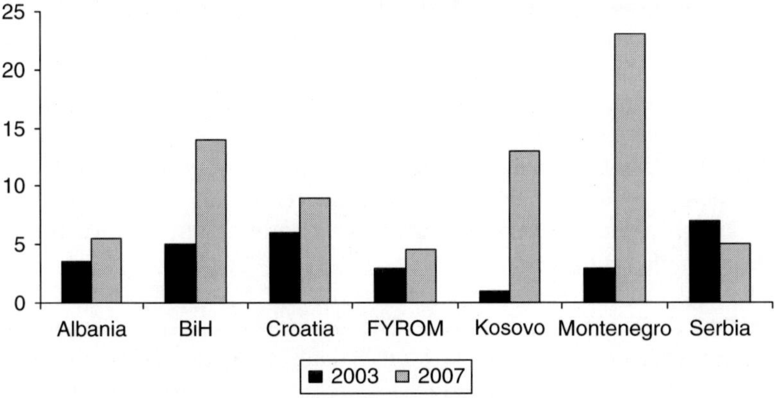

Figure 4.12 Net FDI in the Western Balkans, 2003–2007 (per cent of GDP)
Source: European Commission (October, 2008).

the FYROM, net FDI exceeded, on average, 5 per cent of GDP between 2003 and 2007 (see Figure 4.12). About half of the very high levels of FDI recorded in Montenegro in 2005–2007 went into real estate activities. The coverage of current account deficits with net FDI over the period was reasonably good in Montenegro, the former Yugoslav Republic of Macedonia, Croatia and Serbia.

Conclusion

In describing numerous macroeconomic factors in the EU region, this chapter has highlighted several important points. First, the population of the EU-27 grew from 403 million in 1960 to over 495 million in 2007, and is forecasted to be 504 million in 2035 and to fall to 494 million by 2050. Secondly, the recent synchronized global economic slowdown affected the EU-27 countries, which experienced 0.8 per cent real GDP growth rate in 2008, considerably lower than 2007 (2.9 per cent), and a similar trend is observed in the EU-15 countries with 2.6 and 0.5 per cent in 2007 and 2008, respectively. In contrast, Estonia, Latvia, Lithuania and Slovakia experienced more than 15 per cent recession, and the EU-15 around 7 per cent recession over the 2007–2008 period.

Thirdly, in terms of GDP per capita, the lowest levels were recorded in Bulgaria and Romania, where living standards were approximately 40 per cent of the EU-27 average in 2007. In fact, all the NMS countries had a lower GDP per capita in PPP terms than the EU-15 and MU-16 averages. On the other hand, the Netherlands, Austria, Sweden,

Luxembourg and Ireland recorded the highest GDP per capita figures. Fourthly, much of the weak employment performance of the EU over recent years has been due to the relatively poor labour market performance in Germany and Poland, although recent figures indicate that the situation may be finally turning around. At the same time, many of the southern EU countries remain well below the common EU employment targets, and still tend to exhibit marked gender differences in labour market outcomes, together with large disparities in the performance of labour markets at regional level.

For EU candidate countries, the euro plays a key role in their economic and financial architecture. The widespread use of the euro as an exchange-rate anchor in the Western Balkan economies is a main driver for the other functions played by the euro in terms of trade invoicing, official reserves, and financial and parallel currency. Mainly due to geographic proximity and traditional economic linkages, which are in turn based on large relative comparative advantages, the EU and, in particular, the euro area, represents the most important trading partner of the Western Balkan. In fact, five out of the seven Western Balkan economies are using fixed exchange-rate arrangements. Moreover, the use of the euro as financial currency is extensive in all seven economies, which also reflects a strong process of financial integration between the region and the euro area.

Appendix

Table 4A.1 World population and population projections, 1960–2050 (millions)

	1960	1970	1980	1990	2000	2005	2010	2015	2020	2025	2030	2035	2040	2045	2050	% change 1960–2050
World	3032	3699	4451	5295	6124	6515	6907	7295	7667	8011	8318	8587	8824	9026	9191	203.13
EU-27	403	435	457	470	483	491	498	502	505	506	506	504	501	498	494	22.58
China	657	831	999	1149	1270	1313	1352	1389	1421	1446	1458	1458	1448	1431	1409	114.46
India	446	549	689	860	1046	1134	1220	1303	1379	1447	1506	1554	1597	1632	1658	271.75
Russia	120	130	139	149	147	144	140	136	132	128	124	120	116	112	108	–10.00
US	186	210	231	256	285	300	315	329	343	355	366	376	386	394	402	116.13

Source: Adapted by the author from Eurostat, United Nations, Population Division of the Department of Economic and Social Affairs, various years.

Table 4A.2 Unemployment rates of European countries (females), 2001–2008

	2001	2002	2003	2004	2005	2006	2007	2008	% change 2001–2008
EU-27	9.4	9.7	9.7	9.8	9.6	8.9	7.8	7.5	−20.21
Euro area	9.3	9.5	9.8	10	9.9	9.3	8.4	8.2	−11.83
Belgium	7.5	8.6	8.9	9.5	9.5	9.3	8.5	7.6	1.33
Bulgaria	18.6	17.3	13.2	11.5	9.8	9.3	7.3	5.8	−68.82
C. Republic	9.7	9	9.9	9.9	9.8	8.9	6.7	5.6	−42.27
Denmark	5	5	6.1	6	5.3	4.5	4.2	3.7	−26.00
Germany	7.4	7.9	8.7	9.1	10.1	9.4	8.3	7.2	−2.70
Estonia	12.2	9.7	9.9	8.9	7.1	5.6	3.9	5.3	−56.56
Ireland	3.8	4.1	4.3	4.1	4	4.2	4.2	4.8	26.32
Greece	16.1	15.7	15	16.2	15.3	13.6	12.8	11.4	−29.19
Spain	14.8	15.7	15.3	14.3	12.2	11.6	10.9	13	−12.16
France	9.9	9.7	10	10.3	10.2	10.1	8.9	8.3	−16.16
Italy	12.2	11.5	11.4	10.6	10.1	8.8	7.9	8.5	−30.33
Cyprus	5.3	4.5	4.8	6	6.5	5.4	4.6	4.3	−18.87
Latvia	11.5	11	10.4	10.2	8.7	6.2	5.6	6.9	−40.00
Lithuania	14.3	12.8	12.2	11.8	8.3	5.4	4.3	5.6	−60.84
Luxembourg	2.4	3.5	4.9	6.8	6	6	5.1	6	150.00
Hungary	5	5.4	5.6	6.1	7.4	7.8	7.7	8.1	62.00

Malta	9.3	9.3	9.1	9	8.9	8.7	7.6	6.5	−30.11
Netherlands	2.8	3.1	3.9	4.8	5.1	4.4	3.6	3	7.14
Austria	4.2	4.4	4.7	5.4	5.5	5.2	5	4.1	−2.38
Poland	19.9	21	20.5	20	19.2	14.9	10.4	8	−59.80
Portugal	5.1	6.1	7.3	7.7	8.8	9.1	9.7	9	76.47
Romania	6.1	7.9	6.4	6.9	6.4	6.1	5.4	4.7	−22.95
Slovenia	6.8	6.8	7.1	6.9	7.1	7.2	5.9	4.8	−29.41
Slovakia	18.7	18.7	17.8	19.2	17.2	14.7	12.7	10.9	−41.71
Finland	9.7	9.1	8.9	8.9	8.6	8.1	7.2	6.7	−30.93
Sweden	4.5	4.6	5.2	6.1	7.4 b	7.2	6.4	6.5	44.44
UK	4.4	4.5	4.3	4.2	4.3	4.9	5	5.1	15.91

Source: Adapted by the author from ECB, various years.

Table 4A.3 Unemployment rates of European countries (males), 2001–2008

	2001	2002	2003	2004	2005	2006	2007	2008	% change 2001–2008
EU-27	7.7	8.3	8.4	8.5	8.3	7.6	6.6	6.6	−14.29
Euro area	6.7	7.2	7.7	7.9	8	7.4	6.6	6.9	2.99
Belgium	5.9	6.7	7.7	7.5	7.6	7.4	6.7	6.5	10.17
Bulgaria	20.2	18.9	14.1	12.6	10.3	8.7	6.5	5.5	−72.77
C. Republic	6.7	6	6.2	7.1	6.5	5.8	4.2	3.5	−47.76
Denmark	4.1	4.3	4.8	5.1	4.4	3.3	3.5	3	−26.83
Germany	7.8	8.8	9.8	10.3	11.2	10.2	8.5	7.4	−5.13
Estonia	12.6	10.8	10.2	10.4	8.8	6.2	5.4	5.8	−53.97
Ireland	4.1	4.8	5	4.9	4.6	4.7	4.9	7.5	82.93
Greece	7.2	6.8	6.2	6.6	6.1	5.6	5.2	5.1	−29.17
Spain	7.5	8.1	8.2	8	7.1	6.3	6.4	10.1	34.67
France	7	7.7	8.1	8.4	8.4	8.5	7.8	7.2	2.86
Italy	7.1	6.7	6.5	6.4	6.2	5.4	4.9	5.5	−22.54
Cyprus	2.6	2.9	3.6	3.6	4.3	4	3.4	3.3	26.92
Latvia	14.2	13.3	10.6	10.6	9.1	7.4	6.4	8	−43.66
Lithuania	18.6	14.2	12.7	11	8.2	5.8	4.3	6.1	−67.20
Luxembourg	1.6	2	3	3.6	3.6	3.6	3.4	4	150.00
Hungary	6.3	6.2	6.1	6.1	7	7.2	7.1	7.6	20.63

Malta	6.9	6.6	6.9	6.6	6.4	6.3	5.9	5.6	−18.84
Netherlands	1.8	2.5	3.5	4.3	4.5	3.5	2.8	2.5	38.89
Austria	3.1	4	4	4.5	4.9	4.3	3.9	3.6	16.13
Poland	16.9	19.2	19	18.2	16.6	13	9	6.4	−62.13
Portugal	3.2	4.2	5.6	5.9	6.8	6.6	6.7	6.6	106.25
Romania	7.3	9.2	7.6	9.1	7.8	8.2	7.2	6.7	−8.22
Slovenia	5.7	5.9	6.3	5.9	6.1	4.9	4	4	−29.82
Slovakia	19.8	18.6	17.4	17.4	15.5	12.3	9.9	8.4	−57.58
Finland	8.6	9.1	9.2	8.7	8.2	7.4	6.5	6.1	−29.07
Sweden	5.2	5.3	6	6.5	7.5 b	6.9	5.8	5.9	13.46
UK	5.5	5.7	5.5	5.1	5.2	5.8	5.6	6.1	10.91

Source: Adapted by the author from ECB, various years.

Table 4A.4 Current account balances of EU countries, 2005–2008 (EUR billion)

Countries	2005	2006	2007	2008	% change 2005–2008
Austria	4.9	7.1	8.4	9.8	100.00
Belgium	7.9	6.3	5.7	−8.7	−210.13
Bulgaria	−2.8	−4.7	−7.3	−8.6	−207.14
Cyprus	−0.8	−1.1	−1.8	−3.1	−287.50
C. Republic	−1.3	−2.9	−4	−4.6	−253.85
Denmark	9	6.3	1.6	4.8	−46.67
Estonia	−1.1	−2.2	−2.8	−1.5	−36.36
Finland	5.7	7.5	7.5	3.8	−33.33
France	−10.9	−10.2	−19.7	−36.4	−233.94
Germany	114.6	150.9	191.3	164.8	43.80
Greece	−14.7	−23.7	−32.4	−35	−138.10
Hungary	−6.6	−6.8	−6.5	−8.8	−33.33
Ireland	−5.7	−6.4	−10.3	−8.4	−47.37
Italy	−23.6	−38.5	−37.4	−53.6	−127.12
Latvia	−1.6	−3.6	−4.7	−2.9	−81.25
Lithuania	−1.5	−2.6	−4.2	−3.8	−153.33
Luxembourg	3.3	3.5	3.6	2	−39.39
Malta	−0.4	−0.4	−0.3	−0.4	0.00
Netherlands	37.3	50.4	43.5	44.6	19.57
Poland	−3	−7.4	−14.6	−19.8	−560.00
Portugal	−14.2	−15.6	−15.4	−20.2	−42.25
Romania	−6.9	−10.2	−16.7	−16.8	−143.48
Slovakia	−3.3	−3.7	−3.1	−4.3	−30.30
Slovenia	−0.5	−0.7	−1.4	−2.1	−320.00
Spain	−66.9	−88.3	−105.4	−104.5	−56.20
Sweden	20.4	26.4	28.5	27.4	34.31
UK	−47.8	−66.1	−59	−28.9	39.54

Source: Adapted by the author from ECB, various years.

Table 4A.5 Comparison of macroeconomic structure in EU countries, 2004–2008

Countries	Share of GDP (%)					Share of the total population (%)				
	2004	2005	2006	2007	2008	2004	2005	2006	2007	2008
EU-27	100.00	100.00	100.00	100.00	100.00	100.00	100.00	100.00	100.00	100.00
Euro area	73.88	73.55	73.18	72.21	73.62	67.78	67.85	67.91	64.39	64.71
Belgium	2.75	2.76	2.75	2.71	2.75	2.26	2.26	2.27	2.14	2.13
Bulgaria	n/a	n/a	n/a	0.23	0.27	n/a	n/a	n/a	1.55	1.54
C. Republic	0.84	0.91	0.98	1.03	1.19	2.22	2.21	2.21	2.08	2.09
Denmark	1.87	1.89	1.89	1.83	1.86	1.17	1.17	1.17	1.10	1.10
Germany	21.01	20.45	20.11	19.65	19.95	17.92	17.82	17.72	16.58	16.48
Estonia	0.09	0.10	0.11	0.12	0.13	0.29	0.29	0.29	0.27	0.27
Ireland	1.42	1.48	1.53	1.54	1.48	0.88	0.90	0.92	0.88	0.89
Greece	1.77	1.80	1.84	1.85	1.94	2.40	2.40	2.40	2.26	2.25
Spain	7.99	8.29	8.50	8.50	8.75	9.27	9.38	9.48	9.04	9.15
France	15.77	15.75	15.62	15.33	15.59	13.57	13.61	13.64	12.85	12.87
Italy	13.22	13.04	12.85	12.50	12.57	12.64	12.67	12.68	11.96	12.02
Cyprus	0.12	0.12	0.13	0.13	0.14	0.16	0.16	0.17	0.16	0.16
Latvia	0.11	0.12	0.14	0.17	0.18	0.50	0.50	0.49	0.46	0.45

Table 4A.5 (Continued)

Countries	Share of GDP (%)					Share of the total population (%)				
	2004	2005	2006	2007	2008	2004	2005	2006	2007	2008
Lithuania	0.17	0.19	0.21	0.23	0.26	0.75	0.74	0.73	0.68	0.67
Luxembourg	0.26	0.28	0.29	0.29	0.29	0.10	0.10	0.10	0.10	0.10
Hungary	0.78	0.81	0.78	0.82	0.85	2.20	2.18	2.17	2.03	2.01
Malta	0.04	0.04	0.04	0.04	0.05	0.09	0.09	0.09	0.08	0.08
Netherlands	4.67	4.68	4.67	4.60	4.76	3.54	3.53	3.52	3.30	3.30
Austria	2.21	2.22	2.22	2.19	2.25	1.78	1.78	1.78	1.68	1.67
Poland	1.94	2.23	2.35	2.51	2.89	8.29	8.25	8.20	7.68	7.65
Portugal	1.37	1.36	1.34	1.32	1.33	2.28	2.28	2.28	2.14	2.13
Romania	n/a	n/a	n/a	1.00	1.10	n/a	n/a	n/a	4.34	4.31
Slovenia	0.26	0.26	0.27	0.28	0.30	0.43	0.43	0.43	0.41	0.41
Slovakia	0.32	0.35	0.39	0.44	0.52	1.17	1.16	1.16	1.09	1.08
Finland	1.45	1.43	1.44	1.45	1.48	1.14	1.13	1.13	1.07	1.07
Sweden	2.73	2.69	2.71	2.68	2.62	1.95	1.95	1.95	1.84	1.85
UK	16.84	16.73	16.82	16.54	14.51	13.00	13.02	13.03	12.29	12.31

Source: Adapted by the author from ECB, various years.

5

Recent Structure of European Banking

Introduction

This chapter reviews the key features of the European banking industry: its size, structure and statistics on the technological advances over the period 2001–2008. It is designed to provide readers with an examination and comparison of the overall structure of banks operating in individual EU countries related to different subgroups (that is, the euro area, the EU-27 and NMS) and the banking sector's recent regulatory developments. First it considers the overall size of the European banking sector, with an emphasis on the number of banks, branches and employees both at EU average and individual country levels. Then the focus of attention is shifted to the wave of mergers and acquisitions (M&As) and the application of technological advances in individual EU countries.

Regulatory developments in the EU banking sector

Following the introduction of the euro and the most recent waves of enlargement, during 2004 and early 2005 there were three eye-catching regulatory developments in the European banking sector:

1. ***Implementation of the Basel II***: in an attempt to improve the existing rules of the Basel I, the Basel Committee published the final version of the new capital adequacy rules, known as Basel II, in June 2004. Following this, in July 2004, the European Commission released its own proposals for the new capital adequacy requirements for European banks and investment firms. Specialists agree that the Basel II rules are more risk-sensitive than the Basel I rules, as they require less capital for higher quality loans and more capital for lower quality loans.

2. ***Presentation of the Green Paper on Financial Services Policy covering the period 2005–2010***: this action took place following the completion of the Financial Services Action Plan (FSAP). The objective of the FSAP was to create a single market in financial services and covered 42 legislative measures. The pioneering measures adopted in 2004 changed company law to allow fair value accounting; modernization of accounting provisions, communication and corporate governance; and supplementary supervision of financial conglomerates and financial instruments markets. The other measures were adopted by mid-2005. Moreover, the Green Paper was prepared to introduce a simplified and consolidated version of existing relevant financial regulation and to maintain further supervisory convergence in the EU as well as to maintain implementation of the outstanding FSAP measures.
3. ***Adoption of the new international financial reporting standards (IFRS)***: the IFRS required listed European companies, including banks, to publish their consolidated financial statements in accordance with the new set of accounting standards from 1 January 2005.

Following these regulatory improvements, progress was achieved, particularly in strengthening new corporate governance rules in EU countries aiming for greater accountability and transparency. In fact, strong corporate governance has the potential to enhance the EU banking sector's competitiveness, facilitate the cross-border provision of services and disseminate a more integrated and diversified financial system. In 2007, the EU banking sectors were initiated on areas such as liquidity risk, regulatory capital and accounting as well as a number of new developments that were launched in response to the turmoil in the financial markets.

At the global level, the Financial Stability Forum (FSF) delivered its report containing recommendations to the G7 meeting in April 2008. The FSF recommendations focus, in the short term, on valuation and disclosure as means of rebuilding confidence in the creditworthiness and robustness of financial institutions and facilitating smooth operation of financial markets in terms of liquidity flow and provision of credit. The FSF aims to introduce a number of measures that will reinforce the capital and liquidity barriers of banks, enhance risk management practices and improve competent authorities' assessments, responsiveness and exchange of information.

In the medium term, considerations for policy actions that are expected to take place cover topics pertaining to the current regulatory framework and practices, as well as to market functioning. This will address issues relating to the role of credit rating agencies and market transparency.

In the longer term, policy action will focus on the following areas: (i) enhancing transparency for investors, markets and regulators regarding exposures to structured products and off-balance sheet vehicles; (ii) improving valuation standards, in particular for illiquid assets; (iii) reinforcing the financial sector's prudential framework and risk management by reviewing certain areas of the Capital Requirements Directive (CRD) and enhancing management of liquidity risk; and (iv) improving market functioning and incentive structures, including the role of credit rating agencies.

Finally, the financial stability arrangements (FSA) reached an important milestone with the signing of a Memorandum of Understanding (MoU) in May 2008 by EU Supervisory Authorities, finance ministries and central banks on cross-border financial stability. Since then, emphasis in the area of financial stability arrangements shifted to the implementation of the MoU and clarification of cooperation obligations, which may include possible amendments to the EU legislation.

According to the Banking Supervision Committee (BSC) survey, 2008, which reviewed 112 EU banks, the proportion of banks assigning regulatory risks category the lowest relevant ranking doubled in 2008 compared with 2006 (risk categories range from the lowest, 1, to the highest, 5) (see Figure 5.1). One probable reason for this might be the fact that the uncertainty stemming from key regulatory initiatives

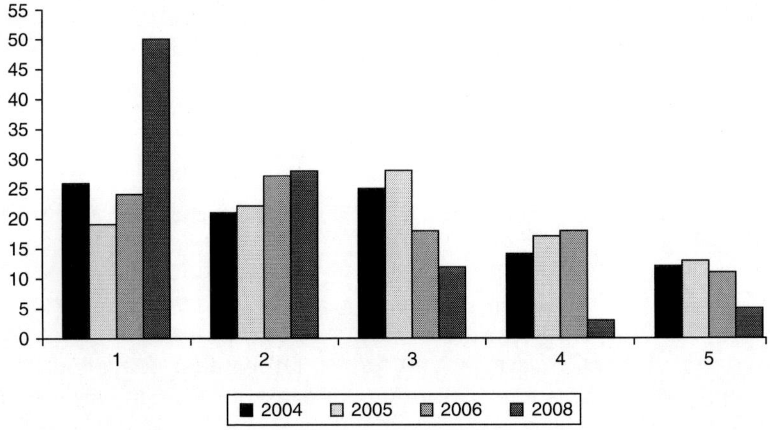

Figure 5.1 Distribution of regulatory risk (per cent)
Source: ECB (2008d), p. 33.

such as the CRD has considerably declined. The individual risks quoted by banks highlight their concerns for the year ahead.

Furthermore, the ECB stated that the pace and scope of regulatory action following market turbulence is important, and implementation issues rather than the development of new regulations are illustrated as a main risk source. The conclusion reached, based on the BSC survey, is that "banks highlight the need to avoid too frequent and possible excessive changes to the regulatory framework as well as the risk of excessive compliance requirements in the form of increasing external controls, corporate governance requirements and reporting burden" (ECB, 2008d, p. 33).

Structural changes in the EU banking sector

This section presents the major trends in the EU in terms of consolidation and M&As (as relevant to changing number of banks and branches), internationalization and intermediation (relevant to branch-level ratios). Note that a number of changes have taken place over the period under investigation, such as the entry of several countries into the euro area as well as the inclusion of Romania and Bulgaria in the group of EU-27 countries.

Trends in number of banks

With regard to the regulatory and structural reforms discussed earlier, a significant decrease in the total number of banks continued, attributable to the huge wave of intra-country and cross-border M&As among several European banks. Figure 5.2 presents a snapshot of the annual figures of the total number of bank in the groups of the EU-27, MU-13 and NMS over the 2003–2008 period.

Owing to the combined effect of regulatory and structural changes as well as the consolidation activities, at the EU-27 level the number of banks declined by 853 between 2001 and 2008 (9.11 per cent) (see Table 5.1). The corresponding figure for the 2006–2007 period was a decline of 175 banks, of which 56 and 55 represent changes in the Netherlands and Cyprus, respectively. In fact, the highest level of decline both in the group of euro-area and EU-27 countries occurred between 2001 and 2002, with 314 and 419 banks closing respectively. In contrast to this, Greece, Ireland, Latvia, Lithuania, Estonia and Italy all reported an increase in the number of banks for several consecutive years.

As of December 2008, the highest share of total number of banks with respect to the EU-27 was observed as 23.37 per cent, 9.61 per cent and

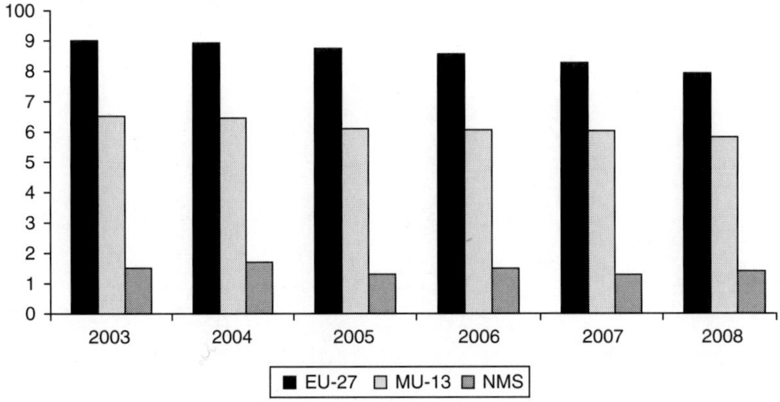

Figure 5.2 Total number of banks in EU countries, 2003–2008 (thousands)
Source: Author's calculations from Bankscope.

8.55 per cent in Germany, Italy and France, respectively. In contrast, the lowest shares are found in Estonia (0.20 per cent), Malta (0.27 per cent) and Slovenia (0.28 per cent). These findings are not surprising given the size of these countries' economies. The share of total number of banks in the NMS constituted 16.53 per cent of the bank population in EU-27, of which 1.91 per cent is in Cyprus and 2.31 per cent in Hungary. In fact, Cyprus and Hungary are important cases because they acquire a higher share than some of the EU-15 countries such as Denmark (2.01 per cent), Portugal (2.06 per cent), Belgium (1.23 per cent) and Greece (0.77 per cent).

Furthermore, over the 2001–2008 period, the total number of banks in the NMS countries increased by approximately 4.5 per cent, from 1346 in 2001 to 1407 in 2008. At the same time the number of banks in the euro area was five times greater than in the NMS in 2008. This was mainly the result of a large number of cooperative and saving banks in Germany, France and Italy. In contrast, the number of banks in the Czech Republic dropped significantly, from 172 in 2001 to 54 in 2008, while substantial increases were observed in Cyprus (from 43 to 163) and Lithuania (from 54 to 84) over the same period.

Branch systems of the EU banking sector

Changing trends in the number of banks was also reflected in the number of bank branches throughout the European banking sector. Even though there was a parallel decline in numerous countries due

Table 5.1 Total number of banks in individual EU countries, 2001–2008

Countries	2001	2002	2003	2004	2005	2006	2007	2008	% share in EU-27 (2008)
Euro area	7213	6899	6623	6427	6271	6157	6128	6569	77.19
EU-27	9363	8944	9054	8908	8689	8514	8348	8510	100
Austria	836	823	814	796	818	809	803	803	9.44
Belgium	112	111	108	104	100	105	110	105	1.23
Bulgaria	n/a	n/a	35	35	34	32	29	30	0.35
Cyprus	43	46	408	405	391	336	215	163	1.92
C. Republic	172	83	77	70	56	57	56	54	0.63
Denmark	203	178	203	202	197	191	189	171	2.01
Estonia	7	7	7	9	11	14	15	17	0.20
Finland	369	369	366	363	363	361	360	357	4.20
France	1050	989	939	897	854	829	808	728	8.55
Germany	2526	2363	2225	2148	2089	2050	2026	1989	23.37
Greece	61	61	59	62	62	62	63	66	0.78
Hungary	230	225	222	217	214	212	206	197	2.31
Ireland	88	85	80	80	78	78	81	501	5.89
Italy	843	821	801	787	792	807	821	818	9.61

Latvia	23	23	23	23	25	28	31	34	0.40
Lithuania	54	68	71	74	78	78	80	84	0.99
Luxembourg	189	177	169	162	155	156	156	152	1.79
Malta	17	14	16	16	19	18	22	23	0.27
Netherlands	561	539	481	461	401	345	341	302	3.55
Poland	711	664	660	744	730	723	718	712	8.37
Portugal	212	202	200	197	186	178	175	175	2.06
Romania	n/a	n/a	39	40	40	39	42	43	0.51
Slovakia	20	20	22	21	23	24	26	26	0.31
Slovenia	69	50	33	24	25	25	27	24	0.28
Spain	366	359	348	346	348	352	357	362	4.25
Sweden	149	216	222	212	200	204	201	182	2.14
UK	452	451	426	407	394	394	396	391	4.59

– MU-13: covers 13 countries in the euro area during 2003–2007; before 2003 EU-12.
– EU-27: covers 27 EU member countries during 2003–2007; before 2003 EU-25.

Source: Adapted by the author from ECB (2008d).

to the recent M&A activities, the total number of branches increased by approximately 15 per cent in the EU-27 between 2001 and 2008. Table 5.2 shows that 11,160 and 31,852 branches were opened in the euro area and EU-27, respectively, over this period. This indicates a 6.37 per cent and 15.44 per cent increase since 2001.

With regard to the euro-area countries, over the period 2001–2008, the highest percentage increases were observed in Spain, France and Italy at approximately 18 per cent, 52 per cent and 17 per cent respectively, and in the majority of NMS, especially Poland, Romania, Lithuania and Bulgaria. This trend continued to increase both in the euro area and the EU-27, despite the downsizing of branch networks in Belgium, Germany (27 per cent), Austria and the UK (14 per cent). This was offset by the significant increase in Spain, France and Italy, and in the majority of the NMS countries, especially Poland, Romania, Lithuania and Bulgaria.

Having discussed the changing trends in the number of branches operating in the European banking sector, the next important step is to stress the effects of foreign bank operations in individual countries. The increasing number of branches discussed above can be attributable to M&A activities and the opening of new branches by banks from Eastern European countries (see Table 5.3).

Employment in the EU banking sector

At this point, it is interesting to investigate if there has been a correlation between the trends in the number of branches and the number of employees among the EU countries (see Table 5.4).

Once again, following financial development and regulatory changes, the number of people employed in the banking system decreased in numerous countries due to the intention of minimizing costs and increasing profitability. Starting from the year 2001, the total number of bank personnel in the EU-27 was 3,177,779; this had decreased by 12 per cent to 2,787,038 by the end of 2008. Of this decline, approximately 12 per cent belongs to Germany and 11.6 per cent to the Netherlands. In contrast, all NMS countries, except the Czech Republic, experienced an increase in the number of bank employees between 2001 and 2008.

Consolidation in the EU banking sector

M&A activity in the EU banking sector is interesting, especially in terms of domestic transactions, which were very high over the 2000–2004 period. In relation to the number of transactions, no clear trend

Table 5.2 Number of branches in individual EU countries, 2001–2008

Countries	2001	2002	2003	2004	2005	2006	2007	2008	% share in EU-27 (2008)
Euro area	175,203	171,706	168,730	168,476	169,644	181,499	183,981	186,363	78.27
EU-27	206,265	202,483	206,956	211,442	214,925	228,601	233,581	238,117	100
Austria	4,561	4,466	4,395	4,360	4,300	4,258	4,266	4,243	1.78
Belgium	6,168	5,550	4,989	4,837	4,564	4,574	4,425	4,316	1.81
Bulgaria[a]	n/a	n/a	5,601	5,606	5,629	5,569	5,827	6,080	2.55
C. Republic	1,751	1,722	1,670	1,785	1,825	1,877	1,862	1,993	0.84
Cyprus	528	521	983	977	951	941	921	923	0.39
Denmark	2,376	2,128	2,118	2,119	2,122	2,152	2,194	2,192	0.92
Estonia	210	198	197	203	230	245	266	257	0.11
Finland	1,571	1,572	1,564	1,585	1,616	1,709	1,638	1,672	0.70
France	26,049	26,162	25,789	26,370	27,075	40,013	39,560	39,634	16.64
Germany	53,931	50,868	47,244	45,331	44,044	40,282	39,777	39,531	16.60
Greece	3,134	3,263	3,300	3,403	3,543	3,699	3,850	4,095	1.72
Hungary	2,950	2,992	3,003	2,987	3,125	3,243	3,387	3,515	1.48
Ireland	970	926	924	909	910	935	1,158	895	0.38
Italy	29,267	29,948	30,501	30,950	31,504	32,334	33,227	34,139	14.34
Latvia	590	567	581	583	586	610	682	658	0.28

Table 5.2 (Continued)

Countries	2001	2002	2003	2004	2005	2006	2007	2008	% share in EU-27 (2008)
Lithuania	156	119	723	758	822	892	970	973	0.41
Luxembourg	274	271	269	253	246	234	229	229	0.10
Malta	58	55	104	99	109	110	104	111	0.05
Netherlands	4,720	4,269	3,883	3,798	3,748	3,456	3,604	3,421	1.44
Poland	4,080	4,302	8,688	8,301	10,074	10,934	11,607	12,914	5.42
Portugal	5,534	5,390	5,397	5,371	5,422	5,618	6,055	6,391	2.68
Romania[a]	n/a	n/a	3,387	3,031	3,533	4,470	6,340	7,375	3.10
Slovakia	1,052	1,020	1,057	1,113	1,142	1,175	1,169	1,258	0.53
Slovenia	717	721	725	706	693	696	711	698	0.29
Spain	39,024	39,021	39,750	40,603	41,979	43,691	45,500	46,065	19.35
Sweden	2,040	2,040	2,069	2,018	2,003	2,004	1,988	2,025	0.85
UK	14,554	14,392	13,646	13,386	13,130	12,880	12,514	12,514	5.26

– Euro area: covers 13 countries in the euro area during 2003–2008; before 2003 EU-12.
– EU-27: covers 27 EU member countries during 2003–2008; before 2003 EU-25.
[a] 2003–2008 change in number of branches.

Source: Adapted by the author from ECB (2008d).

Table 5.3 Number of bank branches in Eastern European countries

Countries	2001	2002	2003	2004	2005	2006	2007	2008	% change 2001–2008
Belgium	35	36	38	36	41	46	49	47	34.29
Bulgaria	n/a	n/a	n/a	4	4	2	3	4	0.00
C. Republic	9	8	8	9	12	13	14	15	66.67
Denmark	9	8	16	15	17	17	18	16	77.78
Germany	59	64	64	62	69	68	66	83	40.68
Estonia	1	1	1	3	6	7	8	11	1000.00
Greece	13	14	14	19	19	20	22	23	76.92
Spain	49	51	49	53	57	62	71	78	59.18
France	55	51	52	55	55	59	64	70	27.27
Ireland	32	31	31	31	31	31	31	31	−3.13
Italy	94	91	49	50	58	65	72	77	−18.09
Cyprus	5	5	5	4	4	4	9	8	60.00
Latvia	1	1	1	1	1	3	2	6	500.00
Lithuania	3	3	2	2	2	2	3	7	133.33
Luxembourg	55	48	41	38	36	34	35	33	−40.00
Hungary	0	0	0	0	3	4	6	10	1000.00
Malta	0	0	0	0	0	0	1	1	100.00
Netherlands	19	19	20	22	22	16	18	30	57.89
Austria	15	15	18	18	25	25	26	30	100.00
Poland	0	0	0	3	7	12	14	18	1800.00

Table 5.3 (Continued)

Countries	2001	2002	2003	2004	2005	2006	2007	2008	% change 2001–2008
Portugal	23	21	22	26	24	23	23	25	8.70
Romania	n/a	n/a	7	6	5	6	10	10	42.86
Slovenia	1	1	1	2	3	2	3	3	200.00
Slovakia	1	1	3	3	5	7	10	9	800.00
Finland	18	19	18	19	19	22	21	20	11.11
Sweden	19	18	15	17	18	16	13	22	15.79
UK	87	85	82	81	81	83	81	81	–6.90
MU-13	467	460	417	431	459	473	501	559	19.70
EU-27	603	591	557	579	624	649	693	768	27.36

– MU-13: covers 13 countries in the euro area during 2003–2008; before 2003 EU-12.
– EU-27: covers 27 EU member countries during 2003–2008; before 2003 EU-25.
– n/a: indicates data "not available".

Source: Adapted by the author from ECB (2008d).

Table 5.4 Number of employees in individual European countries, 2001–2008

Countries	**2001**	**2002**	**2003**	**2004**	**2005**	**2006**	**2007**	**2008**	**% share in EU-27 (2008)**	**% change 2001–2008**
Euro area	2,273,965	2,245,560	2,220,876	2,197,112	2,204,486	2,250,316	2,276,562	2,305,578	69.13	1.39
EU-27	3,177,779	3,134,816	3,130,447	3,129,775	3,124,757	3,181,304	2,787,038	3,335,210	100	4.95
Austria	74,606	74,048	73,308	72,858	75,303	76,323	77,731	78,754	2.36	5.56
Belgium	76,104	75,370	73,553	71,347	69,481	67,957	67,080	65,246	1.96	−14.27
Bulgaria	n/a	n/a	n/a	22,467	22,945	26,738	30,571	34,930	1.05	55.47
C. Republic	42,999	40,534	39,658	38,666	37,943	37,825	40,037	398,852	11.96	827.58
Cyprus	8,200	8,649	10,480	10,617	10,799	10,845	11,286	12,554	0.38	53.10
Denmark	48,538	47,613	46,443	46,372	47,579	46,394	49,644	52,830	1.58	8.84
Estonia	3,949	3,934	4,280	4,455	5,029	5,681	6,319	6,144	0.18	55.58
Finland	26,733	27,190	26,667	25,377	23,644	24,769	25,025	25,699	0.77	−3.87
France	424,615	428,438	435,725	432,326	434,354	474,566	478,615	492,367	14.76	15.96
Germany	772,100	753,950	725,550	712,300	705,000	692,500	691,300	685,550	20.55	−11.21
Greece	59,624	60,495	61,074	59,337	61,295	62,171	64,713	66,165	1.98	10.97
Hungary	34,376	35,232	35,725	35,558	37,527	39,302	41,905	43,640	1.31	26.95
Ireland	40,928	36,585	35,658	35,564	37,702	39,154	41,865	40,507	1.21	−1.03
Italy	343,812	341,584	336,661	336,354	335,726	339,683	340,443	340,463	10.21	−0.97
Latvia	8,172	8,267	8,903	9,655	10,477	11,656	12,826	13,905	0.42	70.15
Lithuania	8,796	8,420	7,557	7,266	7,637	8,624	10,303	11,080	0.33	25.97

Table 5.4 (Continued)

Countries	2001	2002	2003	2004	2005	2006	2007	2008	% share in EU-27 (2008)	% change 2001–2008
Luxembourg	23,894	23,300	22,513	22,549	23,224	24,752	26,139	27,208	0.82	13.87
Malta	3,584	3,459	3,416	3,371	3,383	3,515	3,756	3,915	0.12	9.24
Netherlands	131,230	125,911	120,539	118,032	120,165	116,500	114,424	116,000	3.48	−11.61
Poland	165,225	158,697	154,569	150,037	158,130	162,125	173,955	188,969	5.67	14.37
Portugal	55,538	55,260	54,350	53,230	54,035	58,213	60,979	62,369	1.87	12.30
Romania	n/a	n/a	46,567	49,702	52,452	58,536	66,039	71,622	2.15	53.80
Slovakia	20,118	18,452	19,812	19,819	19,773	19,633	19,779	20,598	0.62	2.39
Slovenia	11,578	11,855	11,816	11,602	11,726	11,838	12,051	12,284	0.37	6.10
Spain	244,781	243,429	243,462	246,236	252,831	261,890	275,506	276,497	8.29	12.96
Sweden	42,001	42,357	44,389	44,242	44,943	47,069	48,457	50,115	1.50	19.32
UK	506,278	501,787	487,772	490,436	461,654	453,045	505,690	495,917	14.87	−2.05

– Euro area: covers 13 countries in the euro area during 2003–2008; before 2003 EU-12.
– EU-27: covers 27 EU member countries during 2003–2008; before 2003 EU-25.

Source: Adapted by the author from ECB (2008d).

appears in recent years, with the exception of the significant increase of M&As by European banks in third countries, the number of which has been higher than that of domestic deals for the 2005–2008 period.

However, in terms of the value of M&As in the EU, the picture is quite different, as an increase has been observed since 2003. This was also the case in 2007, which was the second consecutive year in which the total value of M&A transactions exceeded that of 2000. Compared with 2006, moderate growth was posted following a number of high-profile deals that significantly increased the value of M&As in 2006.

Following high levels of M&A activities in 2000 and 2001, both the number and values of transactions decreased in 2002, while during the period 2002–2004 the number of M&As increased and their values decreased. Values increased again in 2005, but activity remained at much lower levels compared with the period 2000–2002, and has been declining since 2005. In the first half of 2008 the number of M&A transactions remained at the same level as in the same period of 2007, while their value was affected by the acquisition of ABN Amro, Royal Bank of Scotland (RBS), Fortis and Santander. In 2007, the value of outward deals saw a significant increase, mainly due to the acquisition of Finansbank (in Turkey) by the National Bank of Greece (NBG).

Moreover, a number of significant developments took place in 2007 with regard to M&A activity, although some of them did not directly concern EU banks; for instance, sovereign wealth funds acquired material but non-controlling interests in large cross-border banking groups, including Citigroup, UBS, Morgan Stanley and Merrill Lynch, whereas other non-bank investors gained sizable participations in institutions affected by the global financial crisis.

Finally, banks, including those based in the EU, expanded their operations, mainly in emerging markets that had not been so adversely affected by the crisis. For instance, HSBC concluded strategic acquisitions in Taiwan, Korea and Russia; UniCredit acquired a bank in Kazakhstan with the intention of using it as springboard for further expansion into Central Asia; Commerzbank acquired a bank in Ukraine; while Deutsche Bank strengthened its share in Hua Xia bank in China. However, it should be noted that, in most cases, these developments were the outcome of longer term planning and was not motivated by the recent financial crisis.

Market concentration in the EU banking sector

In general, the majority share of total EU banking sector assets is held by the five largest banks in each country. During 2008, changes in the five largest banks' share of total assets increased from 37.8 per cent to 44.1 per cent at the EU-27 level and from 39.1 per cent to 44.7 per cent in the MU-15 (see Table 5.5). On the other hand, smaller countries tend to have more concentrated banking sectors, with the notable exceptions of Austria and Luxembourg, the former having a strong savings and cooperative banking sector, the latter hosting a large amount of foreign credit. Similarly, Germany, Spain, Italy and the UK have more fragmented banking sectors.

In terms of banks' concentration, several EU countries, especially the smaller ones, continued to be characterized by high concentration, as measured by the share of the five largest banks in total banking sector assets. However, based on 2008 figures, concentration remained relatively low in Germany (22.7 per cent), Italy (33 per cent), Luxembourg (27.3 per cent) and the UK (36.5 per cent).

In order to gain a deeper analysis of the structural changes in the banking industries, the Herfindahl-Hirschman Index (HHI),[1] which measures the sum of the squared market shares of the individual institutions, can be considered (see Table 5.6). The HHI is a commonly accepted measure of market concentration. The closer a market is to a monopoly, the higher the market's concentration (and the lower its competition). According to the calculated HHI market concentration ratios, Germany experienced the lowest HHI (158 in 2001 and 191 in 2008), followed by Luxembourg (278 in 2008), Italy (344 in 2008) and the UK (412 in 2008). However, Poland (562 in 2008) had the lowest ratio of the NMS countries.[2] In contrast, the highest level of HHI was observed in Finland, standing at 3160 in 2008, whereas Estonia had the highest ratio of 3120 in 2008 from the group of NMS countries.

Market concentration, as measured by the Herfindahl Index, increased at both the EU-15 and the EU-27 level, reflecting, on one hand, the decline in the number of banks and, on the other, the dynamic growth of certain banking groups, partly as a result of their M&A activity. The results of the HHI measures were similar to the concentration ratios of the largest five. Germany (191) experienced the lowest ratio followed by Luxembourg (278) and Italy (344) in 2008. Once again, in 2008 terms, Finland had the highest concentration ratio (3160) of the EU-15 countries and Estonia (3120) of NMS countries. In conclusion, it can be said that banking industries in smaller countries are more concentrated than those of their larger counterparts.

Regarding the NMS, recent developments in financial intermediation, such as rapid credit expansion and intensifying competition, exerted a downward pressure on concentration indicators, although they still

Table 5.5 Share of the five largest banks in individual EU countries, according to total assets, 2001–2008 (per cent)

Countries	2001	2002	2003	2004	2005	2006	2007	2008	% change 2001–2008
EU-27	37.8	38.3	39.7	40.9	42.1	42.1	44.4	44.1	16.67
Euro area	39.1	39.4	40.5	41.6	42.6	42.8	44.1	44.7	14.32
Austria	44.9	45.6	44.2	43.8	45	43.8	42.8	39	−13.14
Belgium	78.3	82	83.5	84.3	85.3	84.4	83.4	80.8	3.19
Bulgaria	n/a	n/a	n/a	52.3	50.8	50.3	56.7	57.3	9.56
Cyprus	71.5	69.3	57.2	57.3	59.8	63.9	64.8	63.9	−10.63
C. Republic	67.6	65.7	65.8	64	65.5	64.1	65.7	62	−8.28
Denmark	67.6	68	66.6	67	66.3	64.7	64.2	66	−2.37
Estonia	98.9	99.1	99.2	98.6	98.1	97.1	95.7	94.8	−4.15
Finland	79.5	78.6	81.2	82.7	82.9	82.3	81.2	82.8	4.15
France	47	44.6	46.7	49.2	51.9	52.3	51.8	51.2	8.94
Germany	20.2	20.5	21.6	22.1	21.6	22	22	22.7	12.38
Greece	67	67.4	66.9	65	65.6	66.3	67.7	69.5	3.73
Hungary	56.4	54.5	52.1	52.7	53.2	53.5	54.1	54.5	−3.37
Ireland	42.5	46.1	44.4	43.9	45.7	44.8	46.1	55.7	31.06
Italy	28.8	30.6	27.5	26.4	26.8	26.2	33.1	33	14.58
Latvia	63.4	65.3	63.1	62.4	67.3	69.2	67.2	70.2	10.73

Table 5.5 (Continued)

Countries	2001	2002	2003	2004	2005	2006	2007	2008	% change 2001–2008
Lithuania	87.6	83.9	81	78.9	80.6	82.5	80.9	81.2	−7.31
Luxembourg	28	30.3	31.8	29.7	30.7	29.1	27.9	27.3	−2.50
Malta	79.6	82	77.7	78.5	75.3	71.4	70.1	72.8	−8.54
Netherlands	82.5	82.7	84.2	84	84.5	85.1	86.3	86.8	5.21
Poland	54.7	53.4	52	50	48.5	46.1	46.6	44.2	−19.20
Portugal	59.8	60.5	62.7	66.5	68.8	67.9	67.8	69.1	15.55
Romania	n/a	n/a	55.2	59.5	59.4	60.1	56.3	54	−2.17
Slovakia	66.1	66.4	67.5	66.5	67.7	66.9	68.2	71.5	8.17
Slovenia	67.6	68.4	66.4	64.6	63	62	59.5	59.1	−12.57
Spain	44.9	44.3	43.1	41.9	42	40.4	41	42.4	−5.57
Sweden	54.6	56	53.8	54.4	57.3	57.8	61	61.9	13.37
UK	28.6	29.6	32.8	34.5	36.3	35.9	40.7	36.5	27.62

– Euro area: covers 15 countries in the euro area during 2003–2008; before 2003 EU-12.
– EU-27: covers 27 EU member countries during 2003–2008; before 2003 EU-25.

Source: Adapted by the author from ECB (2008d).

Table 5.6 HHI in individual European countries, according to total assets, 2001–2008

Countries	2001	2002	2003	2004	2005	2006	2007	2008	% change 2001–2008
EU-27	506	521	545	567	600	588	628	653	29.05
Euro area	544	553	579	599	642	630	654	687	26.29
Austria	561	618	557	552	560	534	527	454	–19.07
Belgium	1587	1905	2063	2102	2112	2041	2079	1877	18.27
Bulgaria	n/a	n/a	n/a	721	698	707	833	834	15.67
Cyprus	1304	1339	946	940	1029	1056	1082	1024	–21.47
C. Republic	1263	1199	1187	1103	1155	1104	1100	1000	–20.82
Denmark	1119	1145	1114	1146	1115	1071	1120	1229	9.83
Estonia	4067	4028	3943	3887	4039	3593	3410	3120	–23.28
Finland	2240	2050	2420	2680	2730	2560	2540	3160	41.07
France	606	551	597	623	758	726	679	681	12.38
Germany	158	163	173	178	174	178	183	191	20.89
Greece	1113	1164	1130	1070	1096	1101	1096	1172	5.30
Hungary	892	856	783	798	795	823	839	822	–7.85
Ireland	512	553	500	500	600	600	600	800	56.25
Italy	260	270	240	230	230	220	330	344	32.31
Latvia	1053	1144	1054	1021	1176	1271	1158	1205	14.43
Lithuania	2503	2240	2071	1854	1838	1913	1827	1714	–31.52

Table 5.6 (Continued)

Countries	2001	2002	2003	2004	2005	2006	2007	2008	% change 2001–2008
Luxembourg	275	296	315	304	312	294	276	278	1.09
Malta	2163	2390	1580	1452	1330	1185	1174	1236	-42.86
Netherlands	1762	1788	1744	1726	1796	1822	1928	2168	23.04
Poland	821	792	754	692	650	599	640	562	-31.55
Portugal	991	963	1043	1093	1154	1134	1097	1114	12.41
Romania	n/a	n/a	1251	1111	1115	1165	1041	922	-26.30
Slovakia	1205	1252	1191	1154	1076	1131	1082	1197	-0.66
Slovenia	1582	1602	1496	1425	1369	1300	1282	1268	-19.85
Spain	551	529	506	482	487	442	459	497	–9.80
Sweden	760	800	760	854	845	856	934	953	25.39
UK	282	307	347	376	399	394	449	412	46.10

– Euro area: covers 13 countries in the euro area during 2003–2008; before 2003 EU-12.
– EU-27: covers 27 EU member countries during 2003–2008; before 2003 EU-25.
Note: Aggregate concentration figures are weighted averages.
Source: Adapted by the author from ECB (2008d).

remained significantly above the EU-27 average. However, the banking sectors of Bulgaria, Cyprus, Hungary and Poland were characterized by contrasting developments. In these countries, both measures of concentration increased. The reason for this was the ongoing consolidation process in the cooperative bank sector and the increased domestic M&A activity among subsidiaries of foreign banks.

Snapshot of capacity indicators

With respect to the EU banking sector capacity indicators in 2007 (see Table 5.7), the highest number of banks among the EU-27 is observed in Germany (2026) and the lowest in Estonia (15). The highest figures on population per bank is in Romania (512,201) and on population per branch is in the Czech Republic (5541), while the lowest figures are in Luxembourg (3079) and Cyprus (855), respectively.

The number of branches has continued to increase in the EU, despite the continuing downsizing of branch networks in Belgium, Germany, France and the UK in 2008. This was offset by the significant increase in the number of branches in Spain and in the majority of the NMS; especially noteworthy was the expansion of the branch networks in Romania, which was the highest among the NMS countries at 16.32 per cent, followed by Poland by 11.26 per cent from 2007 to 2008. From the group of EU-15 countries, Greece experienced the highest expansion of branch networks at 6.36 per cent from 2007 to 2008. This trend is in line with the continued retail expansion and associated deepening of financial intermediation observed in these countries for years. Along with the expanding branch networks of specific EU countries in 2008, the number of bank employees also increased.

At the same time, the efficiency of the EU banking sector indicated by the ratio of assets per employee in 2007 is highest in Luxembourg (35,022) and lowest in Greece (5923) among the EU-15 countries. On the other hand, among the NMS, the highest figure is identified in Malta (10,066) and the lowest in Bulgaria (1022). Moreover, population per automated teller machine (ATM) can be stated as a measure of technological advance; this is highest in Poland (3837) and lowest in Portugal (721), according to 2007 figures.

However, solely looking at the population per ATM figures may not be an adequate indicator of the progress of technological advances in a banking sector. Therefore, the following section is devoted to a detailed investigation of changing trends relevant to several other cashless transactions in the EU banking sector.

Table 5.7 EU banking sector capacity indicators relative to population, 2007

Countries	Population per bank	Population per branch	Population per ATM	Population per employee	Assets per employee	No. of banks	Total assets (bn)	Total Loans (bn)	Total Deposits (bn)	Capital and reserves (bn)
EU-27	59,401	2,123	1,362	153	12,676	7,162	41,327.69	17,134.54	15,233.4	2,279.83
MU-15	52,098	1,735	1,203	140	12,437	5,676	30,946.96	12,748.73	10,608.39	1,614.44
Austria	10,356	1,949	1,037	107	11,459	867	1,069.32	434.39	328.27	88.56
Belgium	96,564	2,400	756	158	19,347	105	1,350	506.7	512.9	51
Bulgaria	263,456	1,311	2,103	250	1,022	30	35.56	25.05	21.35	4.05
Cyprus	3,663	855	1,474	70	8,076	163	116.03	54.44	56	7.91
C. Republic	184,250	5,541	3,129	258	3,497	37	154.59	77.23	95.51	14.6
Denmark	28,889	2,489	1,758	110	19,700	154	843.81	517.22	191.17	57.11
Estonia	89,493	5,047	1,465	212	3,261	16	21.79	16.62	9.46	3.71
Finland	14,689	3,228	1,606	211	11,497	336	363.22	134.79	107.42	19.4
France	78,679	1,607	1,322	133	13,962	394	7,698.78	1,992	1,540.7	284.17
Germany	40,603	2,068	1,528	119	10,946	2,169	7,892.7	3,227.43	3,067.43	378.2
Greece	177,329	2,902	1,654	173	5,923	66	414.69	225.05	223.26	27.82
Hungary	48,814	2,969	2,643	240	2,589	39	110.2	75.06	46.13	9.14
Ireland	53,613	3,750	1,287	104	31,945	82	1,424.48	665.96	308.67	74
Italy	72,252	1,785	1,349	174	9,755	799	3,687.6	1,977.84	1,349.27	279.38
Latvia	73,402	3,336	2,403	177	2,403	27	32.82	23.42	13.78	2.4

Lithuania	42,194	3,480	2,962	328	2,312	11	25.94	20.64	11.06	1.02
Luxembourg	3,079	2,044	1,086	18	35,022	152	931.56	194.34	286.69	38.67
Malta	18,603	3,935	2,607	109	10,066	21	42	25	15	3
Netherlands	48,026	4,544	2,014	143	19,183	99	2,235	1,002	859	95
Poland	53,086	3,284	3,837	219	1,357	649	248.97	142.26	118.41	19.72
Portugal	60,619	1,759	721	174	7,218	43	450.25	289.48	183.77	22.92
Romania	512,201	3,393	3,575	326	1,092	43	78.17	49.25	37.65	7.07
Slovakia	207,560	4,616	2,702	273	2,544	26	62.88	31.68	40.49	3.83
Slovenia	75,032	2,849	1,321	168	3,609	18	47.62	33.52	20.61	2
Spain	125,696	986	754	163	10,690	362	3,223.7	1,985.8	1,749.4	242.4
Sweden	45,512	4,956	3,235	208	19,202	118	577.92	229.9	179.58	28.33
UK	155,854	4,892	1,002	134	21,783	336	8,188.09	3,177.47	3,860.43	514.4

Note: Population density is expressed as inhabitants per square kilometre. Assets per employee are measured in EUR thousands.
Source: Created by the author from ECB (2007c).

Financial innovation in the EU banking sector

The changeover to the single currency increased the importance of information systems in the European banking industry. Therefore, it can be said that developments in information technology (IT) played an important role in underpinning the process of European financial integration. Financial innovation has enabled banks to manage the rapid development of more sophisticated approaches to risk management, such as the use of credit for derivatives and securitization. These techniques helped to promote the stability of financial systems by spreading risk more widely, although the development posed challenges for supervisors both in monitoring developments and in determining appropriate responses. Analysing the impact of financial innovation in the EU-27 is particularly important in order to shed light on the convergence and financial stability among EU member countries. In fact, the replacement of paper-based payments by electronic methods has significant effects on efficiency gains. These include reductions in employee costs and the closing down of branches in areas of low-level banking activity. Hunter and colleagues (2000) observed that improved IT activities offered the capability for significant development of the relationship between banks and customers from time and cost perspectives, and allowed banks to transfer less profitable customers into lower-cost distribution channels such as automatic teller machines (ATMs) and telephone call centres. Moreover, the introduction of IT to the banking sector created a new market for technically qualified staff, which has been applied all over the world, replacing cash and face-to-face banking transactions. It was emphasized by Inzerillo and colleagues (1999) that changes in the payment system as a means of technological advance have helped to reduce the degree of monopoly relevant to geographic localization. In this respect, Hunter and colleagues (2000) emphasized that each European country reacted to the new technologies differently. For instance, countries with sophisticated national financial markets, such as France and Germany, developed advanced technological applications, whereas smaller economies, such as those of the Netherlands and Portugal, developed customer-oriented technological applications, that is, e-mail credit and chip cards.

The reason that banks invest in IT is that they expect to achieve higher productivity in order to gain competitive advantage in the market. Many academic studies in the literature have proved the positive effects of IT applications in achieving higher productivity levels (Brynjolfson, 1993). However, when analysing the statistics available, it is observed that there have been significant differences across the EU countries, firstly concerning the intensity of cash usage and, secondly, the intensity of using traditional and electronic non-cash payment instruments.[3] Figures on the number of ATMs and point-of-sale (POS) terminals in the EU countries over the period 2001–2008 are summarized in Table 5.8.

ATMs, where 80 per cent of all transactions in developed countries are undertaken, offer access to cash 24 hours a day. The increased popularity of credit card systems since the 1980s, as emphasized by Saarinen (2001), has influenced the level of costs, benefits and risks facing customers in their daily economic transactions. The progress in using ATMs helped banks to increase efficiency in offering services with increased operating hours, minimized waiting time in queues and reduced the chance of processing faulty transactions. With the restructuring process in Europe, the number of ATMs in operation per million people in the EU-27 countries increased by 48 per cent, from 750 in 2003 to 855 in 2008. The euro-area total also experienced a similar increase, of approximately 34 per cent over the same period (from 760 to 977). Among the EU-15, the highest share came from Portugal (1588), Belgium (1456), the UK (1047) and Spain (1353), whilst the lowest were observed in Denmark (561), Sweden (305) and the Netherlands (526).

In the case of NMS countries, the percentage increase in the number of ATMs in operation per million people was significant from 2003 to 2008. The highest levels were experienced in Bulgaria (319 per cent), Romania (257 per cent) and Poland (79 per cent). Also in Table 5.8, a similar trend can be observed in the number of operating POS terminals per million people in EU-27. Despite the increase in the number of POS terminals in all countries, only Denmark experienced a recession of 18.6 per cent from 25,095 in 2003 to 20,029 in 2008.

From another perspective, Electronic Fund Transfers at point-of-sale (EFTPOS) and POS terminals and ATMs can be seen as competitors to some extent. This is due to the fact that EFTPOS terminals might be used to withdraw cash, thus reducing the demand for ATMs. Additionally, EFTPOS terminals for card-based payments represent the most important substitute for cash payments (ECB, 1999n). In 2007, the total number of non-cash payments, using all types of instruments, increased by 5 per cent to 78 billion in the EU. Card payments accounted for almost 40 per cent of all transactions in 2008, while credit transfers and direct debits accounted equally for most of the remainder (see Table 5.9).

Overall, the number of transactions carried out with all payment instruments (excluding cash transactions) grew by 5 per cent in 2008 (see Figure 5.3). This is below the 6 per cent per year that occurred

Table 5.8 Number of ATMs and POS terminals in the EU-27, 2003–2008 (per million inhabitants)

Countries	ATMs					POS terminals				
	2003	2005	2007	2008	% change 2003–2008	2003	2005	2007	2008	% change 2003–2008
Belgium	1,204.57	1,293.01	1,454.15	1,456.51	20.92	10,901.47	9,651.9	11,473.07	11,758.8	7.86
Bulgaria	156.64	360.03	589.04	667.38	326.06	481.2	2,199.58	6,351.33	7,048.91	1364.86
C. Republic	250.45	293.63	325.21	326.6	30.41	n/a	6,122.77	7,648.98	5,536.99	−9.57
Denmark	533.02	553.79	573.08	561.36	5.32	25,095.36	18,753.83	15,882.6	20,029.13	−20.19
Germany	619.6	647.08	864.39	968.31	56.28	6,008.12	6,906.37	6,880.82	7,221.07	20.19
Estonia	550.88	590.72	690.55	692.07	25.63	6,772.86	9,447.12	16,580.01	17,846.22	163.50
Ireland	570.78	709.63	743.63	766.64	34.31	12,528.08	12,052.08	16,368.96	16,629.64	32.74
Greece	496.03	554.31	653.54	692.28	39.56	27,634.97	29,824.49	32,878.94	33,059.49	19.63
Spain	1,237.44	1,298.05	1,350.19	1,353.57	9.38	21,793.83	25,555.16	30,124.04	31,162.13	42.99
France	676.77	759.66	818.22	831.66	22.89	16,118.17	17,392.48	19,489.02	21,469.15	33.20
Italy	678.05	692.36	810.32	913.89	34.78	16,109.36	17,831.33	20,536.77	22,282.6	38.32
Cyprus	507.75	585.91	709.18	n/a	39.67	16,689.26	21,351.28	24,622.45	n/a	47.53
Latvia	373.28	381.22	503.93	562.2	50.61	4,415.68	5,991.71	9,030.8	10,274.04	132.67
Lithuania	287.77	309.29	395.19	438.03	52.22	3,195.24	4,776.97	8,166.84	11,972.78	274.71
Luxembourg	856.95	870.59	927.08	941.85	9.91	16,789.19	17,871.88	18,808.33	19,467.65	15.95
Hungary	293.7	350.05	426.22	460.54	56.81	3,936.3	4,078.89	5,427.23	6,055.01	53.82

Malta	373.93	381.76	394.84	n/a	5.59	14,360.07	18,631.72	21,567.72	n/a	50.19
Netherlands	465.76	456.33	521.8	526.4	13.02	11,481.97	15,457.74	18,699.72	19,232.48	67.50
Austria	923.78	968.02	974.7	916.39	−0.80	9,033.66	10,842.67	12,555.05	12,800.99	41.70
Poland	198.32	229.97	302.81	356.1	79.56	3,474.28	4,348	4,895.84	5,570.84	60.35
Portugal	1,147.87	1,312.01	1,495.05	1,588.76	38.41	12,015.62	13,947.4	19,076.51	21,276.15	77.07
Romania	119.31	201.35	346.29	431.16	261.38	529.04	1,296.25	2,899.12	3,768.74	612.37
Slovenia	621.15	744.7	813.9	848.37	36.58	15,790.35	16,848.15	17,713.12	18,384.2	16.43
Slovakia	279.77	344.16	401.37	416.21	48.77	3,155.41	3,754.9	5,137.52	6,015.14	90.63
Finland	758.68	645.36	608.47	604.37	−20.34	17,648.19	19,637.38	25,526.12	28,797.29	63.17
Sweden	298.73	310.08	307.06	305.13	2.14	12,062.4	19,561.13	20,477.92	21,262.83	76.27
UK	780.15	967.92	1,043.38	1,047.34	34.25	14,463.28	16,175.41	17,286.87	17,942.33	24.05
Euro area	760.56	808.33	925.71	977.71	28.55	13,843.53	15,609.51	17,944.38	19,143.85	38.29
EU-27	749.63	734.47	811.33	855.23	14.09	14,056.09	14,140.87	15,347.84	16,314.04	16.06

Source: Adapted by the author from ECB (2008b).

Table 5.9 Number of transactions per type of payment instrument, 2003–2008 (millions)

Countries	Credit transfers					Direct debits				
	2003	2004	2005	2006	2007	2003	2004	2005	2006	2007
Belgium	730.62	787.96	816.49	840.51	897.56	192.35	211.35	218.98	231.32	239.98
Bulgaria	28.22	35.32	44.74	51.09	50.75	1.62	0.99	1.10	1.20	0.76
C. Republic	362.30	410.01	n/a	n/a	n/a	250.30	269.72	n/a	n/a	n/a
Denmark	241.80	245.13	254.55	266.29	277.63	151.43	157.93	168.09	175.33	185.51
Germany	5,787.58	6,170.89	6,713.15	7,262.19	5,177.66	5,458.84	6,056.02	6,662.10	7,363.34	6,903.66
Estonia	54.60	63.98	71.30	79.81	89.49	8.57	10.34	12.44	14.34	16.13
Ireland	40.90	47.27	134.12	141.33	153.20	37.90	42.21	71.27	92.48	99.86
Greece	12.81	17.00	26.39	29.28	34.52	11.79	13.10	14.96	16.35	17.87
Spain	622.13	731.56	717.53	684.63	733.00	1,382.95	2,118.15	2,181.60	2,103.10	2,222.26
France	2,587.53	2,599.23	2,408.43	2,617.09	2,615.13	2,353.22	2,542.73	2,512.76	2,736.80	2,909.78
Italy	1,018.41	1,048.80	1,048.29	1,066.04	1,094.72	414.35	453.22	463.24	480.03	508.79
Cyprus	4.23	7.39	9.51	11.36	12.93	6.65	8.73	9.46	10.62	11.76
Latvia	68.81	77.15	89.79	107.00	120.02	0.37	0.82	1.37	3.70	4.05
Lithuania	39.38	46.34	52.86	82.05	93.99	1.83	2.86	3.53	6.07	7.20
Luxembourg	13.13	13.04	13.59	51.13	59.72	4.90	5.30	5.77	10.69	12.89
Hungary	139.50	176.85	502.47	612.83	568.36	54.70	55.06	59.79	74.60	78.33
Malta	3.06	3.26	3.77	4.08	4.36	0.40	0.48	0.60	0.73	0.78

Netherlands	1,271.37	1,264.20	1,263.03	1,366.13	1,416.17	1,000.75	1,051.31	1,059.35	1,139.06	1,176.94
Austria	879.10	892.00	933.00	907.00	985.00	647.40	615.80	668.00	682.00	719.00
Poland	619.79	726.61	804.61	917.61	1,037.75	4.43	7.54	11.09	14.54	18.20
Portugal	90.16	75.98	111.12	125.15	131.90	143.05	144.60	139.03	140.35	162.77
Romania	77.02	108.59	128.28	178.11	258.30	9.04	18.49	20.74	24.10	23.07
Slovenia	n/a	159.03	162.29	175.22	177.33	n/a	35.38	35.93	40.12	41.73
Slovakia	128.80	139.57	127.06	171.31	194.77	2.42	2.83	36.77	41.30	116.91
Finland	569.00	573.00	623.00	657.00	701.00	64.00	69.00	72.00	72.00	76.00
Sweden	425.00	462.00	511.00	572.00	645.00	131.00	143.00	160.00	197.00	208.00
UK	2,210.80	2,598.39	2,983.68	3,058.98	3,120.52	2,429.92	2,589.93	2,722.25	2,857.76	2,963.47
EU-15	13,622.74	14,220.94	14,808.13	15,747.48	14,176.91	11,711.49	13,322.78	14,069.07	15,067.52	15,091.54
EU-27	16,500.34	19,336.64	20,381.02	21,806.01	20,650.79	14,423.83	16,607.38	17,290.39	18,503.63	18,725.70

Source: ECB (2008b), p. 13.

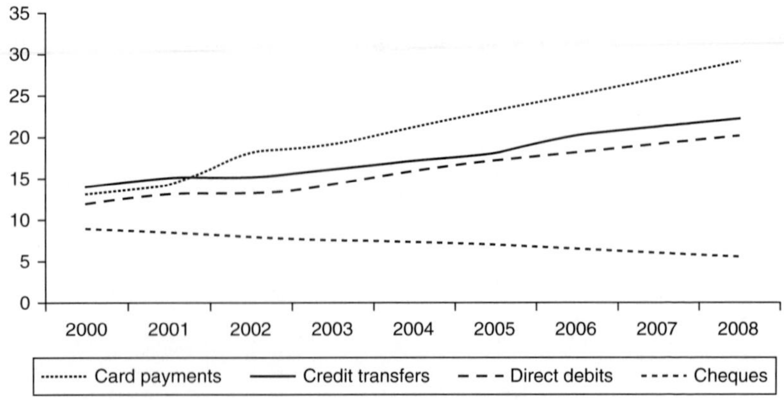

Figure 5.3 Use of payment instruments in the EU-27, 2000–2008 (number of transactions per billion)
Source: ECB (2008b).

between 2000 and 2008. The latter trend was primarily driven by the strong average growth rate of 10 per cent per year for card payments over this period. The use of credit transfers and direct debits grew by 5 per cent and 6 per cent per year respectively. By contrast, transactions using cheques declined by an average of 5 per cent per year over the 2000–2008 period.

Figure 5.6 illustrates that the use of cards and direct debits also increased steadily between 2000 and 2008, at average annual rates of 12 per cent and 8 per cent, respectively. Over the same period the use of credit transfers rose at an average rate of 8 per cent per annum. On the other hand, the use of cheques showed a continuous decline, falling at an average rate of around 5 per cent per annum. There was steady growth in the number of e-money transactions, but these still only accounted for 0.6 per cent of all non-cash transactions in 2007.

In 2008, card payments were the most popular form of cashless payment instrument in the EU-27, accounting for approximately 30 per cent of the total volume of transactions, which reached 73.8 billion in that year (ECB, 2008b). The shares of credit transfers and direct debits were similar, at around 20 per cent each. Finally, cheques, e-money transactions and other cashless payment instruments accounted for less than 10 per cent of the total volume of transactions. Individual country figures are given in Table 5A.2 of the appendix.

At the individual country level, the ECB (2008b) reported that Bulgaria experienced the highest percentage of credit transfers of total payments (81.2 per cent) whilst Portugal had the lowest (9.8 per cent). This is due to the fact that Bulgarian people do not use direct debits (0.6 per cent) or cards (18.2 per cent) as much as credit transfers for their payments. On the other hand, card payments have been very popular in Portugal, representing 64.1 per cent of total transactions followed by 13.7 per cent of direct debits. It is interesting to observe that cheque payments continued to be very popular in the small island economies of Malta and Cyprus, representing 42.6 per cent and 31.1 per cent of total payments, respectively.

In terms of retail payments, the average annual growth in the volume of transactions processed by the EU-27 was 4.7 per cent in 2007. The sharpest increase in transaction volumes was experienced in 2004 due to the inclusion of transactions taking place in the ten NMS, which joined the EU at that time. On the other hand, the average growth in the volume of transactions processed by retail payment systems in the euro area was around 4 per cent in 2004. The value of transactions processed by EU retail payment systems also grew between 2000 and 2007, at an average rate of 5 per cent per annum, while the euro area showed a corresponding growth rate of 3.7 per cent (ECB, 2008b).

Conclusion

By offering a detailed examination of the EU banking sector indicators, this chapter highlighted that the number of bank employees has continued to decrease and alternative distribution channels have gained pace. Some regions, such as Austria, Ireland, Italy, Portugal and Spain, placed a relatively strong emphasis on electronic banking, while others, such as Greece and the Netherlands, have focused more on expanding the services provided through ATMs. The major changes that occurred due to the application of advanced technologies are cost reductions, increased speed and more efficient and effective operation of the financial sector.

In terms of market concentration represented by the Herfindahl Index, we observed an increase at both the EU-15 and EU-27 level, reflecting, on one hand, the decline in the number of banks and, on the other, the dynamic growth of certain banking groups, partly as a result of their M&A activity. Regarding the NMS, recent developments in financial intermediation, such as rapid credit expansion and intensifying competition, exerted a downward pressure on concentration indicators, although they remain significantly above the EU-27 average.

With respect to the EU banking sector capacity indicators, the highest number of banks among the EU-27 was observed in Germany and the lowest in Estonia. The highest figures on population per bank were in Romania and on population per branch in the Czech Republic, while the lowest figures were in Luxembourg and Cyprus. At the same time, the efficiency of the EU banking sector, as indicated by the ratio of assets per employee in 2007, was highest in Luxembourg and lowest in Greece among the EU-15 countries, whilst among the NMS, the highest figure was identified in Malta and the lowest in Bulgaria. Moreover, population per ATM can be stated as a measure of technological advances; this was highest in Poland and lowest in Portugal, according to the 2007 figures.

The number of branches continued to increase in the EU-27 during 2008, despite the reduction of branch networks in Belgium, Germany, France and the UK. This was offset by the significant increase in the number of branches in Spain and in the majority of the NMS; especially noteworthy was the expansion of branch networks in Romania, which was the highest among the NMS. Likewise, from the group of EU-15 countries, Greece experienced the highest expansion of branch networks.

Appendix

Table 5A.1 Country's share in the total number of transactions (per cent)

Countries	Credit transfers					Direct debits					Card payments (except with e-money cards)				
	2003	2004	2005	2006	2007	2003	2004	2005	2006	2007	2003	2004	2005	2006	2007
Belgium	4.43	4.07	4.01	3.85	4.35	1.33	1.27	1.27	1.25	1.28	3.29	3.17	3.18	3.17	3.16
Bulgaria	0.17	0.18	0.22	0.23	0.25	0.01	0.01	0.01	0.01	0.00	0.02	0.03	0.06	0.09	0.04
C. Republic	2.20	2.12	–	–	–	1.74	1.62	–	–	–	0.30	0.40	0.34	0.37	0.47
Denmark	1.47	1.27	1.25	1.22	1.34	1.05	0.95	0.97	0.95	0.99	3.03	3.06	2.87	3.07	3.21
Germany	35.08	31.91	32.94	33.30	25.07	37.85	36.47	38.53	39.79	36.87	10.79	10.57	10.23	9.68	7.62
Estonia	0.33	0.33	0.35	0.37	0.43	0.06	0.06	0.07	0.08	0.09	0.23	0.28	0.35	0.42	0.48
Ireland	0.25	0.24	0.66	0.65	0.74	0.26	0.25	0.41	0.50	0.53	0.76	0.71	0.76	0.81	0.96
Greece	0.08	0.09	0.13	0.13	0.17	0.08	0.08	0.09	0.09	0.10	0.32	0.31	0.29	0.28	0.28
Spain	3.77	3.78	3.52	3.14	3.55	9.59	12.75	12.62	11.37	11.87	6.23	6.31	6.37	6.68	7.14
France	15.68	13.44	11.82	12.00	12.66	16.31	15.31	14.53	14.79	15.54	23.22	21.98	22.61	22.31	22.55
Italy	6.17	5.42	5.14	4.89	5.30	2.87	2.73	2.68	2.59	2.72	5.27	5.23	5.16	4.91	4.88
Cyprus	0.03	0.04	0.05	0.05	0.06	0.05	0.05	0.05	0.06	0.06	0.08	0.08	0.08	0.09	0.09
Latvia	0.42	0.40	0.44	0.49	0.58	0.00	0.00	0.01	0.02	0.02	0.11	0.14	0.17	0.23	0.28
Lithuania	0.24	0.24	0.26	0.38	0.46	0.01	0.02	0.02	0.03	0.04	0.14	0.17	0.22	0.27	0.35
Luxembourg	0.08	0.07	0.07	0.23	0.29	0.03	0.03	0.03	0.06	0.07	0.17	0.16	0.16	0.16	0.17
Hungary	0.85	0.91	2.47	2.81	2.75	0.38	0.33	0.35	0.40	0.42	0.30	0.33	0.37	0.44	0.49
Malta	0.02	0.02	0.02	0.02	0.02	0.00	0.00	0.00	0.00	0.00	0.02	0.02	0.02	0.03	0.03
Netherlands	7.71	6.54	6.20	6.26	6.86	6.94	6.33	6.13	6.16	6.29	6.42	6.12	6.12	6.10	6.17
Austria	5.33	4.61	4.58	4.16	4.77	4.49	3.71	3.86	3.69	3.84	1.05	1.10	1.13	1.15	1.16
Poland	3.76	3.76	3.95	4.21	5.03	0.03	0.05	0.06	0.08	0.10	0.83	0.95	1.14	1.41	1.69

Table 5A.1 (Continued)

Countries	**Credit transfers**					**Direct debits**					**Card payments (except with e-money cards)**				
	2003	**2004**	**2005**	**2006**	**2007**	**2003**	**2004**	**2005**	**2006**	**2007**	**2003**	**2004**	**2005**	**2006**	**2007**
Portugal	0.55	0.39	0.55	0.57	0.64	0.99	0.87	0.80	0.76	0.87	3.61	3.28	3.28	3.14	3.05
Romania	0.47	0.56	0.63	0.82	1.25	0.06	0.11	0.12	0.13	0.12	0.11	0.13	0.18	0.09	0.18
Slovenia	–	0.82	0.80	0.80	0.86	–	0.21	0.21	0.22	0.22	0.44	0.43	0.42	0.41	0.38
Slovakia	0.78	0.72	0.62	0.79	0.94	0.02	0.02	0.21	0.22	0.62	0.13	0.14	0.16	0.17	0.42
Finland	3.45	2.96	3.06	3.01	3.39	0.44	0.42	0.42	0.39	0.41	2.77	2.74	2.91	3.24	3.37
Sweden	2.58	2.39	2.51	2.62	3.12	0.91	0.86	0.93	1.06	1.11	4.12	4.42	4.56	4.73	4.91
UK	13.40	13.44	14.64	14.03	15.11	16.85	15.60	15.74	15.44	15.83	28.95	27.88	27.09	26.72	26.43
MU-15	82.56	73.54	72.66	72.22	68.65	81.20	80.22	81.37	81.43	80.59	63.90	61.68	62.20	61.65	60.90
EU-27	100.00	100.00	100.00	100.00	100.00	100.00	100.00	100.00	100.00	100.00	100.00	100.00	100.00	100.00	100.00

Source: Adapted by the author from ECB (2008b).

Table 5A.2 Relative importance (%) of the main payment instruments in the EU (2008)

Countries	Credit transfers	Direct debits	Cards	Cheques
Belgium	42.2	11.3	42.4	0.4
Bulgaria	81.2	0.6	18.2	n/a
C. Republic	52.9	34.8	10.9	0.1
Denmark	20.1	13.5	65.4	1
Germany	35.2	50	14.1	0.4
Ireland	23.8	14.7	45	16.6
Estonia	37.6	6.7	55.7	0
Greece	21.8	9.5	50.5	17.2
Spain	14.5	42.9	39	2.5
France	17	19	41.2	21.9
Italy	27.9	14.5	36.6	10.1
Cyprus	19.5	14.4	35	31.1
Latvia	54.8	2	42.8	0
Lithuania	52.3	5.2	42.4	0.1
Luxembourg	48.6	10.9	38.7	0.2
Hungary	69.7	8.3	20.4	0
Malta	17.6	3.7	36.1	42.6
Netherlands	31.1	25.8	39.4	n/a
Austria	44.9	37.1	16.1	0.1
Poland	65.7	1.2	33.1	0
Portugal	9.8	13.7	64.1	12.4
Romania	68.1	2.7	25.2	3.9
Slovenia	53.2	12.9	33.8	0.1
Slovakia	52.9	25.3	21.8	0
Finland	40.6	4.5	24.9	0
Sweden	32.3	8.3	59.3	0
UK	20.9	20.2	49.8	9.2

Source: Adapted by the author from ECB (2008b).

6
Performance of European Banks

Introduction

The EU is one of the major global financial players that has been negatively affected by the recent turmoil that swept through global financial markets. Even though the recession in global economies has appeared to abate since mid-2009, there are still uncertainties concerning whether the recovery will be sustainable and whether the impact of the crisis on the EU financial integration will disappear. Today, we should ask, why is it important to monitor the EU financial integration process? The most straightforward answer is that increased competition in the EU economy as a whole has been one of the primary outcomes of the single market, and reducing financial barriers among member countries is expected to increase productivity gains. This will, in turn, generate a more efficient and competitive EU financial sector, which is important not only for the financial sector itself but also for all other sectors that rely on access to competitive sources of funding.

Moreover, as mentioned in previous chapters, the introduction of the euro, technological developments and deregulation have played an important role in fostering competition in the European banking sector since the 1990s (Molyneux, 2003, ch. 10).[1] Additionally, banking structural changes have created variations in the nature of banking industries and their performance levels (Altunbas and Chakravarty, 1998).[2] With this in mind, the chapter first examines the European financial markets. Secondly, in an attempt to identify performance divergence and the level of financial integration among the EU member countries, several financial indicators such as total capital ratio, net interest margin, cost-to-income ratio, return on assets (ROA) and return on equity (ROE) are considered. Finally, income statements and the balance sheet structures of groups of EU countries, that is, the EU-15,

EU-27 and NMS are examined, in an attempt to identify the level of financial integration among them.

Financial integration in the EU

The EU, the US and Japan remain the three major players in global financial markets. Figure 6.1 captures their relative market shares in the key segments of financial services. Some 50 per cent of total bank assets are held by EU financial institutions, followed by approximately 15 per cent by US, 10 per cent by Japan and 25 per cent by others. Insurance premiums have presented a similar pattern of popularity: EU countries cover 38 per cent of total transactions, followed by 31 per cent in the US. Moreover, stock market capitalization and debt securities are highest in the EU and the US, followed by other countries. It is interesting to observe that debt securities have not been popular in the biggest emerging markets, namely, India and China.

Another indicator of an advanced degree of financial integration can be illustrated by the high level of foreign ownership in the European banking sector. Figure 6.2 shows that foreign banks represent more than half of the total assets of national banking markets in most of the EU countries. Tellingly, the highest levels of foreign ownership are mostly found in countries from the NMS, with the highest being in Estonia. In regard to the EU-15, Luxembourg, Finland, Ireland and the UK received the highest levels of foreign capital.

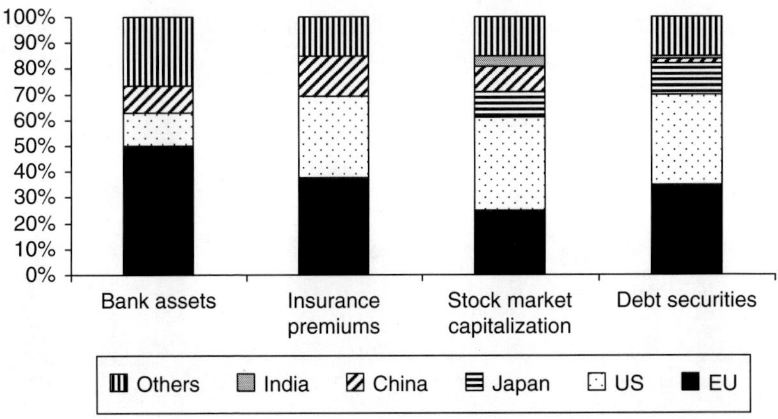

Figure 6.1 EU contributions to world financial activity in 2008–2009 (per cent)
Sources: Adapted by the author from World Federation of Exchanges (2009b), IMF (2008) and SwissRe (2009).

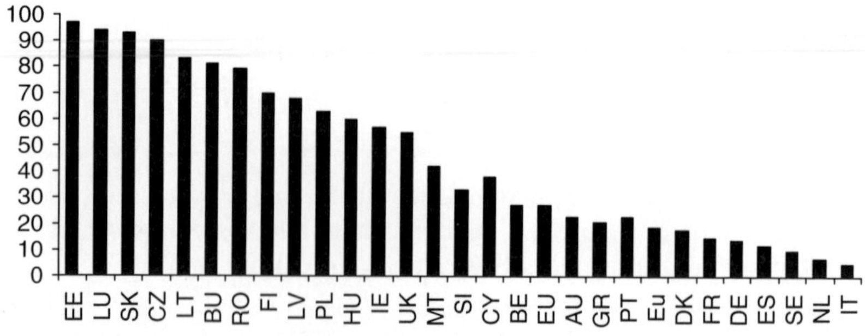

Figure 6.2 Market share of foreign-owned banks in the EU, 2008 (per cent of total assets)
Source: Adapted by the author from ECB (2009a).

European financial markets

Euro-area equity markets

Given the fact that the recent financial crisis had a significant impact on the functioning and competitiveness of global financial markets, equity markets have been hit by falling records of 47 per cent, from USD 60,693 billion to USD 32,575 billion in 2008, back to levels experienced in 2003 (see Figure 6.3).

Parallel to the trend in global equity markets, the euro-area equity markets have also been hit by the market turbulence, by around 50 per cent, whilst emerging markets were hit even harder due to high investor risk aversion and weakened investor confidence in these

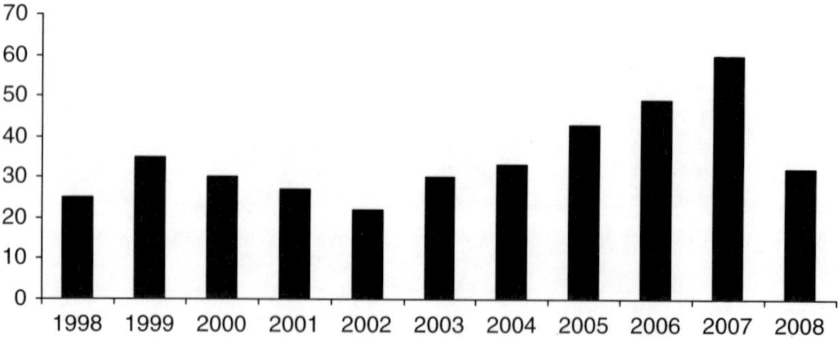

Figure 6.3 Global equity markets domestic market capitalization, 1998–2008 (USD trillion)
Source: World Federation of Exchanges (2009).

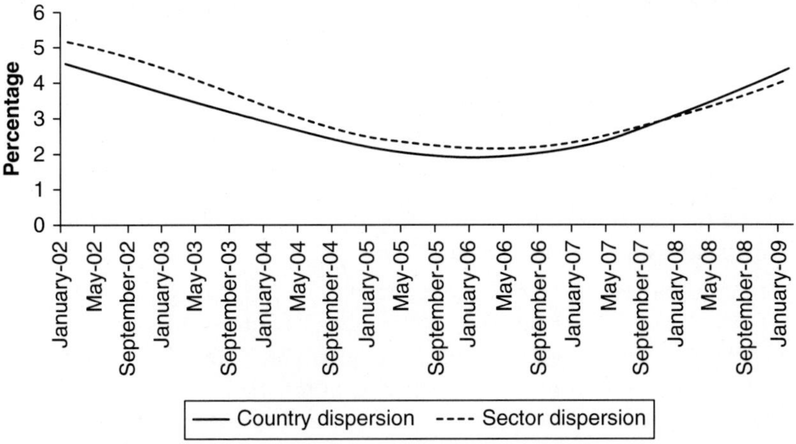

Figure 6.4 Cross-country and cross-sector dispersion of euro-area equity returns
Source: ECB (2009a).

countries. This has resulted in rising cross-country dispersion since October 2007 (see Figure 6.4).

Furthermore, the impact of the turmoil on euro-area equity market integration is confirmed by the increasing relevance of global shocks in explaining equity volatility, in comparison to euro-area events, over the 1973–2008 period (see Figure 6.5). Foreign equity investments in the EU provide evidence of the stagnation of equity investments originating from another EU country since 2004 (see Figure 6A.1 in the appendix).

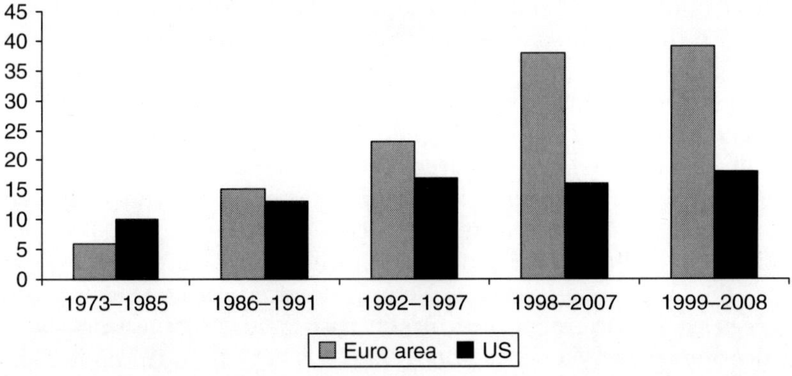

Figure 6.5 Proportion of variance in local euro-area equity returns explained by euro-area and US shocks, 1973–2008
Source: Adapted by the author from ECB (2009a).

By mid-2009, confidence had started to return to European capital markets, and euro-area equity market prices progressively increased with a parallel reduction of price volatility. These developments reflected a positive market attitude among investors as well as reduced uncertainty. This was particularly the case for the European bank equity price index, which launched even more dynamically than the general Eurostoxx Index (Bloomberg, 2009).

European money and bond markets

While they are at different stages of development, money and bond markets in the euro area showed a high level of integration over the last decade, just prior to the financial crisis. In particular, the convergence of prices in the European government bond market has been significant since the introduction of the single currency. Corporate bond and equity markets have also presented a positive integration trend. On one hand, integration is advanced in the euro-area money and bond markets, on the other, there seems to be room for consumers and businesses to benefit from further integration in the NMS.

It can be expected that the financial integration process will gain increasing impetus in the near future as a result of the implementation of the Markets in Financial Instruments Directive (MiFID), the Single Euro Payments Area (SEPA) and the adoption of the euro in an increasing number of EU countries. However, all the above have been negatively affected by the recent financial turmoil. For example, the financial crisis has heavily impacted on the European money market and generated high dispersion on country interest rates in the third quarter of 2008; furthermore, the cross-country standard deviation of EURIBOR exceeded that of the rate for a unified Euro GC Repo Market (EUREPO) (see Figure 6.6).

Secured repo agreements have been less influenced by the crisis. On the other hand, the unsecured money markets of non-euro-area countries have been heavily affected by the financial turbulence. While the share of "other euro area" counterparties for the unsecured segment decreased from 50 per cent to 42 per cent over the period 2007–2008, this remained almost stable in the repo market (see Figure 6.7).

In the case of non-euro-area countries, government bond markets have been heavily influenced by the crisis, and an increasing divergence among non-euro-area bond yields has been recorded since 2007 (see Figure 6.8). The trend shows an inclination in 2009 that suggests that the disintegration experienced might have been a short-term phenomenon linked to the dynamics of the financial crisis.

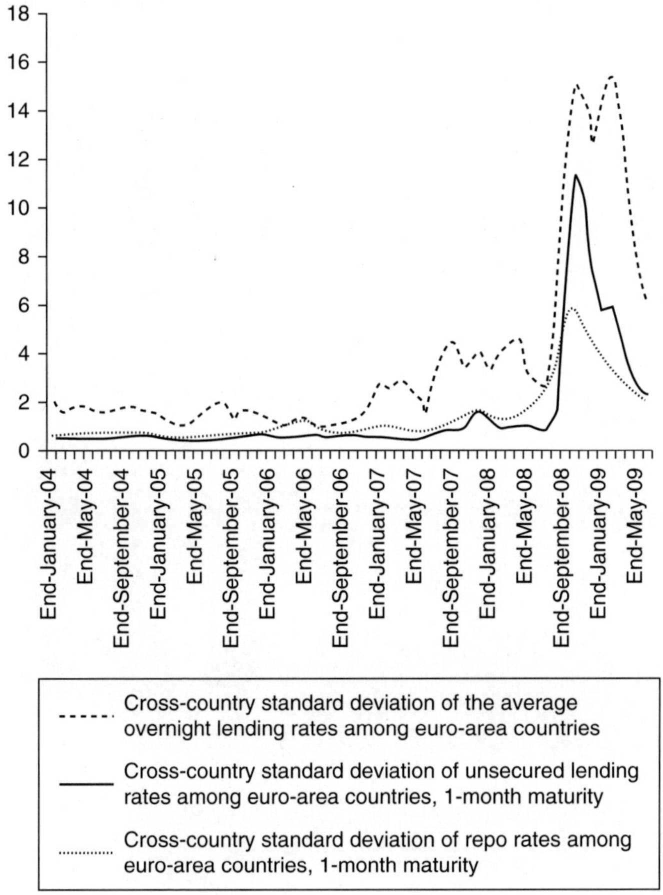

Figure 6.6 Cross-country standard deviation of EURLIBOR and EUREPO rates, 2004–2009 (basis points)
Source: ECB (2009a).

European securities market

Another area where policy had a considerable impact was securitization. Looking at the gross securitization issuance volumes in Figure 6.11, European issuance has been sustained during the turmoil, while US gross issuance volumes have sharply declined. However, when interpreting these statistics, it is important to be aware that primary markets continued to remain almost closed in the first half of 2009. While 81.2 billion EUR was issued in the second quarter in Europe, 99 per cent of all

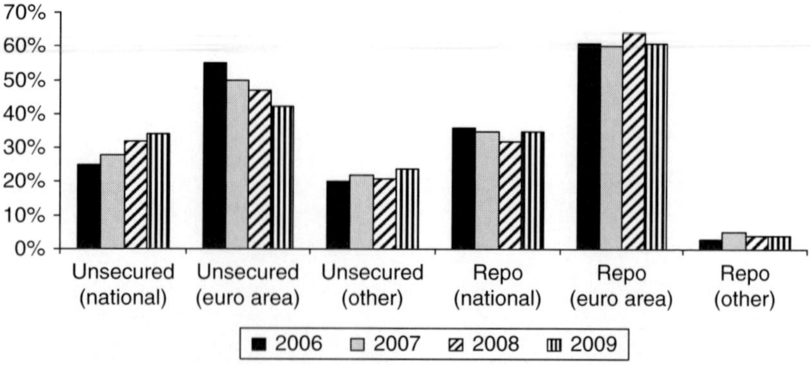

Figure 6.7 Geographical counterparty breakdowns in euro-area money markets, 2006–2009 (per cent)

Note: The data represented herein refers to the second quarter of each respective year.

Source: Adapted by the author from ECB, Financial Stability Reports (2006–2009).

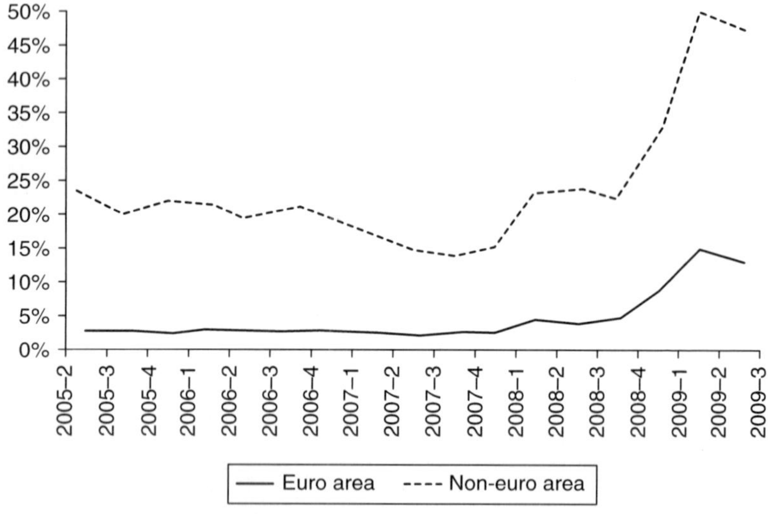

Figure 6.8 Convergence in long-term government bond yield in the EU, 2005–2009

Source: Adapted by the author from Eurostat (2009).

securities were retained on the balance sheet of the issuing banks. This reflected the effort by many central banks to enhance their liquidity and availability of credit by making securitization eligible as collateral for repo funding. In fact, there are signs of improvements in the European

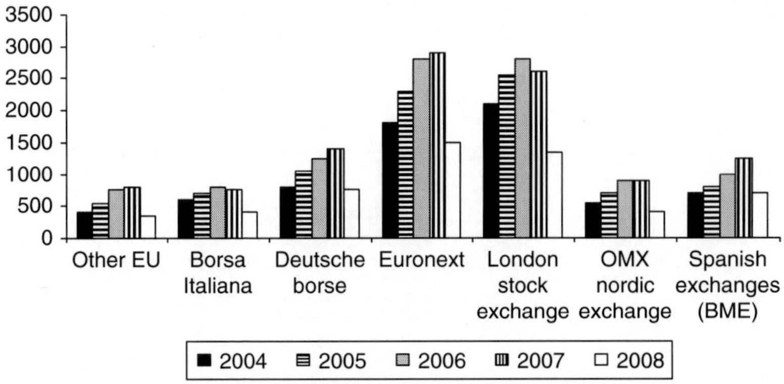

Figure 6.9 Average market capitalization in European stock exchanges, 2004–2008 (EUR billion)
Source: European Commission, European Financial Integration Report, 2008.

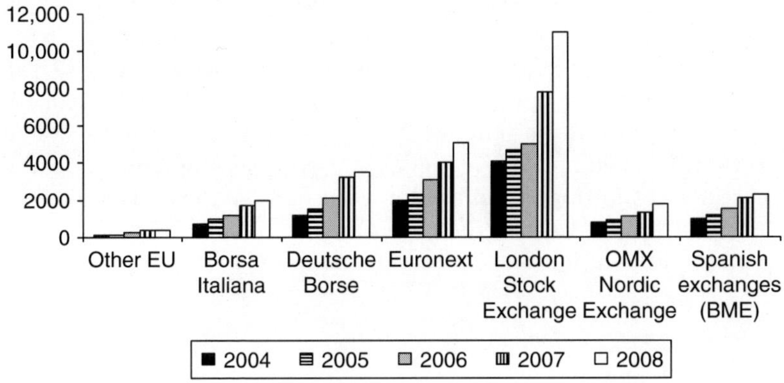

Figure 6.10 Total annual turnover of European stock exchanges, 2004–2008 (EUR billion)
Source: European Commission, European Financial Integration Report, 2008.

securitization market in that market spreads of European securitization started tightening, due to improved market sentiments, from the second quarter of 2009.

Moreover, in line with the global developments, autumn 2008 saw falling European stock markets. As a result, end of the year capitalization of the main European exchanges fell almost half, and by as much as 60 per cent on the smaller markets. Market capitalization in all of the EU stock exchanges experienced sharp recessions from 2007 to

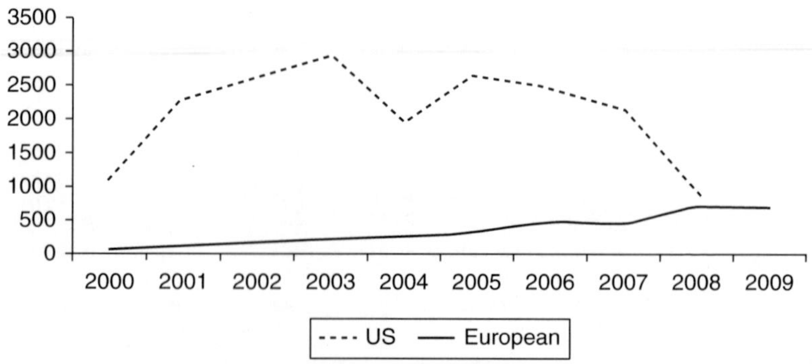

Figure 6.11 Securitization issuance in the EU and US, 2000–2009 (EUR billion)
Source: European Central Bank and Bank of America.

2008, with the highest observed in Euronext, followed by the London Stock Exchange. However, OMX Nordic Exchange was the least affected by the financial turmoil (see Figure 6.9). From 2007 to 2008 total trading volumes continued to grow on the big exchanges, while falling slightly on the other EU markets (from EUR 466 to 451 billion; see Figure 6.10).

It is also worth noting that while a recession in the financial system has been avoided and recent signals are positive, the European banking sector is still fragile and dealing with massive losses. Losses of top European banks have amounted to almost 350 billion EUR due to a combination of mark-to-market losses and credit losses since the beginning

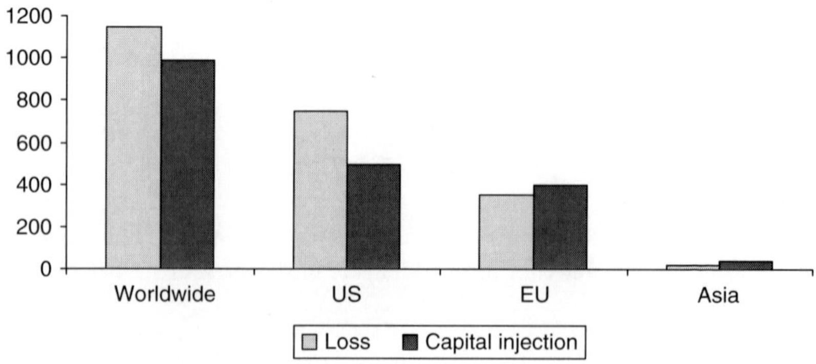

Figure 6.12 Regional breakdown of losses and capital injections in top European banks (EUR billion)
Source: Adapted by the author from Eurostat (2009b).

of the crisis. As a result, capital injections both from private and public sources have been made to fund the bulk of losses and avoid systemic consequences. Thus, many European banks have become dependent on public guarantees, and additional fresh capital could also be needed to bring down banks' leverage ratios further and to finance new credit losses. This would require a considerable effort, since financing costs are more expensive than before due to the downgrading of many banks' credit ratings (see Figure 6.12).

Efficiency and competition in the European banking sector

In an attempt to present an overview and comparison between European and US banks, Figure 6.13 illustrates the average bank profits of the 50 largest banks belonging to these groups in 2006 and 2007. It can be observed that the bank profits of all groups of banks have deteriorated between 2006 and 2007, and that in 2007 European banks achieved higher levels of profit compared with US banks, whilst, among US banks, commercial banks experienced higher profits than investment banks. In fact, the US investment banks achieved the highest profits in 2006. This could be linked with the ability of US investment banks to better exploit economies of scale given the size, scope and level of integration of their domestic market in 2006. However, as the global financial turmoil began in US investment banks, their 2007 profits have shrunk enormously.

Moreover, the reduction in profits observed in the US investment banks ranged from 20 per cent to 7 per cent, followed by 4 per cent

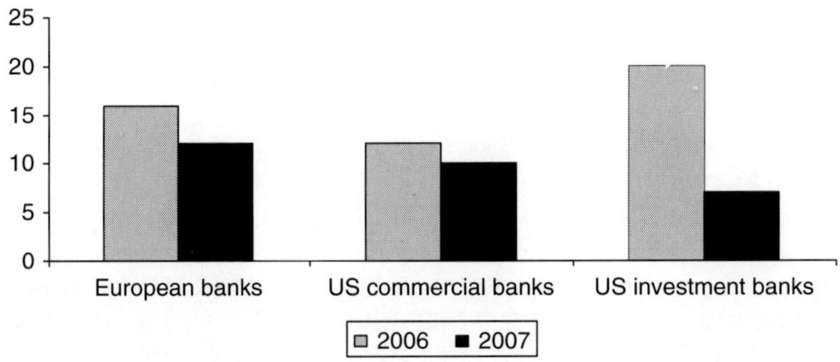

Figure 6.13 Bank profits in largest 50 EU and US banks, 2006–2007 (per cent)
Source: Created by the author from Bankscope.

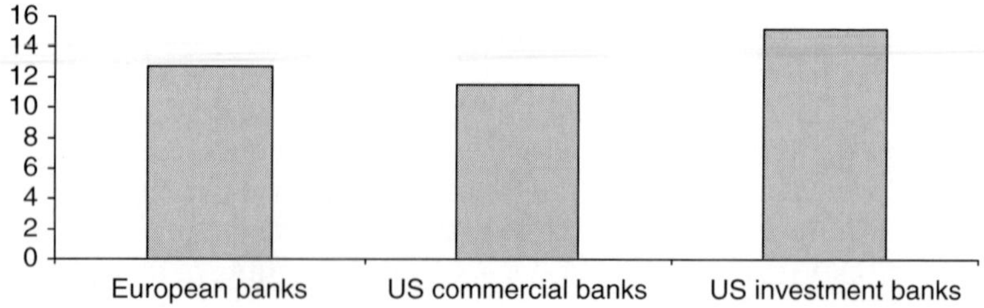

Figure 6.14 Average ROE in largest 50 EU and US banks, 2000–2007 (per cent)
Source: Created by the author from Bankscope.

in the group of European banks (from 16 per cent to 12 per cent) and 2 per cent in US commercial banks (from 12 per cent to 10 per cent). In terms of operational efficiency, average return on equity (ROE) for the same groups of banks is considered over the 2000–2007 period (see Figure 6.14). In this case, the US investment banks were the most efficient, followed by European banks, while US commercial banks were the most efficient of all.

Efficiency indicators

As a consequence of the global financial crisis, business activity in the European financial sector also shrank, and the size of the EU wholesale financial sector fell by 0.3 per cent in 2008, with a further contraction of 6.2 per cent in 2009. Moreover, retail financial services businesses continue to be held back by the high risk aversion of financial institutions. Throughout this section, data gathered from the income statements and balance sheets of European commercial banks and provided by BankScope, Bureau van Dijk, are examined and compared for the groups of EU-15, EU-27 and euro-area countries, which account for 90 per cent of all bank assets for Europe over the 2004–2009 period.

In terms of efficiency, the average ROE in the EU-15 commercial banking sector fell to 4.5 per cent in 2008 from 12 per cent in 2007, whilst the EU-27 performed better than the EU-15 average over the 2006–2008 period. Moreover, all groups of EU countries have been significantly affected by the financial turmoil, with decreasing average ROE figures during 2008 and 2009 (see Figure 6.15).

According to ECB financial stability reports, the EU-15 average was drawn down by numerous countries, such as Belgium, Germany, Denmark, the Netherlands and the UK, which experienced high losses in their financial sectors. In all EU countries, the average ROE witnessed sharp declines in 2008. Austria, Belgium and Latvia, which had the

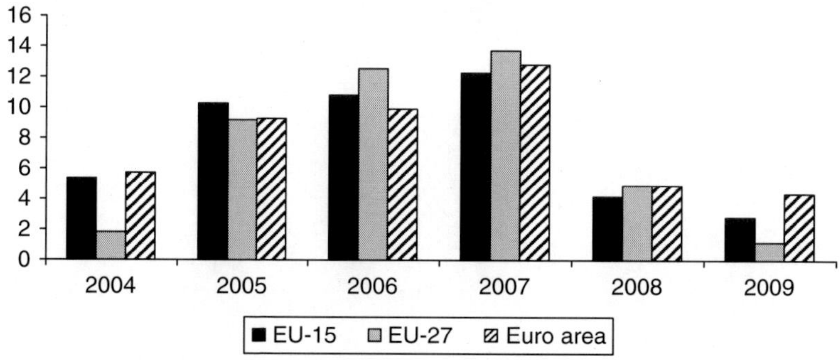

Figure 6.15 ROE of groups of European commercial banks, 2004–2009 (per cent)
Source: Bankscope and author's calculations.

highest figures in 2006, had significant recessions in 2008. Figure 6.16 compares the average annual ROE figures of EU and US large banks. Even though the EU banks tended to be more profitable before the crisis, they experienced higher losses than their US counterparts, resulting in a negative average ROE in 2008. This may be linked with the high exposure of EU's largest banks to US toxic assets.

ROA figures are also examined with particular regard to the evolution of performance in the European banking sector. A comparison of averages for each group of EU countries is presented in Figure 6.17, which

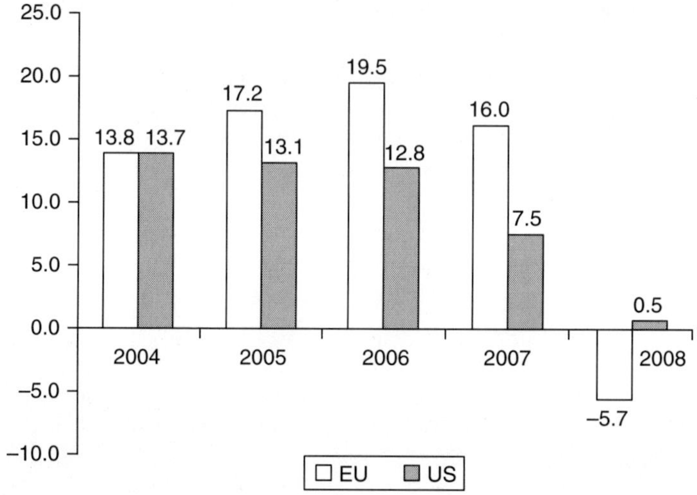

Figure 6.16 ROE of EU and US large banks, 2004–2008 (per cent)
Source: ECB (2005–2009).

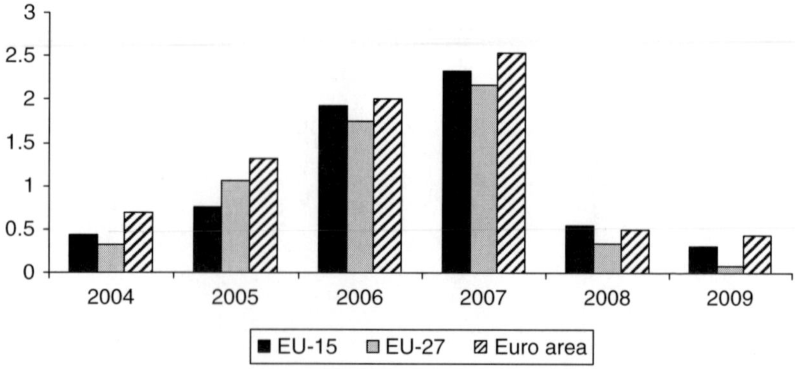

Figure 6.17 ROA of groups of European commercial banks, 2004–2009 (per cent)
Source: Bankscope and author's calculations.

has illustrated similar patterns to the ROE figures with significant recessions in 2008 and 2009. The lowest average ROA are observed in the EU-27 over the crisis period.

In general, EU-15 commercial banks experienced higher levels of ROA than the others, except in 2005, during which euro-area commercial banks achieved the highest level. It can be observed that ROA ratios for EU-27 countries were the lowest among all groups, except in 2005. This can be attributable to the financial help NMS have received from the EU, to ensure successful financial integration when they became EU members in 2004. The improving trend for all groups of banks over the 2004–2007 period experienced a sharp recession with the burst of the financial crisis. In fact, average ROA figures for all groups of banks during 2008 and 2009 were almost lower than 2004. On the other hand, the high ROA ratios identified in all groups of EU commercial banks just before the crisis attracted new competition, which forced a reduction in net interest margins and bank profits (see Figure 6.18). Contrary to the low ROA in 2008 and 2009, all groups of EU commercial banks maintained high net interest margins over the same period.

In terms of competition, the crisis had an influence on the EU banking sector. Various EU governments offered financial support, including partial or full state involvement, to banks that had experienced insolvency risk and other balance sheet problems. Even though government stakes in banks have raised some concerns about cross-border competition, the basic indicators of competition, such as net interest margins,

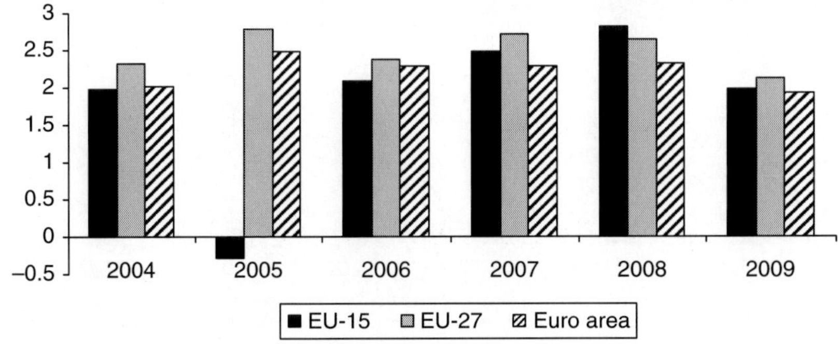

Figure 6.18 NIM of groups of European commercial banks, 2004–2009 (per cent)
Source: Bankscope and author's calculations.

did not show significant movement in 2008, either in the countries that experienced the biggest banking sector problems or in the EU overall.

At this point it can be stated that difficult economic conditions over the crisis period created pressure on banks; such pressure is now expected to motivate them to reduce their expenses by improving cost control, developing M&As or investing more in IT technologies over the medium term. If banks manage to adapt their cost basis to the forecasted slow economic recovery over the next few years, we can expect to observe further efficiency improvements in the EU banking sector.

Similar differences and a general worsening were observed in the cost-to-income ratios (CTI), as a result of higher costs and lower revenues. Following the declining trend recorded in 2005 and 2006, the average CTI increased to approximately 67 per cent in the EU-27, 70 per cent in the EU-15 and even higher in the euro-area countries in 2008 (see Figure 6.19).

At the country level, the highest CTI ratios in 2008 were detected in Austria, Belgium, Germany, Denmark, France and the Netherlands, whilst the lowest were in Estonia and Romania. In an attempt to compare the efficiency levels of EU and US large banks, Figure 6.20 presents the annual average CTI estimates. It shows that a slight recession was observed in the EU banks even before the financial turmoil. Even though their performance worsened dramatically in 2007 compared with their US counterparts, their recovery was very fast in 2008.

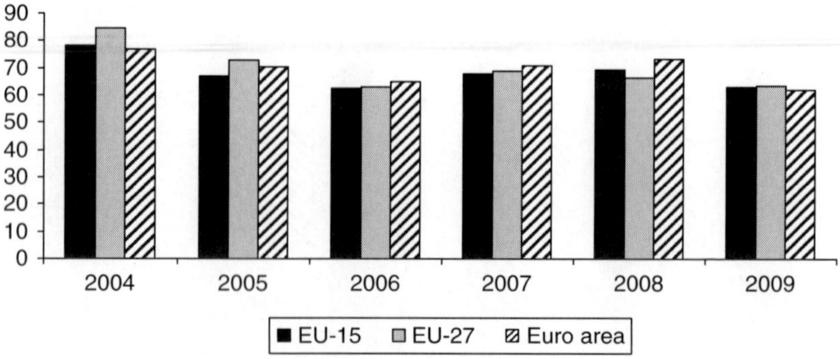

Figure 6.19 CTI ratios of groups of European commercial banks, 2004–2008 (per cent)
Source: Bankscope and author's calculations.

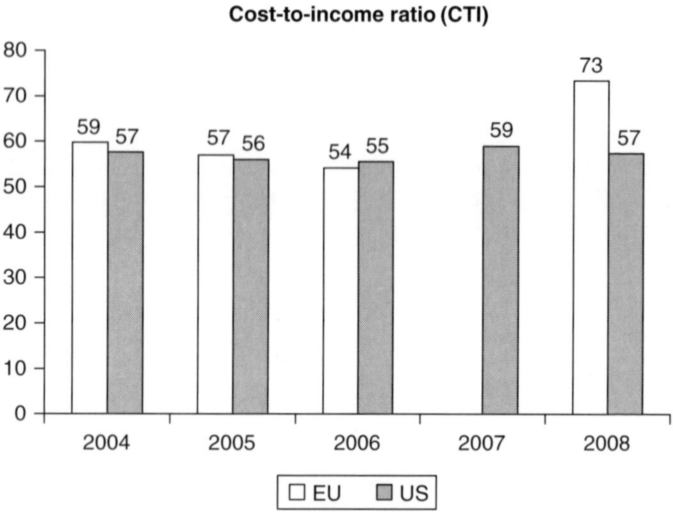

Figure 6.20 CTI of EU and US large banks, 2004–2008 (per cent)
Source: ECB (2005–2009).

Liquidity indicators

The tightening of liquidity due to the crisis has increased the importance of debt securities as a source of alternative finance. One observation from the market during the crisis has been the strength and increased competitiveness of those countries that can provide liquidity to markets such as China and the Middle East. Overall, amounts outstanding rose 16 per cent in 2008 to USD 83 trillion. Moreover, corporate bonds increased to record levels as companies issued bonds as a source of finance at the beginning of 2009; Italy, Germany and France remain the key issuers of public sector debt in Europe.

In fact, the ECB had made liquidity injections into the market since the start of the financial turmoil. The improved liquidity situation, as shown by the ECB survey results, indicated that by mid-2009 the majority of euro-area banks no longer experienced problems in their access to the money market as a result of the turmoil. The increasing net liquidity volumes in the euro-area monetary financial institutions supported this observation (see Figure 6.21).

In terms of the groups of European commercial banks, our dataset indicates that the ratio of liquid assets to customer and short-term funding (CSTF) declined since the financial turmoil in all groups of banks, as compared with the previous years (see Figure 6.22). The euro-area commercial banks presented the highest liquidity ratios during 2007 and 2008, whilst the highest decline was experienced in the EU-15. This is attributable to the fact that, among the EU-15, big countries such as Germany, the UK, Italy and Spain witnessed the most severe liquidity problems in their financial sectors.

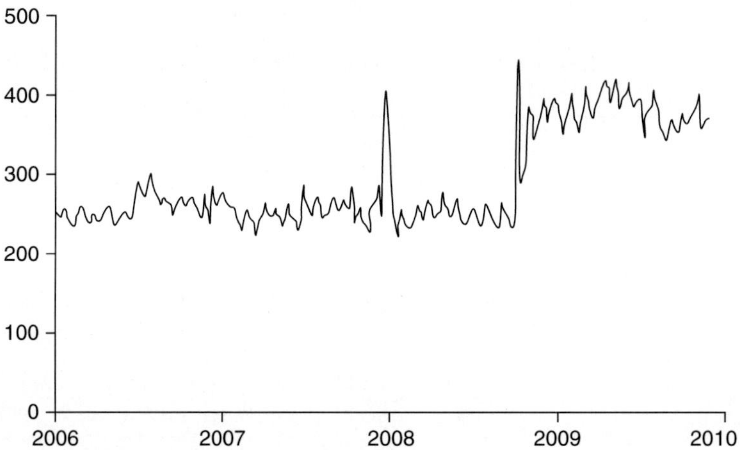

Figure 6.21 Euro-area liquidity indicators, 2006–2009
Sources: ECB; Statistical data warehouse on line.

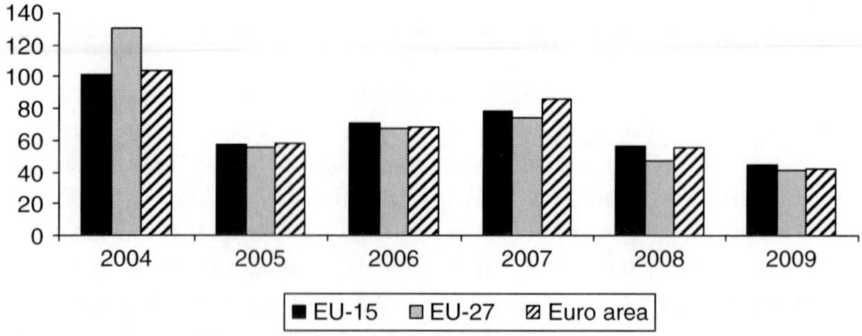

Figure 6.22 Liquid assets to CSTF of groups of European commercial banks, 2004–2009 (per cent)
Source: Bankscope and author's calculations.

In terms of all banks in the EU, Table 6.1 presents the percentage share of individual country figures for cash and short-term government debt to total assets over the 2004–2008 period. As a consequence of the financial turmoil, all EU countries experienced liquidity problems.

Asset quality

The asset quality of EU banks deteriorated in 2008 in all subgroups analysed, although developments in non-performing loans to total

Table 6.1 Cash and short-term debt to total assets ratio, 2004–2008 (per cent)

Country	2004	2005	2006	2008	Mean	% change 2004–08
Austria	8.08	34.41	29.93	7.26	19.92	−10.15
Belgium	0.98	2.37	71.55	20.82	23.93	2024.49
Bulgaria	n/a	n/a	211.91	10.89	111.40	−94.86
C. Republic	12.50	226.48	209.77	17.78	116.63	42.24
Cyprus	14.46	238.28	223.60	8.45	121.20	−41.56
Denmark	0.61	76.18	56.48	0.56	33.46	−8.20
Estonia	7.12	67.94	40.20	13.50	32.19	89.61
Finland	6.81	172.75	180.65	5.04	91.31	−25.99
France	1.45	60.74	62.34	41.18	41.43	2740.00
Germany	1.75	5.79	6.49	17.73	7.94	913.14
Greece	5.77	100.47	107.46	6.58	55.07	14.04
Hungary	17.97	78.76	75.89	n/a	57.54	293.99
Ireland	1.16	59.63	70.26	32.53	40.90	2704.31
Italy	5.71	69.07	74.36	13.13	40.57	129.95
Latvia	4.59	81.00	55.68	7.34	37.15	59.91
Lithuania	14.18	57.41	41.33	5.43	29.59	−61.71

Luxembourg	3.49	5.96	5.65	7.99	5.77	128.94
Malta	4.05	34.83	37.22	2.53	19.66	−37.53
Netherlands	3.28	56.65	62.51	17.84	35.07	443.90
Poland	19.27	191.04	154.88	11.34	94.13	−41.15
Portugal	2.88	82.55	85.94	5.70	44.27	97.92
Romania	n/a	n/a	217.79	25.21	121.50	−88.42
Slovakia	21.90	150.03	191.95	11.14	93.76	−49.13
Slovenia	2.69	9.05	35.46	5.59	13.20	107.81
Spain	1.69	53.87	59.30	2.83	29.42	67.46
Sweden	4.55	33.88	36.89	n/a	25.11	566.37
UK	1.21	9.51	7.34	40.49	14.64	3246.28
Mean	6.73	78.35	89.36	13.56	50.25	101.49

Source: Adapted by the author from ECB, EU Banking Sector Stability (2005–2009).

loans ratio differ significantly across countries (see Table 6A.1 in the appendix). For the EU-15 banking sector as a whole, the ratio of non-performing loans to total outstanding loans increased by 50.9 per cent, from 1.65 per cent to 2.49 per cent from 2007 to 2008 (see Figure 6.23). This was due to both a significant increase in non-performing loans and slowing credit growth following the financial turmoil. The figure experienced in 2008 was the highest since 2003. The EU-26 witnessed the

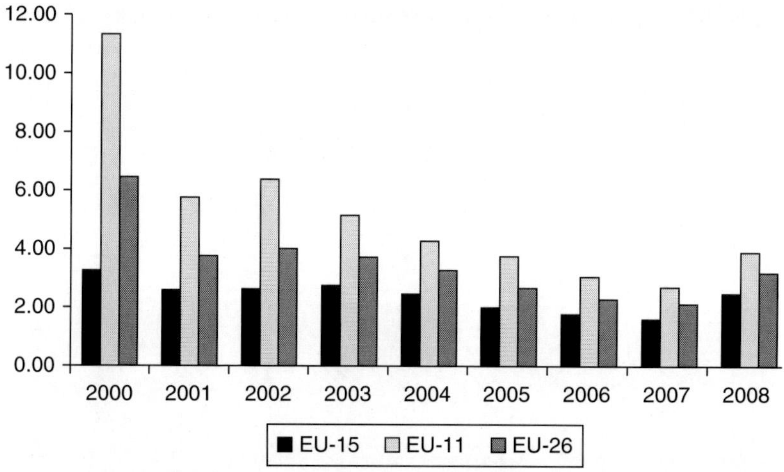

Figure 6.23 Non-performing loans to total loans of groups of European commercial banks, 2000–2008 (per cent)
Note: Data for Cyprus was not available in the group of EU-11.
Source: Bankscope and author's calculations.

highest percentage change (51.17 per cent) from 2007 to 2008 whilst NMS experienced the lowest (43.64 per cent). According to the EU banking sector stability report (2009) the rate of increase in non-performing loans rose further in most of the EU countries during the first quarter of 2009. The declining asset quality was significant in those countries where output contracted the most.

Profits and balance sheet structure of the European commercial banks

Total assets to GDP

Figure 6.24 illustrates that the ratio of total assets to GDP in the EU-27 grew from 319 per cent to 334 per cent between 2006 and 2007. In keeping with the general catching up process, the growth of banking assets in the NMS remained lower, which saw around a 25 per cent increase, reaching 103 per cent, while the EU-15 showed a 10.4 per cent increase, reaching 351.4 per cent, between 2006 and 2007. On average, the fact that the banking sectors in the euro area grew faster than those in the non-euro area is mainly attributable to the economic slowdown in the UK. The total assets of commercial banks in individual EU countries over the 2001–2007 period are indicated in Table 6A.2 of the appendix.

To give an overview and comparison, Figure 6.25 illustrates total assets to home country GDP in the top 25 global banks. The highest ratio is observed in UBS and Credit Suisse, both from

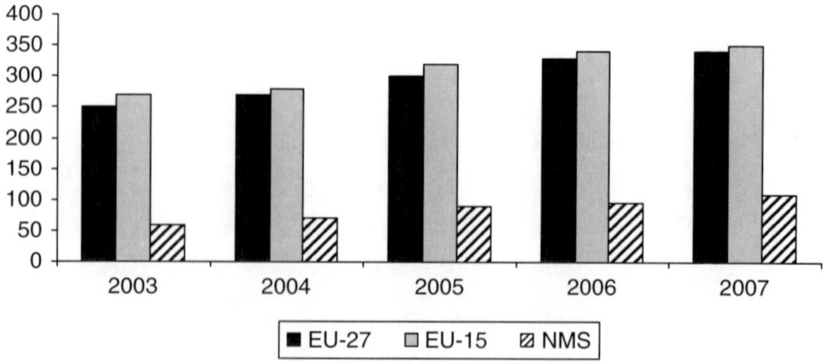

Figure 6.24 Total assets to GDP of groups of European commercial banks, 2003–2007 (per cent)
Source: Bankscope and author's calculations.

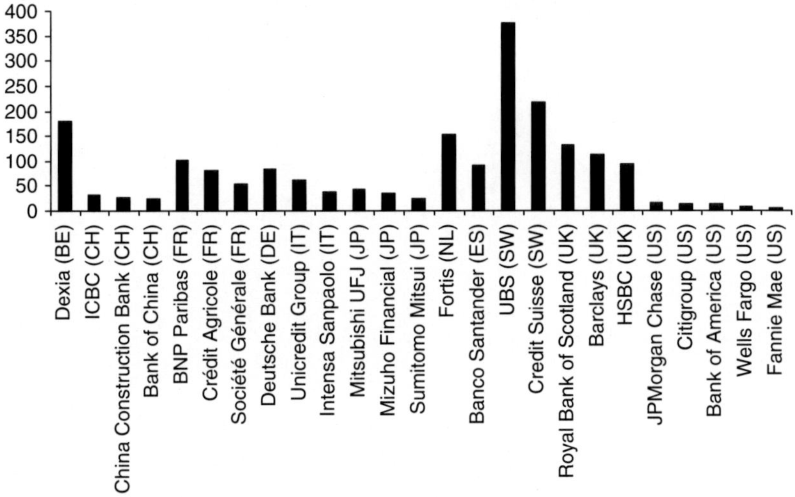

Figure 6.25 Total assets to home country GDP of top 25 global banks, 2009 (per cent)
Source: Adapted by the author from www.zerohedge.com

Switzerland. On the other hand, the lowest ratios are in US banks.

Table 6.2 shows total assets as a percentage of home country GDP in individual EU countries and overall averages over the 2001–2008 period. The whole EU-27 banking sector grew rapidly, reflecting the integration of the EU financial system, that is, the average growth of banks' assets outpaced GDP growth over the 2001–2008 period. In terms of GDP, bank assets in the EU-27 reached 337.5 per cent in 2008 with an increase of approximately 31 per cent since 2001. This indicator was equal to 331.9 per cent as the EU-15 average in 2008 with an increase of around 33 per cent since 2001. Figures indicated that the average difference in the bank asset to GDP ratio among EU-15 and EU-27 was small (approximately 5.6 per cent) in 2008. Thus, the impact driven by the NMS is small. Therefore, it can be stated that NMS banks still have a less significant role than EU-15 banks on the EU-27 average. Among the NMS, Malta and Cyprus were the two small economies with the strongest banking systems, with bank assets amounting to 735 per cent of GDP and 697 per cent of GDP in 2008, respectively. The high share in these two countries was a result of the existence of a efficient banking system.

Table 6.2 Total assets of banks as a percentage of home country GDP, 2001–2008

Countries	2001	2002	2003	2004	2005	2006	2007	2008	% change 2001–2008
EU-27	257.7	254.4	263.2	275.0	299.7	317.7	332.4	337.5	30.97
MU-15	249.8	248.1	251.6	261.6	279.5	293.3	316.8	331.9	32.87
Austria	269.8	253.4	262.6	272.9	295.0	307.0	328.9	378.4	40.25
Belgium	299.8	289.3	301.6	315.7	349.3	352.6	387.5	369.6	23.28
Bulgaria	n/a	n/a	52.1	66.5	79.7	88.4	108.1	107.9	107.10
Cyprus	334.8	304.4	355.5	365.7	444.8	509.2	581.7	697.0	108.18
C. Republic	113.2	99.0	96.4	98.7	100.7	101.3	110.1	104.4	−7.77
Denmark	253.5	274.3	301.8	319.4	359.9	376.5	431.7	467.9	84.58
Estonia	63.2	67.3	72.6	89.0	107.1	117.0	134.9	139.0	119.94
Finland	116.9	115.2	127.5	139.6	149.3	152.7	160.1	206.2	76.39
France	251.7	247.4	250.7	266.2	293.9	317.1	352.7	370.5	47.20
Germany	296.7	297.2	295.5	297.8	304.3	306.7	312.1	316.0	6.50
Greece	138.5	128.7	124.4	124.0	142.2	147.8	168.0	190.2	37.33
Hungary	66.2	65.8	n/a	n/a	88.3	104.1	107.0	118.5	79.00

Ireland	360.8	364.6	412.5	485.0	580.8	664.5	701.6	760.4	110.75
Italy	148.3	156.3	159.2	163.5	175.5	188.0	215.7	230.8	55.63
Latvia	78.1	73.2	85.0	99.9	120.9	141.4	146.0	139.5	78.62
Lithuania	32.1	33.3	39.1	47.1	63.1	72.3	83.8	82.2	156.07
Luxembourg	3194.2	2761.8	2539.2	2525.8	2620.7	2475.1	2514.2	2541.0	–20.45
Malta	317.2	346.2	404.9	461.5	566.7	587.3	691.9	735.4	131.84
Netherlands	282.7	291.6	309.0	341.5	330.2	346.9	387.1	375.9	32.97
Poland	62.9	55.4	58.5	69.3	66.9	69.7	76.0	72.7	15.58
Portugal	272.4	259.7	251.6	239.6	241.5	255.5	269.7	290.2	6.53
Romania	n/a	n/a	28.5	38.0	44.4	53.1	58.2	61.7	116.49
Slovakia	n/a	82.9	80.6	90.6	98.3	93.6	91.7	n/a	10.62
Slovenia	78.3	81.5	83.7	90.1	105.0	112.3	126.2	132.0	68.58
Spain	183.3	184.1	192.0	204.2	236.5	256.1	280.3	308.7	68.41
Sweden	180.0	179.7	188.4	208.4	221.7	246.8	255.4	274.0	52.22
UK	354.8	342.3	381.8	400.5	465.5	509.0	493.2	487.8	37.49

– n/a indicates data not available from the source.
Source: Adapted by the author from ECB, Eurostat and author's calculations.

In the 2001–2008 period, the highest increase in total assets to GDP ratio was observed in Malta (418.1 per cent), Ireland (399.6 per cent) and Cyprus (362.2 per cent), whereas the lowest was in Slovakia (8.9 per cent). In contrast, negative figures were identified in the Czech Republic (–8.9 per cent) and Luxembourg (–653.3 per cent). In the case of the NMS banking industries, Malta was the dominant country in terms of total asset shares in 2008, followed by Cyprus and Latvia. However, countries such as Poland, Romania and Lithuania had significantly lower shares.[3] In general, the financial systems of EU-15 countries were dominated by larger institutions than that of the NMS. Gelos and Roldos (2004) emphasized that the banking systems in NMS were operating in a more competitive environment than that of EU-15 countries. This was mainly due to the removal of financial barriers in the process of becoming an EU member country, changes in the number of banks and financial help from other EU countries.

Capital adequacy

At the end of 2009 the average equity to total assets ratio was almost 7 per cent for the EU-27. On average, the bank capital ratios were higher in euro-area countries than in the EU-15 and EU-27 (see Figure 6.26). The level of capital varies not only with the aim of satisfying prudential regulation and the decisions of the owner and managers but also due to the structural features of the countries' markets as well as the risk of economic shocks (Marques Ibanez and Molyneux, 2001). As a result, banks in countries undergoing economic transition are under pressure to keep

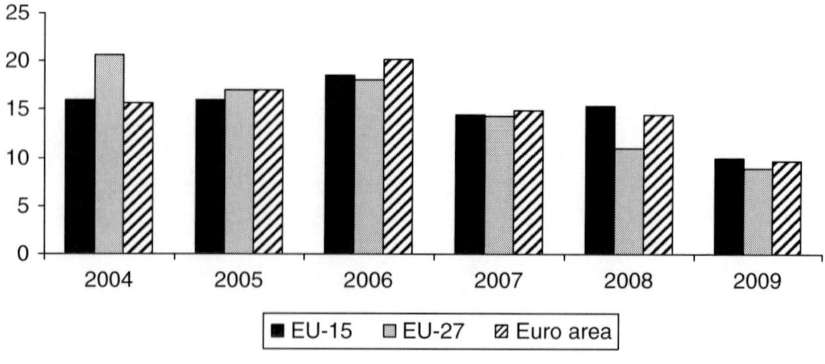

Figure 6.26 Equity to total assets ratio of groups of European commercial banks, 2004–2009 (per cent)
Source: Bankscope and author's calculations.

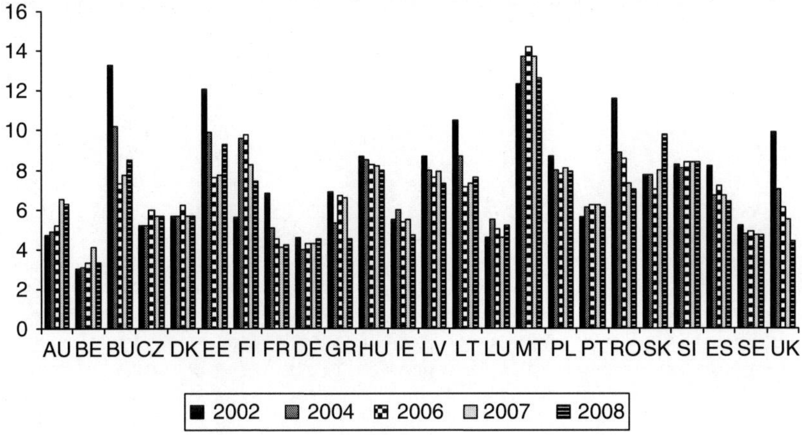

Figure 6.27 Bank capital to assets ratio of selected European countries, 2002–2008 (per cent)
Source: Bankscope and author's calculations.

a high level of capitalization. Additionally, the increase in capitalization can be partly explained by the need to fulfil the new regulations of the BIS Basel Committee.

At the country level, Figure 6.27 illustrates the average bank capital to assets ratio of selected EU countries over the 2002–2008 period. Bulgaria, Estonia, Lithuania and Slovakia experienced increasing figures from 2007 to 2008 among the NMS. On the other hand, Luxembourg, France and Germany are the sole countries experiencing similar trends among the EU-15, albeit with smaller amounts than their NMS counterparts. In contrast, other EU-15 countries experienced a decreasing capital to assets ratio.

Total loans

An analysis of the growth of customer loans in individual EU countries can identify a range of factors associated with banking development in economies. The observed rate of growth in customer loans reflected the demand for banking loans and their supply by individual banks. It is important to recognize that the behaviour of banks and their customers is not necessarily constant across countries and over time. In fact, the supply and demand for bank loans varies according to the progress in banking reforms. These particular factors may have a significant impact on the confidence of banks in the repayment of loans by their borrowers and on the confidence of depositors. In an attempt to present a clear

Table 6.3 Total loans of European banks to home country GDP, 2001–2007 (per cent)

Countries	2001	2002	2003	2004	2005	2006	2007
Austria	137.6	135.2	133.7	137.6	145.4	145.6	149.0
Belgium	105.1	107.5	107.7	107.8	122.9	124.9	127.3
Bulgaria	n/a	n/a	n/a	43.1	52.8	55.9	78.9
Cyprus	n/a	n/a	n/a	n/a	224.3	233.5	281.7
C. Republic	n/a	38.6	40.8	40.4	44.0	49.0	57.0
Denmark	n/a	155.7	161.8	178.5	195.1	212.5	231.0
Estonia	38.4	42.1	37.6	61.2	74.8	90.8	105.5
Finland	62.6	64.4	69.6	73.6	80.7	84.9	88.6
France	97.2	96.3	97.8	100.3	106.8	112.7	122.1
Germany	155.0	151.5	147.9	144.0	142.4	138.7	136.7
Greece	61.2	66.9	71.4	77.8	85.3	90.5	99.4
Hungary	36.0	39.1	38.2	n/a	58.7	70.2	74.2
Ireland	174.3	163.9	157.9	185.6	216.4	239.3	263.4
Italy	82.8	84.5	87.0	88.2	92.7	99.2	115.0
Latvia	32.2	36.4	41.8	51.7	73.2	101.5	103.4
Lithuania	n/a	n/a	n/a	31.2	44.3	54.4	65.8
Luxembourg	661.0	554.8	463.4	440.4	483.4	473.8	530.7
Malta	161.6	167.7	183.9	n/a	233.9	280.7	375.7
Netherlands	149.3	155.4	164.0	178.0	189.3	196.4	195.2
Poland	n/a	34.0	34.5	38.3	37.6	41.4	50.1
Portugal	138.3	141.3	140.4	141.5	146.6	155.9	166.5
Romania	n/a	n/a	n/a	21.8	26.9	38.0	46.4
Slovakia	n/a	n/a	n/a	34.5	39.7	45.6	47.0
Slovenia	n/a	n/a	n/a	59.8	65.7	76.3	92.7
Spain	107.6	111.6	117.3	127.6	149.1	172.5	186.9
Sweden	n/a	n/a	106.5	108.8	121.1	133.2	138.3
UK	143.4	142.5	219.6	228.5	259.9	273.5	293.8
Euro area	119.7	119.0	119.6	121.9	128.8	134.5	142.0
EU-27	118.7	119.2	132.3	136.2	147.1	154.3	163.6

Source: ECB and author's calculations.

identification, a comparison of total loans of banks in individual EU countries is illustrated in Table 6.3.

In general, loans of European banks dominated the aggregate balance sheet figures on the assets side. As expected, large countries such as Germany, Spain, France and Italy provided the highest amount of credit in the EU-27 (see Table 6A.3 in the appendix). On the other hand, Greece, Luxembourg and Finland presented the lowest figures. From the group of NMS, Poland, the Czech Republic and Hungary had the highest figures, while Lithuania, Estonia and Malta had the lowest. The highest percentage change in the amount of total loans in the 2001–2007 period were observed in Spain (168 per cent), the UK (155 per cent) and Greece (153 per cent) in the EU-15. For 2007, Belgium (57 per cent), Sweden (56 per cent) and France (59 per cent) had the lowest level of increase in total loans.

As with the EU-27 average, there was an increase in the lending volume from approximately 119 per cent in 2001 to 164 per cent of GDP in 2007. In terms of EU-15 averages, the highest level of bank lending was observed in Luxembourg at 531 per cent and the UK at 294 per cent GDP in 2007. A high level of banking activity was also observed in Portugal, Spain and the Netherlands. However, in the NMS total loans granted by banks were, on average, significantly lower than they were in the EU-15. This suggested that bank lending was less developed in the NMS. The exception to this was Poland, which was catching up with the figures in Finland and Luxembourg. In contrast, banking activities were low in the Czech Republic, which had the largest banking sector. The ratio of total loans as a percentage of GDP was only about 57 per cent in 2007.[4] Figure 6.28 compares the three groups of commercial banks in the dataset over the 2001–2007 period.

In terms of averages, Figure 6.29 presents total amounts of loans in the euro-area countries over the 1997–2010 period. Since the start of the financial turmoil, the euro-area banking sector witnessed significant sharp declines.

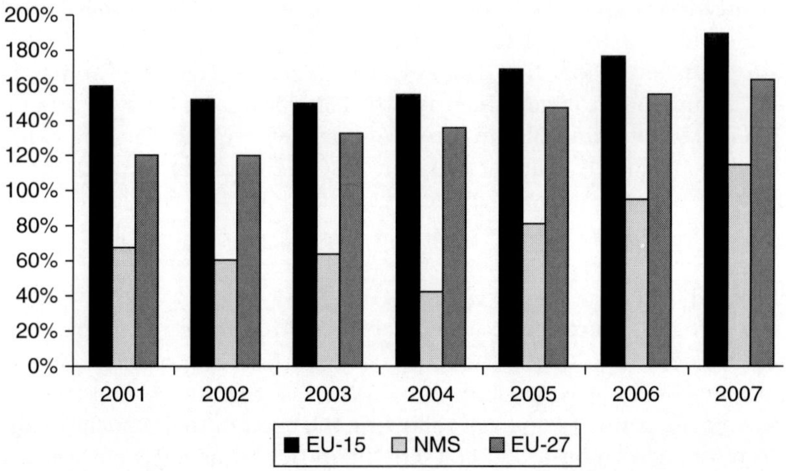

Figure 6.28 Total loans to GDP of groups of European commercial banks, 2001–2007 (per cent)
Source: ECB and author's calculations.

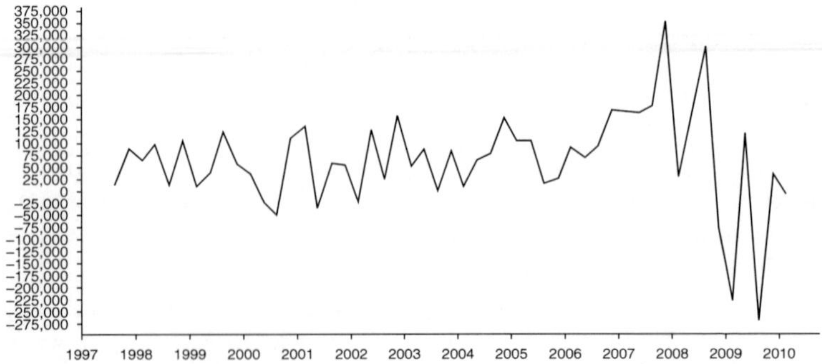

Figure 6.29 Euro-area loans, 1997–2010 (EUR million)
Source: Bankscope.

In terms of cross-border liabilities, EU financial integration, through cross-border M&As, has risen sharply over the past decade and has brought with it a range of benefits to both home and host countries. Benefits range from increased income generation, improvements in technology and risk management, increased access to funds, risk diversification and the deepening of financial markets. The most notable example of the rise in foreign participation in the domestic banking market is found in Central, Eastern and Southern Europe countries (CESE). In many of these markets, the pattern of financial integration has been less diversified and concentrated exposures have developed in individual markets. The majority of CESE countries rely on Western European banks for their funding, with Austria, Germany and Italy accounting for the largest share and the Baltic States (Estonia, Latvia and Lithuania) obtaining funding from Sweden. In terms of lending exposure, Austria has the largest exposure to CESE. The claims of its banks on CESE amount to over 70 per cent of the Austrian GDP and 26 per cent of its banking system assets.

Total deposits

By looking at Figure 6.30, it can be observed that there has been a continuous decline in the total deposits to total assets ratio for the whole euro-area banking sector since 2003. However, the ratio was at its lowest over the period of analysis following the burst of the financial crisis. Moreover, according to ECB (2009c) figures, total deposits constituted around 40 per cent of total assets in 2008. Individual country figures on total amount of deposits from non-credit institutions are shown in Table 6A.4 of the appendix.

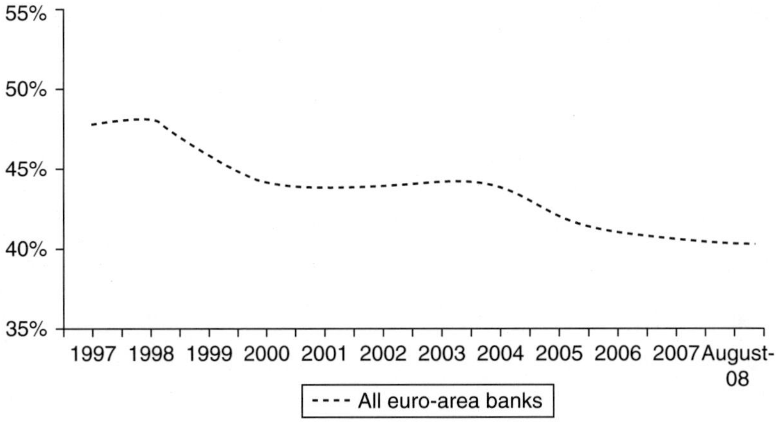

Figure 6.30 Total deposits to total assets ratio, 1997–2008 (per cent)
Source: Bankscope and author's calculations.

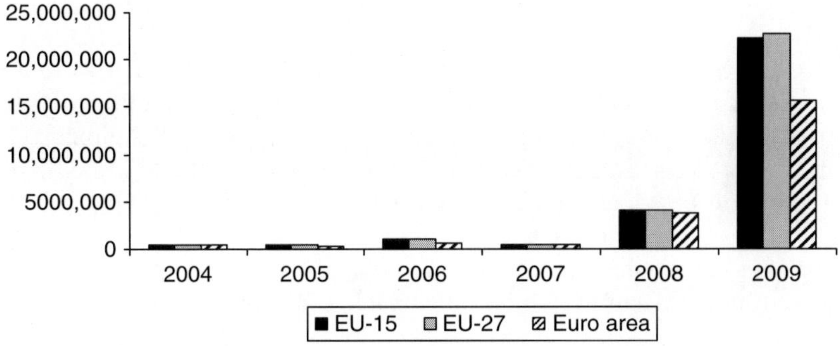

Figure 6.31 Total deposits of groups of European commercial banks, 2004–2009 (USD million)
Source: Bankscope and author's calculations.

In an attempt to identify the divergence of total amount of deposits among the EU-15, EU-27 and NMS commercial banks, Figure 6.31 presents the situation in million USD. The most striking disparity observed among the groups of commercial banks in 2009 was that the lowest amount of total deposits was in the euro area, whereas EU-27 had the highest levels. However, the case was different for EU-15 commercial banks, which acquired similar amounts of deposits to those in the EU-27. This indicates that the total amount of deposits collected in the whole EU banking sector is dominated by the EU-15 countries.

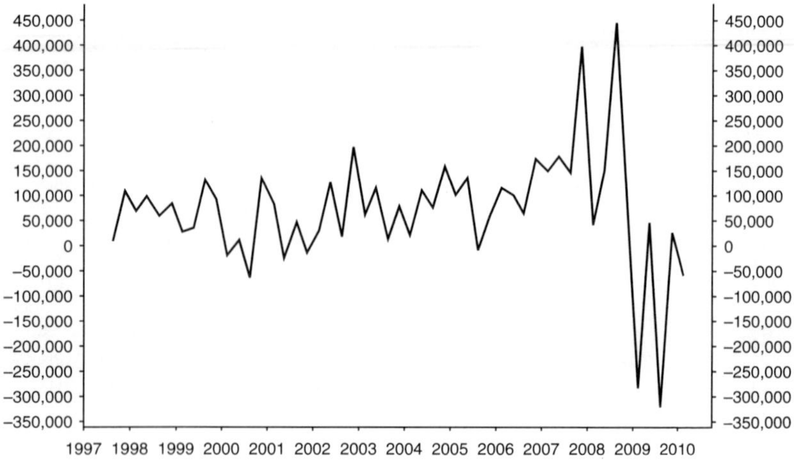

Figure 6.32 Euro-area total deposits, 1997–2010 (EUR million)
Source: Bankscope.

Moreover, general measures reflecting bank positions, such as total household deposits, which constitute the main source of funding for the banking sector in the euro area, are illustrated in Figure 6.32. An increase in the deposit level from less than 50 billion EUR in 1997 to more than 400 billion EUR just prior to the crisis indicated the strong position of the EU banking sector. On the other hand, the impact of the financial crisis is clearly observed to be sharp in the euro-area countries, resulting in significant declines, which have reached negative figures in recent years.

Income and cost structure of the European commercial banks

Once again, as a consequence of the negative impact of the financial crisis, operating income to total assets ratio in the EU countries declined. Obviously, non-interest income accounted for most of the decrease in 2007 and 2008. In contrast, net interest income has been stable and has slightly increased as a share of total assets in 2008. According to the ECB (2009c) stability report, this finding indicates a robust credit growth in most of the EU countries until mid-2008. In fact, the net interest income to total income ratio increased from 55 per cent to 66 per cent during 2007–2008. Moreover, lending margins among

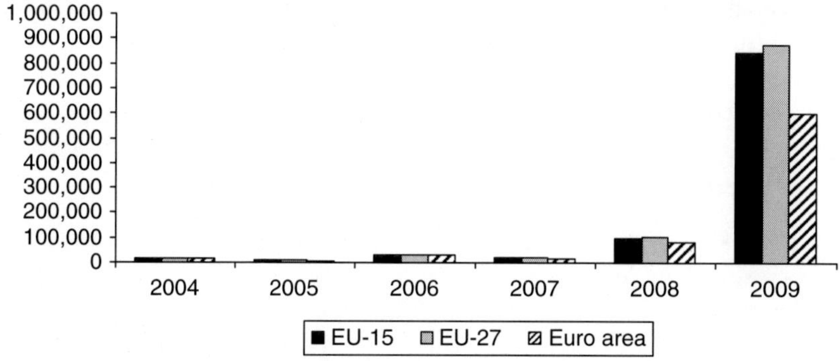

Figure 6.33 Operating incomes of groups of European commercial banks, 2004–2009 (USD million)
Source: Bankscope and author's calculations.

households and non-financial institutions have widened since mid-2008 (see Figure 6A.3 in the appendix).

As a comparison among the groups of European commercial banks, Figure 6.33 indicates total operating income in millions of USD over the 2004–2009 period. The figures state that the operating income in all groups of banks increased during 2008 and reached peak levels in 2009. On the other hand, by looking at Figure 6.34 we observe that net income was negative in 2008. This can be attributed to the banks' huge volume of losses as a consequence of the financial crisis. However, all groups of banks showed a recovery in 2009.

On the cost side, impairment and provisioning costs rose sharply in 2008, following a slight increase in 2007. As emphasized earlier in

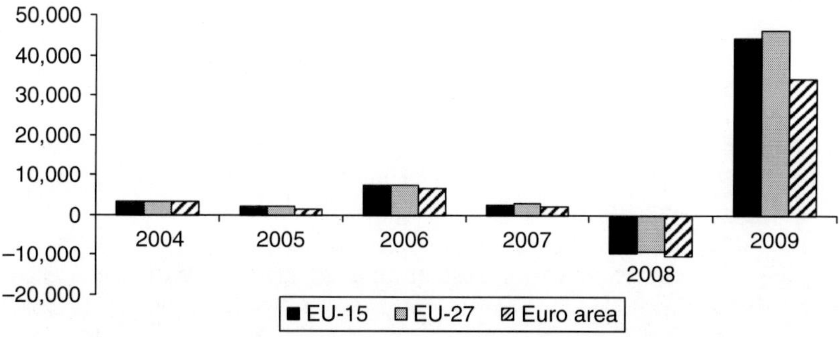

Figure 6.34 Net incomes of groups of European commercial banks, 2004–2009 (USD million)
Source: Bankscope and author's calculations.

this chapter, country-level figures suggest that the amount of non-performing loans increased further in most of the EU countries in 2009. This will, in turn, mean that the asset quality of banks in such countries will deteriorate.

Conclusion

Despite the political and economic convergence in the EU, the financial structures of member countries still remain diverse. This chapter has presented and compared the level of financial integration, performance and balance sheet structures in the EU countries. It illustrated that the current European recession has been showing signs of bottoming out since early 2009 as a result of recovering confidence in the financial sector. However, the downturn is easing more slowly in countries that have experienced steep declines in capital inflows. In particular, Greece and Italy have been left vulnerable because of concerns about their fiscal sustainability, and Hungary and the Balkans due to concerns about large current account deficits.

By analysing performance indicators, it can be observed that the impact of the financial crisis on the process of European financial integration has not been homogeneous. Those segments that had experienced the highest degree of integration over the last decade have been heavily hit by the crisis, and in many cases have seen a sharp reversal in the positive trend over the period 2007–2008. This is especially the case for unsecured money markets, government bond markets and equity markets. However, there is not enough evidence at this stage to assess whether these recent trends can be interpreted as a symptom of increasing long-term market segmentation or if they are linked to a temporary entrenchment by market actors within domestic borders.

In terms of efficiency indicators, the EU-27 had higher average ROE compared with the EU-15 average over the 2006–2008 period. At the country level, the EU-15 average was drawn down by high losses in the Belgian, German, Dutch, Danish and British financial sectors. In terms of ROA, EU-15 commercial banks experienced higher levels than the others except in 2005, during which euro-area commercial banks achieved the highest level. It is observed that ROA ratios for EU-27 countries were the lowest among all groups, with the exception of the year 2005. This can be attributed to the financial help NMS received from the EU, for a successful financial integration process, when they became EU members in 2004. On the other hand, the high ROA ratios identified in NMS countries just before the crisis attracted new competition, which forced a reduction in net interest margins and bank profits, whilst all groups of EU commercial banks maintained high net interest margins over the 2008 and 2009 period.

Similar differences and a general worsening were observed in the cost-to-income ratios. The average CTI increased to approximately 67 per cent in the EU-27 and 70 per cent in the EU-15 in 2008, and has been even higher in the euro-area countries. Moreover, the euro-area commercial banks presented the highest liquidity ratios during 2007 and 2008 whilst the highest decline was experienced in the EU-15. This is attributable to the fact that EU-15 big countries such as Germany, the UK, Italy and Spain witnessed the most severe liquidity problems in their financial sectors. In addition, the asset quality of EU commercial banks also deteriorated in 2008, although developments in non-performing loans to total loans ratio differ significantly across countries.

Appendix

Table 6A.1 Non-performing loans to total loans, 2000–2008 (per cent)

Country	2000	2001	2002	2003	2004	2005	2006	2007	2008
Austria	2.4	2.3	3	3	2.7	2.6	2.1	2.2	2
Belgium	2.8	2.9	3	2.6	2.3	2	1.7	1.1	1.7
Bulgaria	17.3	3.3	2.6	3.2	2	2.2	2.2	2.1	2.4
C. Republic	29.3	13.7	8.1	4.9	4	3.9	3.7	2.8	3.3
Denmark	n/a	0.7	0.9	0.8	0.7	0.4	0.3	0.3	n/a
Estonia	1	1.3	0.8	0.4	0.3	0.2	0.2	0.4	1.9
Finland	0.6	0.6	0.5	0.5	0.4	0.3	0.3	0.3	0.4
France	5	5	4.2	4.8	4.2	3.5	3	2.7	2.8
Germany	4.7	4.6	5	5.2	4.9	4	3.4	2.7	n/a
Greece	12.3	5.6	5.5	7	7	6.3	5.4	4.5	5
Hungary	3	2.7	2.9	2.6	2.7	2.5	2.5	2.5	3
Ireland	1	1	1	0.9	0.8	0.7	0.7	0.8	2.6
Italy	7.8	6.7	6.5	6.7	6.6	5.3	4.9	4.6	4.9
Latvia	4.6	2.8	2	1.4	1.1	0.7	0.4	0.4	3.6
Lithuania	11.3	6.7	5.3	2.4	2.2	0.6	1	1	4.6
Luxembourg	0.5	0.4	0.4	0.5	0.3	0.2	0.2	0.2	n/a
Malta	n/a	n/a	n/a	n/a	6.5	3.9	2.8	1.8	1.6
Netherlands	1.8	2.3	2.4	2	1.5	1.2	0.8	n/a	n/a
Poland	15.5	n/a	21.1	21.2	14.9	11	7.4	5.2	4.4
Portugal	2.2	2.1	2.3	2.4	2	1.5	1.2	1.3	2
Romania	n/a	3.3	n/a	8.3	8.1	8.3	8	9.7	13.8
Slovakia	13.7	11.1	7.9	3.7	2.6	5	3.2	2.5	3.2
Slovenia	6.5	7	7	3.7	3	2.9	2.5	1.8	1.6
Spain	1.2	0.9	1.1	1	0.8	0.8	0.7	0.9	3.4
Sweden	1.6	1.5	1.2	1.9	1.1	0.8	0.8	0.6	1
UK	2.5	2.6	2.6	2.5	1.9	1	0.9	0.9	1.6
EU-15	3.31	2,.61	2.64	2.79	2.48	2.04	1.76	1.65	2.49
EU-11	11.36	5.77	6.41	5.18	4.31	3.75	3.08	2.75	3.95
EU-26	6.46	3.80	4.05	3.74	3.25	2.76	2.32	2.13	3.22

Note: Data on Cyprus was not available.
Source: Bankscope and author's calculations.

Table 6A.2 Total assets of banks in individual EU countries, 2001–2008 (EUR million)

Countries	2001	2002	2003	2004	2005	2006	2007	2008	% Change 2001–2008
Belgium	776,173	774,330	828,557	914,391	1,055,270	1,121,905	1,297,788	1,067,860	37.58
Bulgaria	n/a	n/a	9,254	13,224	17,447	22,302	31,238	1,272,147	13647.00
C. Republic	78,188	79,232	78,004	87,104	100,902	114,878	140,004	36,825	−52.90
Denmark	454,328	506,694	568,848	629,371	746,246	822,024	977,970	118,142	−74.00
Germany	6,268,700	6,370,194	6,393,503	6,584,388	6,826,534	7,120,805	7,562,431	155,056	−97.53
Estonia	4,372	5,221	6,314	8,586	11,876	15,326	20,603	1,091,806	24872.69
Greece	202,736	201,608	213,171	230,454	281,066	315,081	383,293	22,039	−89.13
Spain	1,247,998	1,342,492	1,502,861	1,717,364	2,149,456	2,515,527	2,945,262	383,906	−69.24
France	3,768,943	3,831,610	3,998,554	4,419,045	5,073,388	5,728,127	6,682,335	7,225,140	91.70
Ireland	42,2106	474,630	575,168	722,544	941,909	1,178,127	1,337,357	7,875,402	1765.74
Italy	1,851,990	2,024,156	2,125,366	2,275,628	2,509,436	2,793,244	3,331,830	461,982	−75.05
Cyprus	36,164	33,998	41,890	46,540	60,753	74,709	91,141	124,678	244.76
Latvia	7,279	7,250	8,482	11,167	15,727	22,694	30,816	1,412,191	19300.89
Lithuania	4,361	5,010	6,453	8,553	13,162	17,347	23,817	3,628,272	83098.17
Luxembourg	721,001	662,615	655,971	695,103	792,418	839,564	915,448	32,249	−95.53
Hungary	39,343	46,477	n/a	n/a	78,289	93,679	108,504	26,542	−32.54

Table 6A.2 (Continued)

Countries	2001	2002	2003	2004	2005	2006	2007	2008	% Change 2001–2008
Malta	13,644	15,543	17,901	20,838	27,195	30,034	37,808	931,564	6727.65
Netherlands	1,265,906	1,356,397	1,473,939	1,677,583	1,695,325	1,873,129	2,195,020	42,283	–96.66
Austria	573,384	554,528	586,459	635,348	721,159	789,770	890,747	2,235,179	289.82
Poland	133,476	116,044	112,174	141,571	163,421	189,739	236,008	263,098	97.11
Portugal	352,251	351,773	348,691	345,378	360,190	397,123	440,144	482,332	36.93
Romania	n/a	n/a	15,000	23,200	35,400	51,911	72,095	84,541	463.61
Slovenia	17,782	19,995	21,541	24,462	30,135	34,841	43,493	65,509	268.40
Slovakia	n/a	21,527	23,751	30,834	37,834	41,695	50,318	49,010	127.67
Finland	163,416	165,661	185,846	212,427	234,520	255,055	287,716	3,381,187	1969.07
Sweden	452,289	474,841	519,259	599,682	653,176	773,736	845,958	899,769	98.94
UK	5,830,158	5,854,355	6,288,193	7,085,205	8,526,509	9,868,683	10,093,134	8,840,131	51.63
MU-13	17,614,604	18,109,994	18,909,627	20,454,115	22,670,806	24,962,298	28,312,864	42,208,841	139.62
EU-27	24,685,988	25,296,181	26,605,150	29,159,990	33,158,743	37,101,055	4,107,2278	30,566,597	23.82

Note: Totals in MU-13 and EU-27 since 2003; before MU-12 and EU-25.
Source: Bankscope and author's calculations.

Table 6A.3 Total loans of EU banks to non-banks and consumer credit, 2001–2007 (EUR million)

Countries	2001	2002	2003	2004	2005	2006	2007	% change 2001–2007
Belgium	271,960	287,730	296,007	312,125	371,298	397,412	426,502	56.83
Bulgaria	n/a	n/a	n/a	8,559	11,562	14,101	22,811	166.51
C. Republic	n/a	30,908	33,003	35,695	44,048	55,630	72,511	134.60
Denmark	n/a	287,571	304,974	351,778	404,625	463,963	523,388	82.00
Germany	3,275,038	3,247,073	3,200,535	3,183,757	3,194,049	3,220,752	3,311,351	1.11
Estonia	2,656	3,269	3,269	5,905	8,300	11,903	16,106	506.40
Greece	89,633	104,841	122,404	144,662	168,585	192,903	226,865	153.10
Spain	732,681	813,498	918,454	1,072,820	1,355,154	1,694,291	1,963,790	168.03
France	1,454,613	1,491,502	1,560,142	1,665,527	1,842,655	2,036,192	2,313,561	59.05
Ireland	203,882	213,321	220,227	276,522	350,887	424,303	502,024	146.23
Italy	1,033,668	1,094,177	1,161,515	1,227,066	1,324,685	1,473,435	1,776,940	71.91
Cyprus	n/a	n/a	n/a	n/a	30,640	34,265	44,138	44.05
Latvia	3,001	3,606	4,170	5,783	9,524	16,294	21,822	627.16
Lithuania	n/a	n/a	n/a	5,659	9,242	13,048	18,711	230.64
Luxembourg	149,210	133,103	119,713	121,188	146,171	160,710	193,225	29.50

Table 6A.3 (Continued)

Countries	2001	2002	2003	2004	2005	2006	2007	% change 2001–2007
Hungary	21,406	27,590	28,513	n/a	52,043	63,189	75,200	251.30
Malta	6,950	7,529	8,129	n/a	11,226	14,354	20,527	195.35
Netherlands	668,524	723,117	782,133	874,063	972,103	1,060,394	1,106,662	65.54
Austria	292,410	295,952	298,578	320,297	355,472	374,540	403,422	37.96
Poland	n/a	71,319	66,066	78,268	91,870	112,709	155,662	118.26
Portugal	178,771	191,375	194,549	203,887	218,668	242,334	271,634	51.95
Romania	n/a	n/a	n/a	13,325	21,493	37,167	57,441	331.08
Slovenia	n/a	n/a	n/a	16,228	18,850	23,676	31,969	97.00
Slovakia	n/a	n/a	n/a	11,741	15,262	20,325	25,801	119.75
Finland	87,445	92,632	101,461	111,991	126,690	141,819	159,131	81.98
Sweden	n/a	n/a	293,653	313,147	356,731	417,660	458,039	55.98
UK	2,356,351	2,437,130	3,616,174	4,042,266	4,759,716	5,303,579	6,013,157	155.19
MU-13	8,437,835	8,688,321	8,986,179	9,530,133	10,445,267	11,442,761	12,687,076	50.36
EU-27[a]	11,375,872	11,852,365	13,370,038	14,438,544	16,271,549	18,020,948	20,212,390	77.68

[a]EU-27 total excludes n/a.

Source: Adapted by the author from ECB (2008b).

Table 6A.4 Total deposits of EU banks from non-banks, 2001–2007 (EUR million)

Countries	2001	2002	2003	2004	2005	2006	2007	% Change 2001–2007
Belgium	326,157	345,120	371,244	409,187	462,586	466,168	513,128	57.33
Bulgaria	n/a	n/a	n/a	8,973	11,210	14,875	19,845	121.16
C. Republic	n/a	53,941	52,644	58,919	67,514	77,514	92,985	72.38
Denmark	96,354	102,919	107,112	122,368	143,245	154,405	180,586	87.42
Germany	2,380,289	2,401,168	2,447,673	2,511,278	2,593,143	2,704,740	2,882,321	21.09
Estonia	2,728	3,115	3,415	3,577	6,044	n/a	9,090	233.21
Greece	135,732	133,850	140,040	159,861	187,596	211,069	248,530	83.10
Spain	707,472	752,902	818,322	887,324	1,084,081	1,320,297	1,507,402	113.07
France	1,051,456	1,076,587	1,198,491	1,270,370	1,367,367	1,419,514	1,579,181	50.19
Ireland	131,067	142,956	164,240	186,766	235,966	290,207	327,918	150.19
Italy	681,265	741,211	768,127	807,109	872,933	931,398	1,122,393	64.75
Cyprus	n/a	n/a	28,155	30,062	38,073	43,099	52,514	86.52
Latvia	4,154	5,033	2,647	3,433	8,913	11,054	14,380	246.17
Lithuania	3,007	3,463	4,091	5,616	7,797	9,548	11,644	287.23
Luxembourg	218,233	198,935	207,247	221,952	241,440	288,128	295,787	35.54

Table 6A.4 (Continued)

Countries	2001	2002	2003	2004	2005	2006	2007	% Change 2001–2007
Hungary	26,921	31,208	31,208	n/a	41,164	47,129	51,151	90.00
Malta	7,747	8,675	8,177	8,769	11,237	11,060	14,015	80.91
Netherlands	524,985	537,795	570,573	598,830	684,003	793,700	877,719	67.19
Austria	210,262	211,128	224,844	234,736	254,044	269,476	301,046	43.18
Poland	n/a	81,000	72,000	89,334	105,818	121,634	147,300	81.85
Portugal	134,370	133,804	139,138	147,755	164,029	177,098	192,622	43.35
Romania	n/a	n/a	n/a	15,053	21,623	20,175	38,674	156.92
Slovenia	12,724	13,910	13,910	14,154	16,046	17,555	19,838	55.91
Slovakia	4,232	4,726	n/a	19,659	21,889	26,967	31,459	643.36
Finland	68,977	71,534	76,801	80,829	86,412	89,165	101,154	46.65
Sweden	124,627	131,611	126,556	130,210	153,444	182,526	189,905	52.38
UK	1,851,098	1,819,959	3,394,740	3,815,204	4,581,326	5,155,527	5,857,150	216.41
MU-13	6,570,265	6,746,990	7,140,650	7,530,151	8,249,646	8,978,515	9,969,039	51.73
EU-27[a]	8,703,857	9,006,550	10,971,395	11,841,328	13,468,943	14,854,028	16,679,737	91.64

[a]EU25 total excludes n/a.

Source: Adapted by the author from ECB (2008d).

Table 6A.5 Long-term debt securities by non-financial companies, 2001–2007 (EUR million)

Countries	**2001**	**2002**	**2003**	**2004**	**2005**	**2006**	**2007**	**% Change 2001–2007**
Belgium	6,716	3,499	8,591	8,608	2,674	5,091	9,203	37.03
Bulgaria	n/a	n/a	n/a	41	55	126	162	295.12
C. Republic	126	382	389	250	221	436	1,057	738.89
Denmark	n/a	n/a	n/a	n/a	n/a	6,780	1,518	−77.61
Germany	6,948	15,850	21,615	28,626	22,769	15,969	6,068	−12.67
Estonia	6	13	16	48	70	163	296	4833.33
Greece	63	87	452	1,162	4,571	4,513	3,325	5177.78
Spain	379	572	1,427	1,319	1,061	341	2,757	627.44
France	55,599	30,777	58,827	34,360	33,095	39,388	35,365	−36.39
Italy	15,170	10,288	7,474	17,160	6,009	6,099	14,098	−7.07
Latvia	n/a	n/a	36	0	4	25	9	−75.00
Hungary	n/a	n/a	128	0	101	0	13	−89.84
Malta	4	119	58	24	0	30	75	1775.00
Netherlands	15,725	3,931	8,016	2,805	5,264	8,266	11,629	−26.05
Austria	1,955	1,913	6,482	4,001	7,798	4,000	8,309	325.01
Poland	n/a	n/a	293	563	385	710	1,756	499.32
Portugal	1,649	392	1,142	1,190	2,676	3,169	3,325	101.64
Romania	n/a	n/a	551	334	292	87	2	−99.64
Slovenia	236	113	17	130	205	25	34	−85.59
Finland	1,938	1,236	2,109	2,343	1,604	3,983	2,025	4.49
Sweden	15,472	12,949	2,708	2,523	3,340	3,366	5,630	−63.61
UK	54,376	30,808	53,302	52,291	49,687	71,213	59,344	9.14

Source: Adapted by the author from ECB (2008d).

Table 6A.6 Short-term debt securities by non-financial companies, 2001–2007 (EUR million)

Countries	2001	2002	2003	2004	2005	2006	2007
Belgium	45,338	38,305	58,661	55,984	47,888	42,725	73,472
Bulgaria	n/a	n/a	n/a	n/a	n/a	n/a	n/a
C. Republic	n/a	n/a	n/a	n/a	n/a	n/a	n/a
Denmark	n/a	n/a	n/a	n/a	n/a	4,563	4,590
Germany	123,476	116,629	197,879	237,986	219,474	184,345	248,624
Estonia	13	34	8	10	27	62	102
Greece	n/a	n/a	n/a	24	n/a	n/a	7
Spain	10,095	9,815	7,293	7,020	6,963	7,785	6,453
France	545,855	449,687	409,773	490,148	480,900	581,644	810,139
Ireland	n/a	n/a	n/a	n/a	n/a	n/a	n/a
Italy	5	2	20	2	1	18	n/a
Cyprus	0	0	n/a	n/a	n/a	n/a	n/a
Latvia	n/a	n/a	0	0	0	0	6
Lithuania	n/a	n/a	n/a	n/a	n/a	n/a	0
Luxembourg	n/a	n/a	n/a	n/a	n/a	n/a	n/a
Hungary	n/a	n/a	0	0	0	0	6
Malta	n/a	n/a	n/a	n/a	n/a	n/a	0
Netherlands	1,263	1,703	3,452	550	604	141	429
Austria	18	370	778	784	796	516	503
Poland	n/a	n/a	n/a	10,030	9,306	11,241	13,646
Portugal	33,227	42,649	54,870	70,599	98,211	105,134	127,182
Romania	n/a	n/a	43	75	221	606	n/a
Slovenia	n/a	n/a	n/a	n/a	n/a	n/a	n/a
Slovakia	n/a	n/a	n/a	n/a	n/a	n/a	n/a
Finland	58,481	57,940	63,028	68,261	90,545	100,548	94,455
Sweden	8,813	8,532	n/a	n/a	n/a	n/a	n/a
UK	n/a	n/a	66,498	65,306	61,897	96,765	81,138

Source: Adapted by the author from ECB (2008d).

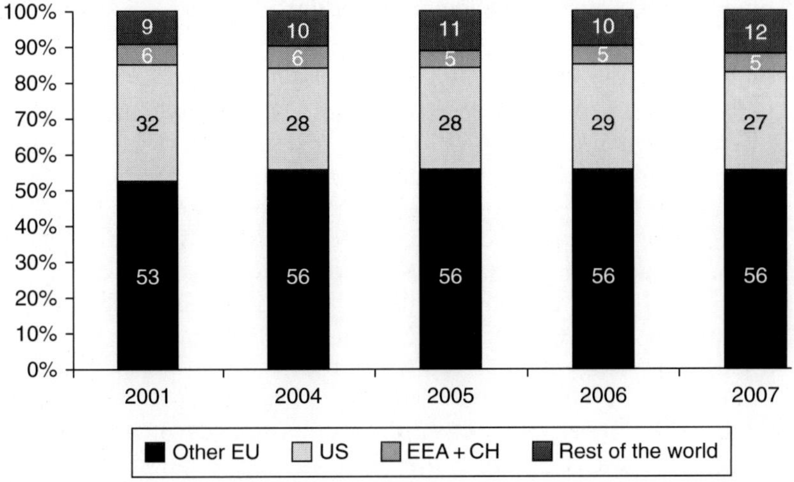

Figure 6A.1 Equity investments in EU by origin of investors, 2001–2007 (per cent)

Source: Europa (2009), European Financial Integration Report 2008, p. 10.

Appendix 6B: policy achievements in 2009

1. In 2009, and in the wake of the financial crisis, the Commission launched a comprehensive review of the EU regulatory and supervisory framework for financial services. This review was based on two Strategic Initiatives included in the Commission Legislative and Work Programme: "Financial Markets for the Future Package", which aimed at filling regulatory gaps, and "Supervision of EU Financial Markets", which took forward the recommendations of the de Larosière group that was established in late 2008.
2. Individual policy initiatives aimed at addressing the problems highlighted by the crisis were outlined in the Programme for Financial Market Reform, which accompanied the Commission Communication "Driving European Recovery" that was adopted on 4 March 2009. The main elements of the Programme were devoted to supervision, alternative investment management, remuneration, prudential requirements for banks, and measures to strengthen consumer and investor confidence. They were largely consistent with the global agenda for reform outlined by the G20.
3. Apart from this new Programme, the Commission continued with the implementation of policy initiatives started in previous years, such as the Economic and Financial Affairs (ECOFIN) Roadmaps ("Actions taken in response to the financial turmoil", "Review of the Lamfalussy process" and "Strengthening EU arrangements for financial stability"), the SEPA, and the simplification and the administrative burden reduction exercises.

Financial market supervision

1. Implementing the conclusions of the Lamfalussy process carried out in 2007, the revised Commission decisions establishing the EU Committees of Supervisors were adopted in January 2009. The Centre for Economic and Social Rights (CESR), Committee of European Banking Supervisors (CEBS) and Committee of European Insurance and Occupational Pensions (CEIOPS) status were strengthened and their tasks updated and aligned. At the same time, the Commission adopted a proposal for a European Parliament and a Council decision establishing a Community financial grant programme to support the Level 3 Committees' activities as well as the work of the International Accounting Standards Committee Foundation (IASCF), European Financial Reporting Advisory Group (EFRAG) and

the Public Interest Oversight Body (PIOB) in the field of financial reporting and statutory audit. The EP and the Council adopted this proposal in September.

2. The President of the European Commission set up the High Level Group on financial supervision in the EU under the chairmanship of Jacques de Larosière in October 2008. The Group delivered its report in February 2009. It recommended the reform of the EU supervisory architecture based on two pillars: one for macro- and the other one for micro-prudential supervision, aimed at enhancing financial stability in Europe and ensuring a level playing field for the financial services industry. The report also included a number of recommendations for regulatory reform of the EU framework for financial services.
3. The Commission endorsed the de Larosière Group's recommendations in the Communication of 4 March and subsequently developed the policy proposals that were presented in the Communication "European financial supervision" of 27 May. The Commission proposed the creation of a European Systemic Risk Council (later renamed "Board") for monitoring risks to macro-financial stability, and a European System of Financial Supervisors as a network of new European Supervisory Authorities and national supervisors to ensure the most effective and efficient organization of micro-prudential supervision. On 19 June the European Council largely endorsed the 27 May Communication, inviting the Commission to prepare the respective legislative proposals.
4. The Commission adopted a package of measures to establish the European Systemic Risk Board (one Regulation and one Council decision) and the European System of Financial Supervisors (three Regulations establishing, respectively, the European Banking Authority, the European Insurance and Occupational Pensions Authority and the European Securities Markets Authority) on 23 September 2009. The package also included a working document outlining the planned changes in legislation to make the new authorities operational.
5. The so-called "Omnibus" proposal for a Directive, including changes to a series of sectoral directives to define the scope of powers of the new European Supervisory Authorities, was adopted by the Commission in October. It is expected that the new system for financial supervision will become operational in 2011, following the co-decision negotiations and the adoption by the European Parliament and the Council.

Prudential legal framework

1. Following the amendments to the Capital Requirements Directives that were adopted in October 2008 (the CRD II package) that introduced rules on securitization retention, in July 2009 the Commission adopted a proposal to further amend the CRD (the CRD III package). The proposed amendments address capital requirements for the trading book and re-securitizations, disclosure of securitization exposures and remuneration policies. They aim at reinforcing the prudential framework for banks in those areas that were linked with causes of the crisis. In July 2009 a public consultation was launched on possible changes to the Capital Requirement Directive (the CRD IV package) relating to the following areas: through-the-cycle expected loss provisioning, specific incremental capital requirements for residential mortgages denominated in a foreign currency, and the removal of national options and discretions.
2. In October 2008, the Commission published a Communication on EU framework on cross-border crisis management in the banking sector, scoping out a broad range of issues that need to be addressed at the EU level to ensure the stability of the banking sector and create the conditions under which failure of a cross-border banking group can be effectively handled. An operational framework would provide the necessary safety net and, as such, would fully complement the reform of the EU system of financial supervision. After adoption the Communication was submitted to a public consultation.
3. In June 2009, the Commission published a report on compliance with the Anti-Money Laundering Directive. The report analyses how banks belonging to a group of companies comply, as a group, with their obligations pursuant to the AML Directive in a cross-border context and the difficulties they face.
4. In April 2009, the European Parliament and Council adopted the Solvency II Directive on the take-up and pursuit of insurance and reinsurance business. The formal adoption took place a few months later, pending the legal revision of the texts. In the meantime, the Commission, together with national supervisors, worked on the preparation of implementing (Level 2) measures.
5. In April 2009, the Commission published a report on Institutions for Occupational Retirement Provision (IORP) Directive focusing on the calculation of technical provisions, application of investment rules, adaptation of national supervisory systems and cross-border custodianship.

6. The Regulation on Credit Rating Agencies, proposed by the Commission in November 2008, was adopted in September 2009. The CRA Regulation, covering the operation and supervision of credit rating agencies in the EU, entered into force in December.
7. Under the "Better Regulation" principles, in September, the Commission proposed amendments to the Prospectus Directive. The changes were aimed at increasing legal clarity and efficiency, enhancing investor protection and eliminating unnecessary administrative burdens.
8. In April 2009, the Commission adopted a proposal for a Directive on Alternative Investment Fund Managers (AIFM). The proposal covered all types of non-Undertakings for Collective Instruments in Transferable Securities (UCITS) funds such as hedge funds, private equity and other types of institutional funds, and thus filled an important gap in EU regulation. The managers of such funds would have to be authorized and subject to ongoing supervision to ensure that the funds were transparent, had appropriate governance standards and had robust systems in place for the management of risks, liquidity and conflicts of interest. The proposal differentiated between various types of funds to address inherent risks in the different business models.

Retail financial services

1. The financial crisis underscored the need for a regulatory environment that provided a sound basis for informed decision-making, one in which investors are confident about the information and services they receive. In April 2009, the Commission adopted a Communication on Packaged Retail Investment Products, which outlined the need to update the current EU regulatory framework in this area and to introduce new legislation on product disclosure and selling processes. The overarching aim of this policy initiative was to foster consistency in the approach taken for different packaged investment products, such as investment funds, insurance-based investments and the various types of structured products.
2. The recast of the UCITS Directive (2009/65/EC) was published in the *Official Journal of the European Union* on 17 November 2009. The new Directive introduced provisions that will increase the efficiency of the EU-regulated investment fund framework, enhance consumer protection and strengthen supervisory mechanisms.
3. The crisis has demonstrated that a lack of retail clients' trust in their banks can have dramatic consequences. In October 2008,

the Commission proposed amendments to the Deposit Guarantee Scheme Directive, increasing the coverage levels to €50,000 (€100,000 in the long term) and shortening the pay-out period. These amendments were adopted by the European Parliament and the Council in March. Throughout 2009, the Commission services have continued to examine ways to further enhance effectiveness and resilience of the deposit protection system in the EU. Over the same period, preparatory work has been carried out for a review of the Investor Compensation Schemes Directive, as well as in view of possible policy proposals on Insurance Guarantee Schemes.

4. The Commission services pursued several other work strands aimed at enhancing the confidence of consumers and investors, based on the Programme set out in the 4 March Communication. These included preparatory work on responsible lending and borrowing, an analysis of rules and practices to avoid mortgage foreclosure procedures, and the preparation of initiatives to strengthen consumer stakeholder groups' capacity to provide input to policymaking at the EU level. The Commission services also continued to pursue initiatives started in previous years in the areas of financial education, financial inclusion, customer mobility and credit, including work with member states to prepare for the national implementation of the Consumer Credit Directive before 11 June 2010.

Financial market infrastructure

1. The Commission services continued to monitor the implementation of the Code of Conduct for Clearing and Settlement that was signed in 2006. In 2009 the Monitoring Group met on three times a year (February, July and October) and the Commission services reported to the ECOFIN in November.
2. In October, the Commission – building on the findings of the Fiscal Compliance (FISCO) Group regarding the fiscal barriers for clearing and settlement, better known as "Giovannini Barriers 11 and 12" – adopted a Recommendation on withholding tax relief procedures. The purpose of the Recommendation was to make it easier for investors resident in one EU member state to claim entitlements to relief from withholding tax on securities income (mainly dividends and interest) received from another member state. The Recommendation also provided guidance in how to ensure that procedures to verify entitlement to tax relief do not hinder the functioning of the single market.

3. The developments during the financial crisis showed that the lack of central counterparties for clearing over-the-counter (OTC) derivatives, particularly credit default swaps (CDS), exposed the financial system to serious risks. Therefore, the Commission services fostered work on improving safety in OTC derivatives markets, especially regarding CDS. A report was published in July 2008, looking at the role played by derivatives in the financial crisis, their benefits and risks, and assessing how these risks could be reduced. This was followed by a public consultation. In October 2008, the Commission issued a Communication presenting the operational conclusions based on the report and on the consultation, and signalling appropriate legislative initiatives to be pursued going forward.
4. In 2009, the Commission services, following a request of the ECOFIN Council in December 2008, prepared a draft for a future "Securities Law Directive". The instrument is designed to enhance legal certainty in securities holding and transactions in the financial market and to strengthen the investor's position regarding the exercise in a cross-border context; furthermore, central securities depositories are granted freedom to provide their services throughout the Internal Market. A public consultation was held in the first half of the year as part of the impact assessment procedure.
5. In September 2009, the Commission adopted a Communication outlining the Roadmap 2009–2012 to complete the implementation of the Single Euro Payments Area (SEPA). The Communication identified a series of actions to be undertaken by the EU and national authorities, industry and users, grouped under six priority objectives: to (i) foster migration, (ii) increase SEPA awareness and promote SEPA products, (iii) design a sound legal environment and strengthen SEPA compliance, (iv) promote innovation, (v) ensure necessary standardization, interoperability and security, and (vi) clarify and improve SEPA governance. Throughout the year the Commission also worked through other means to foster migration towards SEPA, in particular through its benchmarking surveys on SEPA preparedness and migration by public authorities and the major public consultation on possible end-dates for SEPA migration. As from 2 November 2009, European banks started, for the first time, to offer customers, both consumers and businesses, the new SEPA Direct Debit, which can be used for national and cross-border euro direct debits throughout the 32 SEPA countries (the EU-27, Iceland, Liechtenstein, Norway, Switzerland and Monaco). The Commission supported this launch by providing the necessary

legal platform for SEPA, in particular for SEPA Direct Debit, through the Payment Services Directive. In addition, the new Regulation on cross-border payments provided the legal clarity needed to launch the SEPA Direct Debit. Both the Payment Services Directive and the new Regulation on cross-border payments entered into force on 1 November 2009.

Corporate environment

1. The financial crisis raised serious questions about the adequacy of existing corporate governance practices in financial institutions. Taking into account the lessons of the crisis, in April 2009 the Commission adopted a Communication and two complementary Recommendations on remuneration policies. The objective of the Recommendation on remuneration in the financial services sector was to encourage financial institutions to develop remuneration policies for risk-taking staff that are consistent with sound and effective risk management. The Recommendation on the regime for the remuneration of directors of listed companies promoted appropriate remuneration policies to link pay with performance and to stimulate directors to ensure the medium- and long-term sustainability of their company.
2. To give effect to the principles set out in the Recommendations, in July the Commission proposed the relevant amendments to the Capital Requirements Directive (see above). The purpose of these amendments was to bring remuneration policies in banks within the scope of the supervisory review so that supervisors would be able to check whether remuneration policies and practices of credit institutions were consistent with sound risk management. In the future, the Commission services will also examine analogous measures in relation to non-banking financial services.
3. In November 2009, the Commission adopted a progress report and a Green Paper on the interconnection of the European business registers. The objective of the initiative was to explore, in the context of a public consultation, ways to improve access to business information and facilitate direct communication between registries. The Paper also examined the need for legislative action and outlined options for follow-up.
4. In February 2010, the Commission adopted proposals for amendments to the 4th Company Law Directive to exempt micro-enterprises from accounting requirements. The proposal would allow member states to exempt the EU's smallest companies from the

requirement of the Accounting Directives. This would alleviate the regulatory burden: the total cost reduction potential was estimated at around €6.3 billion or €1200 per year per individual company.

5. The crisis raised serious concerns about some aspects of international accounting standards. A number of important accounting issues were examined at the global level, in particular the use of fair value measurement in distressed market conditions, the potential pro-cyclical effects of fair value reporting, the reporting requirements for off-balance-sheet items and loan loss provisioning. In line with progress of the G20 work, the Commission, assisted by the Accounting Regulatory Committee, endorsed new IFRS standards and interpretations throughout the year.
6. In September 2010, the European Parliament and the Council adopted the decision on the financing of the International Accounting Standards Committee Foundation (IASCF), the European Financial Reporting Advisory Group (EFRAG) and the Public Interest Oversight Body (PIOB) (see also above). The purpose of the EU funding was to increase independence and effectiveness of these bodies in fulfilling their statutory tasks.
7. In July 2010, the Commission services published a summary report of the responses to the public consultation on control structures of audit firms, launched in November 2008. The stakeholders recognized the need to open up the market for the audit of international companies to more suppliers and favoured removing all barriers that may prevent new firms from entering the market.

International regulatory dialogues

1. In 2009, the Commission continued to be active in deepening international financial services regulatory dialogues with the US, Japan, Russia, India and China. A number of meetings took place. The work on those dialogues also benefited from the Commission's membership in the G20 and the Financial Stability Board (FSB), which was created by the decision of the April 2009 London Leaders Summit. The FSB was instrumental in ensuring the delivery of the G20 commitments in the run up to the Pittsburgh Summit in September. The Commission actively contributed to the meetings of the Board and its various subgroups. It also monitored the implementation of the G20 commitments in the EU, whilst promoting the EU regulatory framework at a global level, driven by the objective of achieving a level playing field.

2. The EU–US Financial Markets Regulatory Dialogue (FMRD) was impacted by global developments in 2008 and 2009. When it comes to the substance of the dialogue, the proposals in the area of financial regulation currently discussed in the EU and US have fully reflected the G20 commitments to the extent that they go in the same direction and present the same ambitions (in particular in relation to credit rating agencies, alternative investment managers or OTC derivatives). However, it has been essential to ensure that the implementation of these commitments in the EU and the US are compatible, and do not create overlaps, duplication or even extraterritorial effects, with the ultimate effect of fragmenting investor protection or markets, imposing unnecessary burdens on economic players or damaging the level playing field. The FMRD, as in the past, has continued to be the forum of choice for identifying upstream issues and come forward with solutions, subject to political and/or legislative validation.

7
Global Financial Crisis and European Banking

Introduction

The last months of 2008 witnessed the worst global financial crisis since the Great Depression of 1929–1930. The first indications of a serious crisis appeared on 15 January 2008, with the news of a sharp drop in profits of the Citigroup, which led to a significant fall on the New York Stock Exchange.[1] This was followed by a spectacular fall in share prices in all major world markets and, as a result, a number of US and EU banks declared massive losses in their 2007 end-of-year financial statements. In fact, the global financial crisis, which started in the US and expanded its area of impact by spilling over to Europe and Asia, entered a new phase when Lehman Brothers, one of the leading investment banks in the US, filed for bankruptcy protection in September 2008. The situation, which emerged as a liquidity problem in the inter-bank markets during the early stages of the crisis, gradually turned into concerns regarding the reliability of financial institutions.

Causes of the global financial crisis 2008–2009

Up to 2008, the world had experienced a remarkably long and strong period of economic growth, which began to dip downwards in 2008 (see Figure 7.1). The recession in the EU countries did not differ much from that in other advanced economies.

There is no doubt that the world economy has already experienced one of the most serious recessions in modern times. Due to the entry of India, China and the countries from the former Soviet Union (since

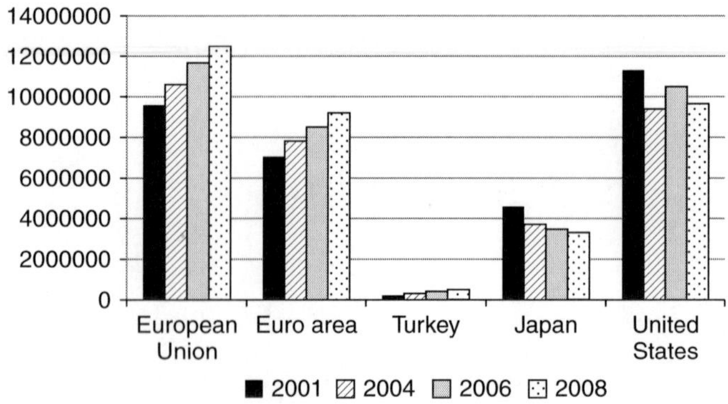

Figure 7.1 Annual GDP of selected countries, 2001–2008
Source: Adapted by the author from Eurostat (2009).

the early 1990s) into the global trading and production system, the first truly global recession has been witnessed. Moreover, global imbalances were expressed as massive current account deficits in some countries, especially the US, and correspondingly high surpluses in others (particularly China). In terms of monetary policy, interest rates were pushed further down into negative figures in both the US and the EU, and fuelled both a remarkable increase in asset prices and private and corporate debt. The availability of cheap money created a risky strategy of borrowing short to lend long.

One obvious problem was that retail banks retained no risk on the loans they had made and there was no direct link between the original borrowers (for example, homeowners in the UK) and the final holder of the mortgage (for example, a hedge fund in Germany). Another problem was the feasibility of insurance in highly integrated global financial markets. Even though the basic principle of insurance is independent risk, the case of all insurance takers claiming at the same time will collapse any insurance system.

Another weakness was the fact that the premium paid to individuals was based on the short-term performance of financial firms approved by boards of the companies and not sanctioned by the regulatory authorities. As the financial bubble inflated, these rewards were enormous, sufficient to lead to the individual's disregard of any feasible penalty, such as dismissal, when the bubble finally burst. Leverage grew to historically unprecedented levels, with even some commercial banks lending up to 30–40 times their capital, though, in many cases their structural investment vehicles were formally placed in unregulated offshore locations.

In particular, the immediate reason behind the financial crash was the collapse of the housing boom in the US, where house prices had increased by 50 per cent between 2000 and 2005, the largest boom in US history. It began to falter by mid-2006, and financial turmoil was then triggered by the rise in defaults by sub-prime mortgage borrowers, followed by an implosion of the market for securitized assets backed by such loans. It can be stated that the crisis had its roots in real estate and the sub-prime lending crisis as a consequence of enormous increase in values of real estate during 1990s and 2000s (see Figure 7.2).

Moreover, increasing housing prices coincided with a period of government deregulation that not only allowed unqualified buyers to take out mortgages but also helped blend the boundaries between traditional investment banks and mortgage lenders. Real estate loans were spread throughout the financial system in the form of collateralized debt obligations (CDOs) and other complex derivatives in order to disperse risk. However, the failure of rising home values and mortgage payments of homeowners forced banks to acknowledge huge write-downs and write-offs. These write-downs resulted in several banks having insolvency problems, with many being forced to raise capital or go bankrupt. Given the fact that many people were taking advantage of the housing boom in

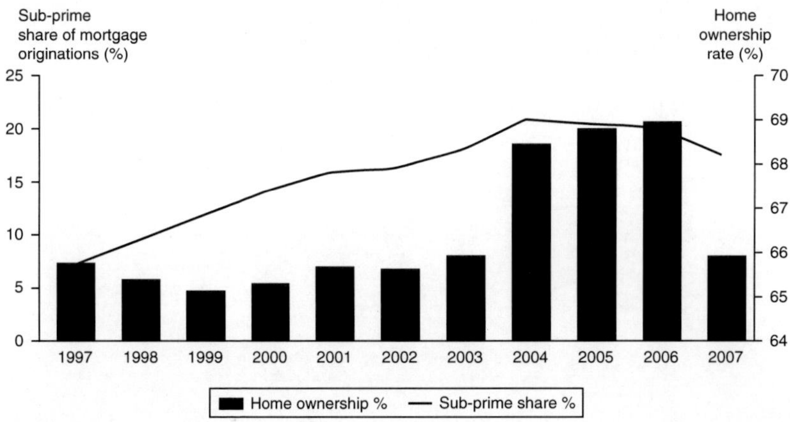

Figure 7.2 US sub-prime lending, 2004–2007
Source: US Census Bureau, Harvard University, State of Nation's Housing Report, 2008.

the US, both investors and mortgage companies ended up having financial problems as a consequence of this situation. Figure 7.3 illustrates the median and average sales prices of new homes sold in the US between 1963 and 2008.

As can be seen from this figure, housing prices in the US experienced a continuous increase over the 1963–2007 period, particularly since the beginning of 1990s. The sharp decline from the early months of 2007 was the main reason for the global financial crisis. Later on, a commodity price bubble was created following the decline in the housing bubble. The price of oil nearly tripled from USD 50 to USD 147 between early 2007 and 2008, which forwarded the flow of money from housing and other investments into commodities. As a result, increasing oil prices diverted a larger share of consumer spending into petrol, which created downward pressure on economic growth in oil-importing countries, as wealth flowed to oil-producing countries.

In the autumn of 2008, several US and some European banks failed or would have failed had they not been supported by the monetary authorities. The dramatic fall of the 158-year-old US investment bank

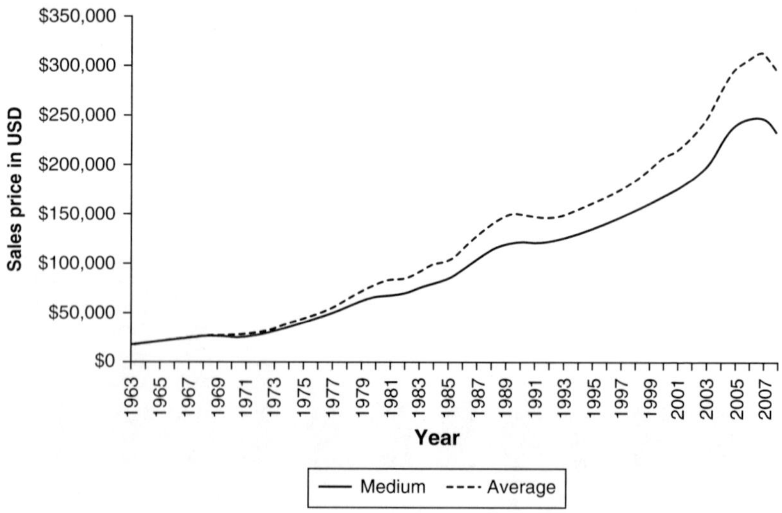

Figure 7.3 Annual median and average sales prices of new homes sold in the US, 1963–2007

Source: US Census Bureau, Harvard University, State of Nation's Housing Report, 2008.

Lehman Brothers, the takeover of the stock broking firm and investment bank Merrill Lynch and the move by Goldman Sacks and Morgan Stanley to seek banking status in order to receive protection from bankruptcy set the world's financial system into panic. In order to stop further collapse, the US government made its most dramatic interventions in financial markets since the 1930s. Only the infusion of hundreds of billions of dollars into the US banking system, followed by similar interventions in Europe, staved off an entire crash of the world's financial markets.

Furthermore, as US households and financial institutions had become increasingly indebted or overleveraged during the years preceding the crisis, this ended up increasing their vulnerability to the collapse of the housing bubble and worsened the ensuing economic downturn (see Figure 7.4). The leverage ratios of the top five US financial institutions increased significantly in 2007 compared with previous years, in particular with regard to Lehman Brothers and Merrill Lynch.

As illustrated in Table 7.1, investors in risky stocks lost over USD 1 trillion of market cap value as a result of the mortgage securitization process being based on securitizing risky loans and allowing excessive leverage to acquire such assets.

The effect of the financial turmoil on an already wavering real economy was severe. GDP declined rapidly, not only in the developed world

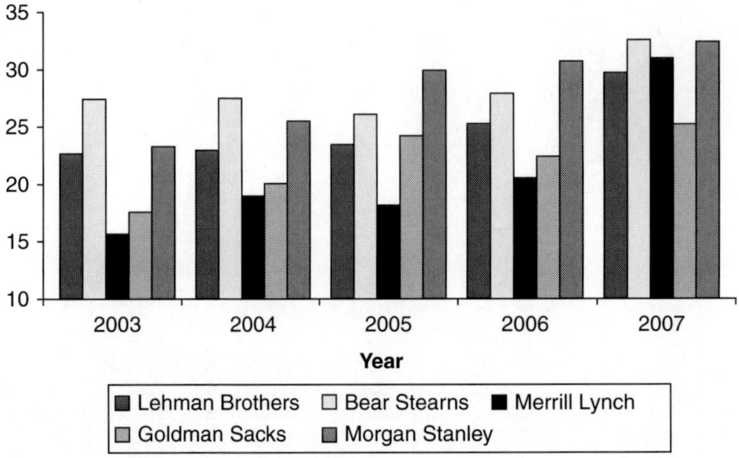

Figure 7.4 Leverage ratios for major investment banks, 2003–2007
Source: Created by the author from company annual reports.

Table 7.1 Change in the prices and market capitalization values of some risky stocks, 2000–2009 (USD million)

Mortgage companies	**Mid-2000s**			**March 2009**		
Company	**Price**	**No. of shares**	**Mkt cap**	**Price**	**Mkt cap**	**Notes**
Fannie Mae	80	1,000	80,000	0.40	400	Government conservatorship
Freddie Mac	50	1,400	70,000	0.17	238	Government conservatorship
Washington Mutual	45	1,700	76,500	0.05	85	Bankruptcy banking ops sold to JPMorgan Chase (JPM)
Countrywide Financial	52	580	30,160	6.00	3,480	Acquired by Bank of America
New Century Financial Corp.	–	–	1,750	–	55	Bankruptcy
Investment banks	**Mid-2000s**			**March 2009**		
Goldman Sachs Group	240	460	110,400	100	46,000	No longer an investment bank
Bear Stearns Companies	133	135	17,955	2	270	Acquired by JPMorgan Chase (JPM)

Citigroup	52	5,450	283,400	2	10,900	No longer an investment bank
Merrill Lynch	92	2,000	184,000	6	12,000	Acquired by Bank of America (BAC)
Lehman Brothers	60	689	41,340	0.04	28	Bankruptcy
Other financial institutions		**Mid-2000s**			**March 2009**	
Bank of America	52	5,000	260,000	6	30,000	Received USD 45 bn in bailout funds
American International Group	72	2,500	180,000	0.35	875	Received USD 180 bn in bailout funds
Combined Mkt cap of above financial institutions			1,335,505		104,331	1.2 trillion in Mkt cap lost

Source: Adapted by the author from annual company reports.

but also globally. The global nature of the recession is also shown by the historical decline in world trade, which some claim has been greater even than that during the Great Depression in the 1930s. It certainly is by far the greatest decline in trade in the Organisation for Economic Co-operation and Development (OECD) area since the early 1960s. In February 2009, the year-on-year decline in trade was 33 per cent, whereas the last previous low was 14 per cent in October 1982.

Employment during the recession

Employment in the EU declined by 2.5 million persons between the first quarter of 2008 and the first quarter of 2009. From the end of the second quarter of 2008, the European Restructuring Monitor (ERM) began to report significantly higher levels of declared job losses due to bankruptcy, which peaked around the end of 2008. The impact of the recession has already been significant for most EU countries in terms of job losses and rising unemployment. However, experience of previous recessions indicates that the labour market may continue to decrease when account is taken of the large number of temporary employment maintenance measures that have been implemented across Europe.

The recession in question started in some parts of Europe well before others. In the year up to the first quarter of 2008, GDP grew at over 2 per cent in the EU as a whole, and much more in some of the NMS. At this point, recession had already hit Ireland, where GDP fell by over 1 per cent during this period; in contrast, in Denmark it remained virtually unchanged (see Table 7.2). In all countries, even in these two, employment increased significantly, illustrating the lagged effect of any downturn in economic activity on jobs.

Over the first quarter of 2009, the recession was well under way in most countries, and GDP declined by around 5 per cent in the EU-15 and by slightly less in the NMS, largely because of continued GDP growth in Poland, Greece and Cyprus. The decline in GDP was especially significant in Lithuania (12 per cent), Latvia (19 per cent), Slovenia (9 per cent), Ireland (8 per cent) and Germany (7 per cent).

The decline in GDP was only partly reflected in employment, which fell by just under 1.5 per cent in the EU as a whole, again reflecting the lagged effect of the downturn on jobs and implying a marked reduction in value added per person employed. This reduction was evident in Slovenia, Germany and Luxembourg, where GDP also declined by more than the EU average. In contrast, Spain witnessed a decline in GDP (which was less than the EU average) that seems to have fed through

Table 7.2 Changes in GDP and employment, 2007–2009 (per cent)

Countries	**GDP**			**Employment**		
	Quarter 1		**Quarter 2**	**Quarter 1**		**Quarter 2**
	2007–2008	**2008–2009**	**2008–2009**	**2007–2008**	**2008–2009**	**2008–2009**
EU-15	2.1	−4.9	−4.9	1.5	−1.3	n/a
EU-25	2.3	−4.7	−4.8	1.8	−1.4	n/a
EU-27	2.4	−4.7	−4.8	1.8	−1.3	n/a
Austria	2.9	−3.5	−4.4	2.2	−0.3	−1
Belgium	1.9	−3.1	−3.8	1.9	0.1	n/a
Cyprus	4.2	0.8	−0.7	n/a	n/a	n/a
C. Republic	3.8	−3.4	n/a	2.6	−0.5	n/a
Denmark	−0.1	−4.3	n/a	1.5	−1.8	n/a
Estonia	0.8	−14.7	n/a	1.9	−7	n/a
Finland	3.3	−6	n/a	2.7	−0.9	n/a
France	1.9	−3.4	−2.6	1.1	−0.7	−1.1
Germany	2.9	−6.7	−5.9	1.6	0.4	−0.1
Greece	3.2	0.3	−0.2	1.5	−0.9	n/a
Hungary	1.8	−5.6	−7.4	n/a	n/a	n/a
Ireland	−1.3	−8.4	n/a	2.2	−7.5	n/a
Italy	0.4	−6	−6	1.2	−0.9	n/a
Latvia	2.8	−18.6	−18.2	5.9	−8.5	n/a
Lithuania	7	−11.6	−22.6	0.6	−5.6	n/a
Luxembourg	1	−5.4	n/a	5.2	2.6	n/a
Malta	3.9	−2.3	n/a	n/a	n/a	n/a
Netherlands	4	−4.2	−4.9	2	0.3	n/a
Poland	6.4	1.9	n/a	n/a	n/a	n/a
Portugal	0.9	−3.7	n/a	0.9	−1.6	n/a
Slovakia	8.2	−5.7	−5.4	3.2	0	−0.9
Slovenia	5.9	−9	n/a	3.2	0.5	n/a
Spain	2.7	−3	n/a	1.7	−6.3	n/a
Sweden	2.2	−6.3	−6.3	n/a	n/a	n/a
UK	2.5	−4.9	−5.6	1.5	−1	−1.9

Source: Adapted by the author from Eurostat and national accounts.

almost immediately into employment, which fell by over 6 per cent. This fall in employment was greater than in any other country apart from Ireland, where the downturn began earlier, and Estonia and Latvia, where the fall in GDP was much larger than anywhere else. In each country, the decline in employment was much smaller than the decline in GDP, implying that jobs have been maintained despite the reduction in output. This again is especially evident in Germany, where the decline in employment during 2008–2009 was only marginal, even though GDP fell by 6 per cent. The larger EU countries figure prominently on the list of declared job losses. In 2008–2009 Poland (20,583) and Ireland (11,172) recorded very substantial job losses.

Global contagion

The crisis rapidly developed and turmoil spread throughout the global economy, resulting in a number of European bank failures, declines in various stock indexes and large reductions in the market value of equities and commodities. Both mortgage-backed securities (MBS) and CDO were purchased by corporate and institutional investors globally. Derivatives such as credit default swaps also increased the linkage between large financial institutions. Moreover, the de-leveraging of financial institutions, as assets were sold to pay back obligations that could not be refinanced in frozen credit markets, further accelerated the solvency crisis and caused a decrease in international trade. At the end of October 2008, a currency crisis developed, with investors transferring vast capital resources into stronger currencies such as the yen, the USD and the Swiss franc, which has forced numerous emerging economies to seek aid from the IMF.

The Brookings Institution Report (June 2009) stated that US consumption accounted for more than a third of the growth in global consumption between 2000 and 2007, indicating that the US economy has been spending too much and borrowing too much for years and that the rest of the world depended on US consumers as a source of global demand. Therefore, a recession in the US and the increased savings rate of US consumers was expected to lead to declining economic growth rates in other countries. For instance, the annualized GDP was 14.4 per cent in Germany, 15.2 per cent in Japan, 7.4 per cent in the UK, 18 per cent in Latvia, 9.8 per cent in the euro area and 21.5 per cent in Mexico during the first quarter of 2009.

Moreover, some developing countries who had seen strong economic growth ended up with significant slowdowns. For instance, growth rates in Cambodia fell from more than 10 per cent in 2007 to close to zero in 2009, and Kenya saw only 3–4 per cent growth in 2009, down from 7 per cent in 2007. According to the research by the Overseas Development Institute, reductions in growth can be attributed to falls in trade, commodity prices, investment and remittances sent from migrant workers. Moreover Arab countries had lost USD 3 trillion due to the crisis by March 2009. In May 2009, the United Nations (UN) reported a drop in foreign investment in Middle Eastern economies due to a slower rise in demand for oil, and the World Bank (WB) predicted a tough year for the Arab states. In September 2009, Arab banks reported losses of nearly USD 4 billion since the onset of the global financial crisis.

Global financial crisis and the EU

While various researchers and organizations view the crisis from different perspectives, one way to view it is as a series of policy events proceeding through four periods where the policy responses differed. *The first phase* of the crisis represents the early build-up to the crisis in which policymakers responded in an ad hoc manner to assist individually troubled banks and financial institutions. *In the second phase*, national governments, primarily through central banks, moved to address issues of liquidity that arose from widespread concerns over the viability of the financial system, rather than the more narrow concerns of individual institutions. *In the third phase*, government finance ministries adopted policies to address issues of solvency as banks and other financial firms attempted to de-leverage their positions by reducing their holdings of troubled assets, and as credit markets essentially shut down. *In the fourth phase*, governments, through finance ministries and legislative bodies, shifted to address growing concerns over the economic downturn, which had worsened the financial crisis.

According to the IMF and ECB reports, many factors that led to the financial crisis in the US created a similar crisis in the EU. Essentially, low interest rates and an expansion of financial and investment opportunities that arose from aggressive credit expansion, growing complexity in mortgage securitization and a loosening in underwriting standards spurred a broad expansion in credit and economic growth. This rapid rate of growth pushed up the values of equities, commodities and real estate. The combined effect of higher commodity prices and rising housing costs squeezed consumers' budgets, and resulted in a reduction in their expenditures.

One consequence of this drop in consumer spending was a slowdown in economic activity and, in turn, the decline in the prices of housing led to a large-scale downgrade in the ratings of sub-prime mortgage-backed securities and the closing of a number of hedge funds with sub-prime exposure. Concerns over the pricing of risk in the market for sub-prime mortgage-backed securities spread to securities and the inter-bank money markets. In particular, Iceland was hard hit by the financial crisis, with major Icelandic banks completely shutting down for a period of time. On 19 November 2008, Iceland and the IMF signed a stabilization programme supported by a USD 2.1 billion two-year standby arrangement. Following the IMF decision, Denmark, Finland, Norway, and Sweden agreed to provide an additional USD 2.5 billion.

Interest rates

On 8 October 2008, central banks in the US, the euro area, the UK, Canada, Sweden and Switzerland agreed on a coordinated cut in interest rates to improve liquidity. Soon after, the US Treasury, in coordination with the Federal Reserve, announced its Capital Purchase Program as part of its Troubled Asset Relief Program and arranged for an injection of capital, in exchange for equity shares, into eight major US banks. On 29 October 2008, the US Federal Reserve cut key interest rates by half a percentage point, something which has been followed by China and Norway.

In response to these cuts, on 6 November 2008, the Bank of England cut its key interest rates by 1.5 percentage points to 3 per cent; three times larger than any cut seen since the Central Bank's monetary policy committee was established in 1997. At the same time, the ECB cut its interest rates by half a percentage point to 3.25 per cent. The Czech Central Bank also cut its rates by a larger than expected three-quarters of a percentage point, while the Swiss National Bank lowered its rates by one-half of a percentage point.

Currency swap facilities

In addition to reducing interest rates and providing liquidity by injecting capital directly into banks, the Federal Reserve and other central banks in Europe expanded short-term bilateral currency swap facilities by USD 180 billion to compensate for a dollar liquidity crisis. Most financial institutions outside the US have relied on inter-bank and other wholesale markets to obtain dollars. However, as credit markets seized up, these institutions, in particular the European banks, ended up having no access to short-term dollar financing.

Preceding the financial crisis, European banks had vastly expanded their accumulation of dollars in the inter-bank market and had acquired dollar-denominated assets from official monetary authorities. In essence, European banks borrowed dollars short term in the inter-bank market in order to finance a rapid growth in investments in dollar-denominated assets with varying maturities held by non-banks, such as asset-backed commercial paper, which left European banks with large short-term US dollar funding requirements. Such constant refinancing contributed to the squeeze in liquidity and to problems in obtaining dollars in the foreign exchange market and in cross-country currency swap markets.

The principal tool the Federal Reserve and the ECB used to counter the currency shortage was a temporary currency swap, which allowed central banks to borrow currency from each other in order to re-lend the currencies to banks in their jurisdictions. Typically, inter-central bank foreign exchange swap arrangements are used to support foreign exchange market intervention, rather than to alleviate shortages of foreign exchange in the short-term funding market. In addition to shortages of dollars, there have also been shortages of euros and Swiss francs. During the period when the ECB was concluding swap arrangements with the Federal Reserve, it was also establishing currency swaps with the Czech Central Bank, the National Bank of Denmark and the National Bank of Poland. Central banks in Europe responded to the currency shortage by providing currency from their own foreign exchange reserves and by borrowing from other central banks, principally from the central bank that issued the currency.

Depositor guarantees

The IMF approved a short-term liquidity facility to assist banks facing liquidity problems and, in this respect, Ireland, Greece and Germany increased their guarantees to deposit holders to improve liquidity in the financial system. On 4 December 2008, the ECB initiated another round of cuts in interest rates by three-quarters of a percentage point to 2.5 per cent, representing the largest one-day rate move in the bank's ten-year history. In turn, the Bank of England and Sweden's Central Bank cut their key rates to 2 per cent. However, this was just the beginning of this process. On 8 January 2009, the Bank of England reduced its Official Bank Rate by 0.5 percentage points to 1.5 per cent and, on 5 February 2009, by 0.5 per cent more to 1.0 per cent to stimulate economic growth.

In this unstable economic environment, the first bank to experience a collapse was the UK-based Northern Rock, which was nationalized in February 2008 by the British government after failing to raise sufficient capital to meet its borrowing requirements. The government covered all Northern Rock's debt obligations (approximately 90 billion pounds), signalling the first major UK bank intervention since the 1970s.

The European Framework for Action (EFA)

On 29 October 2008, the European Commission released its "European Framework for Action" as a way to coordinate the actions of the EU-27 in addressing the financial crisis. On 16 November 2008, the Commission announced a more detailed plan that brought together short-term goals to address the current economic downturn with the longer-term goals on growth and jobs that are integral to the Lisbon Strategy for Growth and Jobs that was adopted by the EU in 2000 and recast in 2005. The short-term plan focuses on a three-part approach to an overall EU recovery action plan.

Part I: A new financial market architecture at the EU level: The basis of this architecture involves implementing the measures that EU members have announced, as well as providing for: (i) continued support for the financial system from the ECB and other central banks; (ii) rapid and consistent implementation of the bank rescue plan that has been established by the members; and (iii) decisive measures that are designed to contain the crisis from spreading to all the members. As the financial system is stabilized, the next step is to restructure the banking sector and to return banks to the private sector. Proposals include: deposit guarantees and capital requirements, regulation and accounting standards, credit rating agencies, executive pay, capital market supervision and risk management.

Part II: Dealing with the impact on the real economy: The policy instruments that can be employed to address the expected rise in unemployment and decline in economic growth are in the hands of EU members. Nevertheless, the EU can assist by adding short-term actions to its structural reform agenda, while investing in the future through: (i) increasing investment in research and development (R&D) innovation and education; (ii) promoting "flexibility" to protect and equip people, rather than specific jobs; (iii) freeing up businesses to build markets at home and internationally; and (iv) enhancing competitiveness by promoting green technology, and overcoming energy security constraints and achieving environmental goals. In addition, the impact of the financial crisis on the real economies of the EU countries will require adjustments to be made in the fiscal and monetary policies. The Stability and Growth Pact of the EU members should serve as the key for members facing higher than expected levels of fiscal or monetary stimulus, so that such policies can be accompanied by structural reforms. Such reforms should aim to sustain domestic demand in the short run, ease transitions within and into the labour market and increase potential growth by directing investment into areas that will sustain employment and advance productivity. Reforms in the finance sector should focus on enhancing the competitive positions and the needs of small and medium-sized firms.

Part III: A global response to the financial crisis: The crisis has raised questions concerning global governance that are related to the financial sector and to the need to maintain open trade markets. The EU used the 15 November 2008 Multi-nation Economic Summit in Washington DC to promote a series of measures to reform the global financial architecture. The European Commission argued that the measures should include strengthening: (i) international regulatory standards; (ii) international coordination among financial supervisors; (iii) measures to monitor and coordinate macroeconomic policies; and (iv) developing the capacity to address a financial crisis at the national regional and multilateral levels. A financial architecture plan should also include three key principles: (i) efficiency; (ii) transparency and accountability; and (iii) inclusion of representation from key emerging economies.

In relation to the EFA, several EU countries, such as Germany, France, Italy, Austria, the Netherlands, Portugal, Spain and Norway announced plans to recapitalize banks and to provide government debt guarantees. European leaders agreed to increase the role of the IMF in preventing a future financial crisis. As a consequence, the leaders set a 100-day deadline to draw up reforms for the international financial system and asked the Bank for International Settlements (BIS) to develop a set of guidelines to ensure that banks hold enough capital to reduce the risks of a similar financial crisis.

On 7 January 2009, the BIS responded to the request by the G20 by publishing a first draft of its proposed guidelines for "stress testing banks", or assessing the impact of various large shocks on the ability of banks to absorb losses. Stress testing is a risk management tool that is used by banks to assess the financial position of a bank under a severe but plausible scenario, to absorb the impact of unexpected risks on the bank's capital position, which is comprised of common stock and retained earnings. Banks do not loan out their capital directly to borrowers, but use it as a cushion to help them absorb losses from loans and other banking activities.

Currently, banks are required to engage in periodic stress testing as a risk management tool. The BIS guidelines provide a set of recommendations for bank supervisors as they review the conduct of stress tests within their banks in order to overcome shortcomings in the present system that failed to assess such risks as the behaviour of complex structured products, risks in relation to hedging strategies, securitization risk, contingent risk and funding liquidity risk.

European economic recovery plan

On 27 November 2008, the European Commission proposed a USD 256 billion Economic Recovery Plan (ERP) that would fund cross-border projects, including investments in clean energy and upgraded telecommunications infrastructure. The ERP is comprised of two parts. First, each EU member is asked to contribute an amount equivalent to 1.5 per cent of their GDP to boost consumer demand. Second, members are tasked to invest in energy-efficient equipment to create jobs and save energy, invest in environmentally clean technologies to convert such sectors as construction and automotive industries to low-carbon sectors, and to invest in infrastructure and communications. The members of the European Council approved the plan in a meeting on 12 December 2008. As Table 7.3 indicates, most European countries have announced some form of economic stimulus package.

As part of the ERP, budget rules imposed by the Stability and Growth Pact are to be loosened to allow EU members to adopt economic stimulus plans to support their declining economic growth rates. The plan is intended to engage with the goals and objectives outlined in the Lisbon Strategy to improve the rate of economic growth among EU members and propose official support measures to increase the rate of employment.

Financial help for troubled countries

As mentioned earlier in this book, the emerging countries in Europe have also been sharply hit by the global financial crisis due to their trade and financial links with the rest of Europe, which resulted in falling export demand and capital inflows. In particular, countries that relied on extraordinary capital inflows and experienced very fast credit growth before the crisis faced the need for significant adjustment. In this respect, the IMF, working with the EU and other multilateral institutions, provided joint help to close external financing gaps created by the crisis. Therefore, assistance has been provided to these countries since April 2009 (see Table 7.4).

Table 7.3 Announced and planned/proposed stimulus packages

Date announced	Country	$ in billions	Status, package contents
12 December 2008	EU	256	Fund cross-border projects including clean energy and upgraded telecommunications architecture. Each EU member to contribute an amount equivalent to 1.5% of GDP to boost consumer spending
13 January 2009	Germany	65	Infrastructure, tax cuts, child bonus, increase in some social benefit, $3250 incentive for trading in cars more than nine years old for a new or slightly used car
24 November 2008	UK	29.6	Proposed plan includes a 2.5% cut in the value added tax for 13 months, a postponement of corporate tax increases, government guarantees for loans to small and midsize businesses, spending on public works, including public housing and energy efficiency. Plan includes an increase in income taxes on those making more than $225,000 and an increase in National Insurance contributions for all but the lowest income workers
5 November 2008	France	33	Public sector investments and loans for carmakers. Does not include the previously planned $15 billion in credits and tax breaks on investments by companies in 2009
16 November 2008	Italy	52	Three-year programme. Measures to spur consumer credit, provide loans to companies, and rebuild infrastructure. Sixth February announced a $2.56 billion stimulus package that was part of the three-year programme that includes payments of up to $1950 for trading in an old car for a new, less polluting one and 20% tax deductions for purchases of appliances and furniture
22 November 2008	Netherlands	7.5	Tax deduction to companies that make large investments, funds to companies that hire temporary workers and creation of a programme to find jobs for the unemployed

Table 7.3 (Continued)

Date announced	Country	$ in billions	Status, package contents
11 December 2008	Belgium	2.6	Increase in unemployment benefits, lowering of the value added tax on construction, abolishing taxes on energy, energy checks for families, faster payments of invoices by the government, faster government investment in railways and buildings and lowering of employers' fiscal contributions
27 November 2008	Spain	14.3	Public works, help automobile industry, environmental projects, research and development, restoring residential and military housing and funds to support the sick
14 January 2009	Portugal	2.89	Funds to be provided to medium and small businesses, money for infrastructure, particularly schools, and investment in technological improvement
20 November 2008	Israel	5.4	Public works to include desalination plants, doubling railway routes, adding R&D funding, increasing export credits, cutting assorted taxes, and aid packages for employers to hire new workers
21 December 2008	Switzerland	0.59	Public works spending on flood defense, natural disaster and energy-efficiency projects
5 December 2008	Sweden	2.7	Public infrastructure and investment in human capital, including job training, vocational workshop, and workplace restructuring; extension of social benefits to part-time workers
26 January 2009	Norway	2.88	Investment in construction, infrastructure and renovation of state-owned buildings, tax breaks for companies

Note: Amounts are in USD. Currency conversions to USD were done in the news articles or by using current exchange rates.
Source: Adapted by the author from various news articles.

Table 7.4 IMF support to European countries affected by the current crisis (as on 4 September 2009)

Country	IMF loan size, approval date	Key objectives and policy actions	Additional information
Hungary	$15.7 billion, November 2008	Address the main pressure points in public finances and the banking sector: • Substantial fiscal adjustment, to provide confidence that the government's financing need can be met in the short- and medium-term • Upfront bank capital enhancement, to ensure that banks are sufficiently strong to weather the imminent economic downturn, both in Hungary and in the region • Large external financing assistance, to minimize the risk of a run on Hungary's debt and currency markets	In addition to financial assistance from the IMF, the programme is also supported by $8.4 billion from the EU and $1.3 billion from the World Bank. The second review of the programme was completed in June 2009. Available via the Internet: http://www.imf.org/external/country/HUN/index.htm
Ukraine	$16.9 billion, November 2008	• Help the economy adjust to the new economic environment by allowing the exchange rate to float, aiming to achieve a balanced budget in 2009, phasing in increases in energy tariffs and pursuing an incomes policy that protects the population while slowing price increases	Since the programme's adoption, the global economic environment has deteriorated markedly, hitting Ukraine harder than expected. This has required a recalibration of economic policies. The second review of the programme was completed in July 2009

Table 7.4 (Continued)

Country	IMF loan size, approval date	Key objectives and policy actions	Additional information
		• Restore confidence and financial stability (recapitalizing viable banks and dealing promptly with banks with difficulties) • Protect vulnerable groups in society (an increase in targeted social spending to shield vulnerable groups)	Available via the Internet: http://www.imf.org/external/country/UKR/index.htm
Iceland	$2.1 billion, November 2008	• Prevent further sharp króna depreciation by maintaining an appropriately tight monetary policy and temporary restrictions on capital outflows • Develop a comprehensive and collaborative strategy for bank restructuring by (i) putting in place an efficient organizational structure to facilitate the restructuring process, (ii) proceeding promptly with the valuation of banks' assets, (iii) maximizing asset recovery in the old banks, (iv) ensuring the fair and equitable treatment of depositors and creditors of the intervened banks, and (v) strengthening supervisory practices and the insolvency framework	The first review of the programme, initially scheduled for the first quarter of 2009, was delayed, to allow the authorities to fully articulate their policy plans. The Government of Iceland and IMF staff reached agreement in early August on policies to underpin the first review. The agreement is being reviewed by IMF management and will need to be presented to the IMF's Executive Board for its consideration and approval. Available via the Internet: http://www.imf.org/external/country/ISL/index.htm

Latvia	$2.35 billion, December 2008	• Take immediate measures to stem the loss of bank deposits and international reserves • Take steps to restore confidence in the banking system in the medium-term and to support private debt restructuring • Fiscal measures to limit the substantial widening in the budget deficit and prepare for early fulfilment of the Maastricht criteria • Implement incomes policies and structural reforms that will rebuild competitiveness under the fixed exchange rate regime	The first review of the programme was completed in August 2009 Available via the Internet: http://www.imf.org/external/country/LVA/index.htm
Belarus	$2.5 billion, January 2009; augmented to $3.5 billion in June 2009	• Facilitate an orderly adjustment to external shocks and address pressing vulnerabilities • Adopt a new exchange rate regime – a step devaluation of the ruble against the dollar of 20% and a simultaneous switch to a currency basket with a trading band of ±5% – to improve external competitiveness • Support policies to strengthen monetary framework, balance budget and impose strict public sector wage restraint	The first review and an augmentation of the programme was completed in June 2009. Available via the Internet: http://www.imf.org/external/country/BLR/index.htm

Table 7.4 (Continued)

Country	IMF loan size, approval date	Key objectives and policy actions	Additional information
Serbia	$0.5 billion, January 2009; augmented to $4.0 billion in May 2009	• Tighten the fiscal stance in 2009–2010, with the 2009 general government deficit limited to 1.75% of GDP, followed by further fiscal consolidation in 2010. This involves strict incomes policies for containing public sector wage and pension growth and a streamlining of non-priority recurrent spending, which helps create fiscal space to expand infrastructure investment • Strengthen the inflation-targeting framework while maintaining a managed floating exchange rate regime	Since the programme was designed, Serbia's external and financial environment has deteriorated substantially. In response, the authorities have: (i) raised fiscal deficit targets for 2009–2010, while taking additional fiscal measures; (ii) received commitments from main foreign parent banks that they would roll over their commitments to Serbia, and keep their subsidiaries capitalized; and (iii) requested additional financial support from international financial institutions and the EU. The first review was completed in May 2009. Available via the Internet: http://www.imf.org/external/country/SRB/index.htm

Romania	$17.1 billion, May 2009	Cushion the effects of the sharp drop in private capital inflows while implementing policy measures to address the external and fiscal imbalances and to strengthen the financial sector: • Strengthen fiscal policy to reduce the government's financing needs and improve long-term fiscal sustainability • Maintain adequate capitalization of banks and liquidity in domestic financial markets • Bring inflation within the Central Bank's target	Allocations for social programmes will be increased, as well as protection for the most vulnerable pensioners and public sector employees at the lower end of the wage scale. IMF support is coordinated with that of the EU and the World Bank. Available via the Internet: http://www.imf.org/external/country/ROU/index.htm http://www.imf.org/external/country/ROU/index.htm
Poland	$20.6 billion Flexible Credit Line, May 2009	The Flexible Credit Line (FCL) is an instrument established for European Fund member countries with very strong fundamentals, policies, and track records of their implementation. Access to the FCL is not conditional on further performance criteria	The arrangement for Poland was the second commitment, after Mexico, under the IMF's FCL, created in the context of a major overhaul of the Fund's lending framework. Available via the Internet: http://www.imf.org/external/country/POL/index.htm
BiH	$1.57 billion, July 2009	Safeguarding the currency board arrangement by a determined implementation of the fiscal, income and financial sector policies	Available via the Internet: http://www.imf.org/external/country/BIH/index.htm

Source: IMF (2009f), p. 20.

While there is heterogeneity across countries, adjustment efforts are broadly paying off, with some countries making good progress in normalizing access to private sources of financing. Strengthening the banking sectors was and continues to be a priority in most cases. Even though the troubled countries received financial help from the IMF, it is expected that the crisis will still lift the debt level through two channels. One is the cyclical deterioration of the budget, which for the 2008–2010 period the *World Economic Outlook* estimates at a cumulative 16 per cent of GDP for advanced and 10 per cent of GDP for emerging European countries, though with considerable cross-country variation. The other is the extensive use of the public balance sheet to shore up the financial system, including direct support measures such as capital injections and asset purchases and guarantees.

As of June 2009, the estimated fiscal impact of upfront financial sector help varies between 0.7 per cent of GDP in Italy and 13.6 per cent in the Netherlands, with an average for euro-area countries of about 5 per cent (Horton *et al.*, 2009). The net fiscal costs of these measures, which exclude Central Bank support, could be lower should the actual demand for support continue to fall short of what governments have offered. In principle, the possible impact of fiscal guarantees is higher, with many countries having extended guarantees between approximately 10 and 30 per cent, and reaching about 200 per cent of GDP in Ireland. Although the fiscal implications of guarantees are particularly difficult to evaluate, they have been estimated to fall between 2 and 5 per cent of GDP (IMF, 2009d). Either way, however, the debt impact of the crisis is likely to create a sizable need for fiscal adjustment. In addition, it is also likely to influence the size of the adjustment necessitated by the growth effects of the crisis.

Risks facing the European banking sector

In the BSC (2008) risk survey, EU banks assigned the first rank in importance to risks originating from the financial markets, whilst they allocated a strong second rank to risks from macroeconomic developments. Financial market-related risks were viewed by around 49 per cent of the banks as a major source of risk during 2007–2008 (a considerable increase from around 20 per cent in the 2006 survey and a similar level in 2005), followed by risks related to the macroeconomic environment, rated as the main risk source by around 39 per cent of the banks. According to the results, the general uncertainty in various segments of credit markets and their spillover effect on financial markets have had a direct impact on banks' financial performance and capital standing, while risks related to macroeconomic conditions currently appear more distant. The potential spillover effects of macroeconomic factors on financial markets could be seen as one of the reasons why banks consider the general economic developments as a source of risk.

Moreover, a large proportion of responding banks view risks from regulatory developments or from individual strategic developments as the least important. The percentage of banks viewing regulatory risks as least important broadly doubled from 24 per cent in the previous survey to 50 per cent, while the percentage of banks viewing strategy risks as the least important increased by more than 10 percentage points compared with the 2006 survey, to reach 41.1 per cent. Though competition remains fierce in most banking markets, banks see the possibility of a loss in market share or in efficiency as currently less decisive than other risk factors.

Moreover, according to the BSC (2008) survey, the shift towards considering financial market risks as prevalent are most striking for EU-15 banks. Approximately 57.6 per cent of respondents view this source of risk as most important compared with 21.3 per cent in the 2006 report. Banks in NMS view risks from the economy as most important in 45.3 per cent of the responses (a significant increase from 29.8 per cent in the previous survey), followed by 39.6 per cent of banks viewing financial markets risks as most significant. This could be attributed to economic growth as a result of a catching-up process in the NMS, including a possibility of overheating, or to NMS banks' lower direct exposure to the structured finance markets. On the other hand, it could also reflect concerns about the negative impact of a decline in the economic activity of developed economies on the economic activity in NMS, and thus the profitability and quality of NMS banks' portfolios. Still, the second-round effects of the turmoil led to a doubling of the percentage of NMS banks being most concerned with financial market risks compared with the 2006 survey.

Conclusion

The financial crisis has underscored the growing interdependence between financial centres and has tested the ability of EU countries to cooperate in developing an EU-wide response. The financial interdependence between the US and the EU means that the EU and the US share common concerns over the global impact of the financial crisis and the economic downturn. It also means that they both support and hope to benefit from efforts by national governments to stimulate their economies. These common concerns may eventually work to spur EU members to build a common consensus regarding the necessity of providing financial assistance to the Eastern European countries (EEC).

In addition to these concerns, the US and the EU members share common concerns over the organization of financial markets domestically and abroad, and seek to improve supervision and regulation of individual institutions and of international markets. Extensive cross-border banking activities by a number of EU countries has demonstrated that serious problems in one country can have a substantial impact on the financial system elsewhere, while governments may face potentially large liabilities that are associated with branches in another country. One solution being considered is that of developing organizational structures within national economies that can provide an oversight of the different segments of the highly complex financial system. Such an oversight is viewed by many as critical, because financial markets are generally considered to play an indispensable role in allocating capital and facilitating economic activity.

The financial crisis has also revealed extensive interdependency across financial market segments both within many of the advanced national financial markets and across national borders. As a result, the US and the EU have shared mutual interests in solving both the financial crisis and the economic recession, because the two crises have become negatively reinforcing events. A coordinated systemic action has become necessary as financial markets in the US and EU have become highly integrated as a result of cross-border investment by banks, securities brokers and other financial firms. As a result of this integration, economic and financial developments that affect national economies are difficult to contain and are quickly transmitted across national borders, as attested to by the financial crisis of 2008. As financial firms react to a financial crisis in one area, their actions can spill over to other areas as they withdraw assets from foreign markets to shore up their domestic operations. For instance, banks and financial firms in the EU have felt the repercussions of the US financial crisis as US firms operating in the EU, and European firms operating in the US, have adjusted their operations in response to the crisis.

8
Turkey as an Accession Country

Introduction

This chapter focuses on the legal and structural changes, as well as current developments, in the Turkish banking sector. In becoming an EU accession country, Turkey had to adjust its legislation and regulatory environment to that of the EU by adopting the EU *acquis communautaire* during the convergence process. The first section of this chapter reviews the restructuring strategy of Turkey over the last decades. Following this, the chapter examines the recent structure and assesses the increasing foreign presence in the Turkish banking sector, specifically comparing it to its Central and Eastern European counterparts. Then, the focus of attention switches to the EU accession process, by discussing Turkey's long-standing EU membership negotiations as well as the likely pros and cons both for Turkey and the EU. Finally, Turkey's readiness and the impact of the Basel II Accord directives on the current levels of capital adequacy of Turkish banks, and the institutional preparations of Turkish banking and financial systems towards adapting EU regulation and systems are discussed.

Restructuring strategy of Turkish economy and banking sector

Turkey's accession negotiations with the EU are highly dependent on the progress the country makes with political and economic reforms; in particular, issues related to the banking sector are of the utmost importance. This is due to the fact that the total assets of the banking sector account for more than 90 per cent of the Turkish financial system. To achieve the progress required, Turkey adopted comprehensive restructuring programmes, supported by the IMF and the EU over the last decades, to deal with macroeconomic instability, public sector debt, systemic alterations created by state banks, and inadequate risk assessment and management systems as well as a lack of independent and effective supervision. These can be suggested as the major factors contributing to weaknesses in the Turkish banking system in the past. Thus, Turkey needed to create a good structuring strategy, considering the burden of financial crises experienced in the country as well as Turkey's hopes of satisfying the requirements of the IMF and the EU. Figure 8.1 summarizes the most striking features of the Turkish financial sector, and the key amendments and aims of the reform programmes.

Looking back about three decades, Turkey entered 1980 with an IMF stabilization programme following one of the worst balance of payments crises in its history. As a result, on 24 January 1980, the Structural Adjustment and Stabilization Program (SASP) was implemented, beginning the policy restructuring period. The first result of this programme was the deceleration of the inflation rate from 86 per cent at the end of 1980 to 30 per cent at the end of 1981. In order to deal with declining GDP growth in 1983, monetary policy was relaxed, and the economy began to grow, with inflation remaining in the range of 30–50 per cent until 1987. Even after this progress,

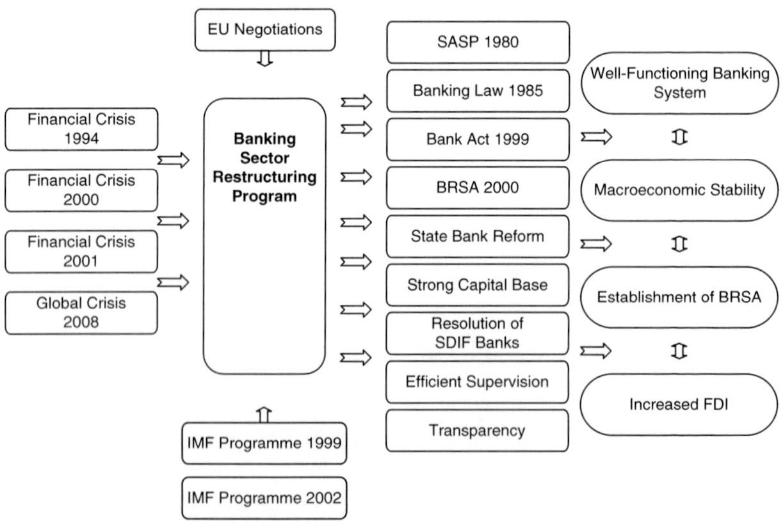

Figure 8.1 Restructuring strategy in Turkey
Source: Created by the author.

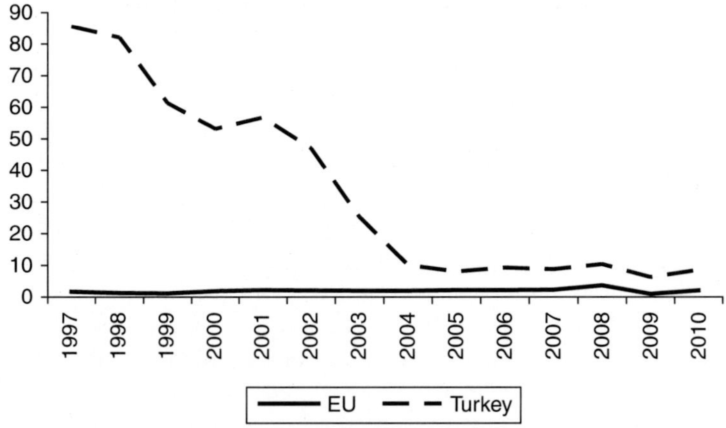

Figure 8.2 Annual inflation rates: Turkey and the EU, 1997–2010 (per cent)
Source: Created by the author from Eurostat.

the inflation rate was still extremely high compared with the EU average (see Figure 8.2).

Without question, Turkey's implementation of liberalization policies changed the structure of the economy. Exports grew from less than USD 2.9 billion in 1980 to USD 10 billion in 1987 and to more than USD 30 billion in the mid-1990s. However, this successful performance under the regime of the aggressive real devaluation of the Turkish lira (TL) only lasted until 1988; the following year the government shifted its priorities to control inflation by allowing real appreciation of the currency. Moreover, the inter-bank market operations, initiated in 1986, allowed banks to lend and borrow from each other for overnight facilities. On the other hand, the Istanbul Stock Exchange was reopened and became a fundamental part of the financial system.

From the perspective of interest rates, Onis and Aysan (1999) suggested that a systematic increase in the domestic debt and short-term domestic borrowing requirements created an upward bias in interest rates. Thus, the financial sector emerged as a major gainer in terms of high interest earnings. Indeed, it became possible to realize annual returns as high as 47 per cent on the dollar in 1989, 25 per cent in 1990, 18 per cent in 1992 and 18 per cent in 1993. By the end of 1993 it became apparent that the rapid growth of the Turkish economy in the early 1990s had not been based on strong foundations.

Furthermore, Altinkemer (2003) proposed that one of the main weaknesses of the Turkish economy was the exceptional treatment of state banks in terms of assigning certain non-bank activities to them, thereby creating duty losses that were to be financed by the central government's budget. The problem imposed on the state banks was due to non-strict regulation, which created additional financial distortions in the market against private banks. Furthermore, as a result of the capital account liberalization, banks' ability to get short-term foreign credits helped to postpone fiscal adjustments and increase the budget deficit and the domestic debt stock even further with shortening maturity. All these concerns eventually resulted in the 1994 crisis, with inflation reaching 106.3 per cent and interest rates rising to 158.1 per cent for the year.

Additionally, pressures on exchange and interest rates as well as the open position of the banking system (around 5 billion USD) increased demand for the US dollar, which generated a run from the TL. Banks rushed to foreign exchange markets to close their foreign exchange position, which ended up with the intervention of the Central Bank of Turkey (CBT). As a result, the CBT lost half of its reserves and overnight interest rates reached a record level. The open position of commercial banks declined to 1.1 billion USD in June 1994, which caused a devaluation of the TL from 15,000 TL/USD in January 1994 to 38,000 TL/USD by the first days of April 1994 (Kibritcioglu *et al.*, 1998). The real effective exchange rate indices over the 1980–2009 period are presented in Figure 8.3.

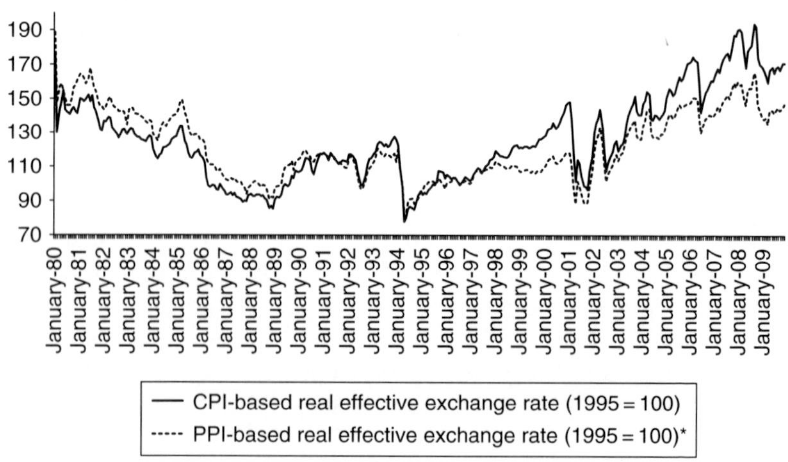

Figure 8.3 Real effective exchange rate indices, TL/USD, 1980–2009
Source: Central Bank of Turkey, Quarterly Bulletins and State Planning Organization Main Economic Indicators, various years.

Looking at another important issue in more depth, sustaining economic growth was very difficult in an environment characterized by over-expansion of public expenditure and inadequate increases in public revenues. It was clear in retrospect that the rising current account deficit, covered by inflows of primarily short-term capital flows, could not provide a basis for sustainable growth. In order to break the vicious circle of domestic borrowing with high interest rates, at the beginning of 1994 the government adopted the low interest-rate objective and implemented it by relying heavily upon the resources of the Central Bank.

Onis and Aysan (1999) highlight that a major component of the base money created by the CBT was channelled as bank credit to the public sector. These policies, combined with the reduction of the investment rating of Turkey, precipitated the crisis in 1994. This, in turn, generated a major outflow of short-term capital. Thus, the financial crisis manifested itself as a major balance of payments crisis leading to a massive depreciation of the exchange rate in the early months of 1994. Since the 1994 economic crisis, Turkey has been trying to maintain economic stability measures with assistance from the IMF. Starting in 1994, subsequent reform packages were introduced to provide confidence in the banking sector. The Turkish government changed its policy from a limited coverage case to a full coverage case.[1]

It is certainly the case that the Banks Act of 1999 represented a fundamental turning point in the evolution of bank regulation in Turkey. Obviously, the IMF was once again heavily involved. But there were some doubts about its involvement due to the fact that the Asian crisis of 1997 had resulted in a radical rethinking of IMF policies. The IMF has been subjected to severe criticism due to its misjudgement of the Asian crisis, in which bank failures seem to have played a fundamental role. It is open to discussion whether the IMF might be right in insisting on tighter regulations of the banking sector in emerging market countries such as Turkey. However, the major problem is that the IMF insists on rapid adjustment to international norms and fails to take into account the costs involved in the transition period, given the depth of disequilibrium that has built up over the years.

In 1999, the Russian financial crisis of 1998 (Russia was Turkey's second most profitable trade partner after Germany)[2] and a major earthquake in August 1999 hit the Turkish economy, resulting in a 4.7 per cent decline in GDP growth rate. In addition, high public sector deficits continued and once again the Turkish economy was in need of an urgent stabilization policy.[3] Following this, in December

1999 the Turkish government launched a three-year IMF-supported pegged exchange rate-based stabilization programme (fixed exchange rate regime) that aimed to decelerate the inflation rate. The economic stabilization programme included a reduction in the budget deficit, economic structural reforms and currency stabilization.[4] The first nine months of the stabilization programme appeared to be successful and the economy gained public confidence,[5] with a recovery of 7.4 per cent GDP growth in 2000. However, the high budget and trade deficit and high public sector deficit still continued during this period.

In September 2000, the Banking Regulation and Supervision Agency (BRSA) began to operate as an independent institution with responsibility for regulating and supervising the banking sector. Soon after, in May 2001, the BRSA announced the Banking Sector Restructuring Program (BSRP), which aimed to eliminate distortions in the financial sector and adopt regulations to promote an efficient, globally competitive and well-functioning banking sector. The restructuring programme was based on four main pillars: (i) restructuring the state banks, (ii) seeking prompt resolution for banks experiencing financial problems, (iii) strengthening the financial position of private banks, and (iv) strengthening the regulatory and supervisory framework.

Thereafter, Turkey entered into the twenty-first century with another IMF-supported programme, which was based on firm monetary and exchange rate policies. The new IMF standby agreement included a USD 4 billion credit to be disbursed over a three-year period, and set goals to reduce the inflation rate from around 70 per cent in December 1999 to single-digit figures by the end of the year 2002. The programme was once again accompanied by measures of strong fiscal performance and structural reforms to provide a nominal anchor for reducing inflation, maintain sounder public finance, and liberalize and modernize the economy (see Figure 8.4). Even though significant progress was made during 2000, the programme was seriously impaired after only 11 months with a severe liquidity crunch that exposed long-standing structural weaknesses in the banking system. As a result, a banking crisis blew up in late November 2000, accompanied by a massive capital outflow, and the programme was finally abandoned three months later, in February 2001.

As a result of the uncertain and fragile characteristics of the Turkish banking system as well as its incapability to fix the burden of high interest rates, the CBT had to abandon its guarantee to a fixed exchange rate regime (see Figure 8.4). Devaluation led to an increase in the inflation rate, reversing the CBT's major achievement and contributing to the

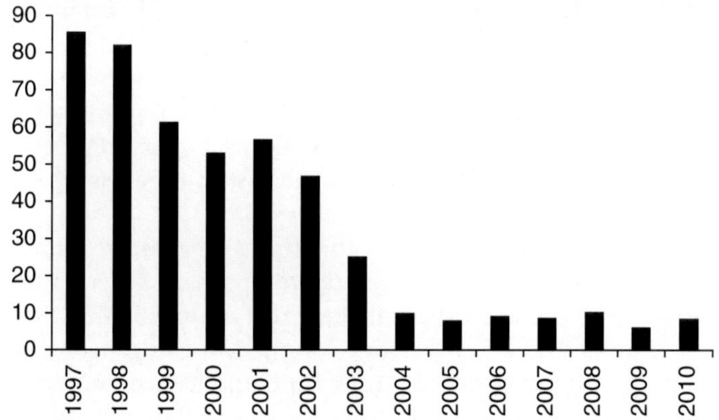

Figure 8.4 Annual inflation rate in Turkey, 1997–2010 (per cent)
Source: Created by the author from Eurostat

2001 financial crisis. However, it is promising to observe that Turkey's inflation rate has been kept mostly in single digits since 2004.

At this point, I would like to summarize a list of factors that contributed to the emergence of the 2000–2001 financial sector distress in Turkey:

(i) The financial liberalization programme resulted in an increase in the number of private banks.
(ii) Excessive public deficit increased Turkey's dependence on foreign loans, which were vital for financing the budget deficit. As a result of sharp real-exchange-rate depreciation, high interest rates, high inflation and trade deficit, bank balance-sheet assets deteriorated quickly.
(iii) Bank profitability is an important factor that indicates the health of a financial system. In order to prevent closure, insolvent banks in Turley faked their balance-sheet problems to depositors by rolling over non-performing loans or increasing their deposits. The incentive of insolvent banks was to reflect healthier balance sheets by hiding the true values of their assets and deposits, which led to an inaccurately determined market value. In other words, although debts were not performing, for many years banks covered up their bad debts.[6]
(iv) Turkey could not maintain a well-functioning financial system, which is important for the efficient identification of, and allocation of funds to, the most productive and innovative activities.

(v) Political and institutional forces played an important role in explaining the inability to implement proper banking sector regulations over lengthy periods of time. The Turkish experience in the aftermath of capital account liberalization leading to the financial crises of 2000–2001 can be suggested as a case study for highlighting the relevance of political and institutional variables in the process of bank regulation.

(vi) The entry of new banks into the Turkish banking sector during the crisis period on the basis of mainly political criteria is another important issue. Even though the entry of new banks should not be interpreted as a negative development, it can generate harmful outcomes on the overall economy if bank licences are granted by political intervention. This can be illustrated with the failure of six banks within a decade of their commencement, banks which were allowed entry into the banking sector during and immediately after the 1991 elections.

(vii) The presence of foreign banks has been minor in Turkey. In a well-regulated and closely supervised banking system, foreign banks contribute to increasing the efficiency and development of domestic financial markets. This can be due to the transfer of know-how and foreign banks' established modern electronic systems. However, in a country that fails to have a well-regulated and supervised banking sector, only certain types of foreign banks can be expected to be willing to enter.[7]

Furthermore, Oney and Suphi (2001) argued that bank-specific factors, such as a lack of consideration for the adequate capitalization of the banking system, poor asset quality mainly based on the quality of a bank's credit evaluation, low profitability, high liquidity and the credit risk of banks were also connected to the banking failure in Turkey. Credit risk primarily corresponds to non-performing loans, which was one of the reasons for the bank failures. This can be attributed to the idea that loans were illegally transferred to the bank owners, managers, the bank's business partners' relatives and to related businesses without a request for any collateral.

Gunay and Tektas (2006) stressed the significance of a sound and well-functioning banking sector for macroeconomic stability and sustainable economic growth, and highlighted a lack of revenue diversification, inadequate capital, mismanagement of credit risk and rapid rise of non-performing loans as the main factors leading to banking crises in Turkey. The 2000–2001 twin economic crises in Turkey once again confirmed the strong association between a poorly functioning under-regulated banking system and the sudden outbreak of macroeconomic crises. Indeed, the Turkish experience showed that both public and private banks contribute significantly to the occurrence of economic crises. It can be argued that private commercial banks played an influential role in the first of the Turkish twin crises experienced in November 2000, whilst public banks emerged as the central actors in the background of the following crisis of February 2001.

In May 2001, a new strengthened economic programme was launched in order to overcome the negative impact of the crises and achieve sustainable economic growth. Following this, a revised three-year plan was adopted in February 2002, covering the 2002–2004 period. The new plan contained provisions for fiscal adjustment to help bring about debt sustainability, reform of the banking sector through an operational and financial restructuring of public banks, and regulation and supervision of private banks.

However, the early general elections on 3 November 2002 dramatically changed the political climate in Turkey. The established single-party government asked the IMF to make minor changes in the programme, which had two overriding goals: (i) to manage the crises and increase the resilience of the economy to shocks, and (ii) to ensure growth with disinflation. In order to achieve these targets, strong structural adjustment policies focusing on the elimination of problems in the banking sector, the enhancement of transparency in economic management, and improvement of governance in both public and private sector were adopted.

Large IMF loans tied to the implementation of ambitious economic reforms enabled Turkey to stabilize interest rates and the currency, as well as meet its debt obligations. In 2002 and 2003, the reforms began to show results. With the exception of the period preceeding the Iraq War, inflation and interest rates have fallen significantly, the currency has been stabilized and confidence has begun to return.

Interest of foreign investors in the Turkish banking sector

Many banks striving to increase their shares in the global arena have expanded their operations beyond the borders of their local markets. A driving force of such expansion and internationalization of the banking sectors was the liberalization of financial markets both in developed and developing countries.[8] The Turkish financial sector has been open to foreign institutions, especially after the financial liberalization in the early 1980s, when foreign firms became eligible to form partnerships with their Turkish counterparts and purchase a 100 per cent stake.

However, foreign banks were not prevalent in the Turkish banking system until after the reforms, which were implemented following the 2001 financial crisis.

The BRSA and State Banks Joint Management Board worked hard on a successful implementation of the reform programme, which reduced financial risk and strengthened the capital structure of Turkish banks, allowing for increase in profits and growth. As in many developing countries, foreign banks in Turkey have the opportunity to gain a high market share due to the low market value of banks, and make profit due to less effective domestic competition compared to developed countries. In particular, banks under the management of the Savings Deposits Insurance Fund (SDIF) in 2001 were merged under a single name and some of them were sold to foreign financial institutions.

Various factors, both positive and negative, have led to significant structural changes in the Turkish banking sector in the last two decades, including the deregulation and liberalization of the sector as well as the consecutive financial crises of 1994 and 2000–2001. In addition, the feedback from the IMF as part of the restructuring programme signed in 1999 has been an important factor in the recent transformation of this sector. These changes also caused the facilitation of foreign bank entry into Turkey's banking system and resulted in a consolidation process, with a remarkable increase in competition and pressure on domestic banks to improve their operational efficiency.[9]

Since 2005, Turkey has attracted an unprecedented amount of investment from foreigners – in total around USD 33 billion – and a significant amount of this flow has been directed to the banking sector. The most probable reasons for this increase are positive economic and regulatory developments as well as the opening of negotiations with the EU in 2005. Thus, a significant number of foreign banks raised their shareholdings in large and medium-sized Turkish banks over the 2005–2006 period. Most of the investors were leading banks in the global arena, and were of European origin (see Table 8.1).

The earliest entrant to this market was HSBC, which started its financial activities there in 1990. HSBC expanded its operations in Turkey through the acquisition of Demirbank, which was the fifth largest private bank in 2001. In 2007 HSBC announced its goal of 100 per cent organic growth of its investments in Turkey, which would be achieved by 2010 via opening 200 new branches and employing 4000 more people.

In 2002, the 50/50 shareholder partnership agreement between Koçbank (the sixth largest private bank at the time of the deal) and UniCredito of Italy (one of the Europe's largest banks) was the first

Table 8.1 Entry of foreign banks into the Turkish banking sector, 2001–2006

Year	No. of M&As	Targeted bank	Investor bank	Origin of investor	Stake bought	Value of deal (USD million)
2001	1	Demirbank	HSBC	UK	100	350
2002	1	Koçbank	UniCredito	Italy	50	240
2005	6	YKB	UniCredito/ Koçbank	Italy–Turkey	57	1,495
		TEB	BNP Paribas	France	50	217
		Dışbank	Fortis	Belgium	89	1,051
		Garanti bank	GE Capital Corporation	USA	26	1,556
		C Bank	Bank Hapoalim	Israel	58	113
		Finansbank	National Bank of Greece	Greece	46	2,800
2006	5	Tefkenbank	EFG Eurobank	Greece	70	185
		Denizbank	Dexia Bank	Belgium	75	2,400
		Şekerbank	BTA	Kazakhstan	34	255
		MNG Bank	Arab Bank/ Bank Med	Lebanon/ Jordan	91	160
		Akbank	Citigroup	USA	20	3,100
Total	13	13	12	10		13,922

Source: Adapted from Altunbas *et al.* (2009), p. 183.

foreign partnership established in the Turkish financial sector. In 2005, the Koçbank/UniCredito joint venture bought a majority share of Yapı Kredi Bankası, one of the largest and best-established private banks, as the biggest merger project in the history of Turkish banking.

Following UniCredito, BNP Paribas bought a 50 per cent stake in Türkiye Ekonomi Bankası (TEB) while Fortis of Benelux acquired 89 per cent of Dışbank, a privately owned medium-sized bank. The largest deals in terms of value were those of Citigroup, National Bank of Greece (NBG), Dexia Bank of Belgium and General Electric Capital Corporation. Citigroup and GE Capital Corporation, both US-based financial institutions, preferred to be minor shareholders and strategic partners of Akbank and Garanti Bankası.

Many reasons have been identified in the literature as factors attracting foreign investors into a banking sector. I would like to list here some of the possible factors relating to Turkey. The regulatory changes in Turkey are one, following the external financial liberalization process that started in 1984. These regulatory changes cover:

(a) Reforms in the investment area.
(b) Equal treatment of domestic and foreign banks.
(c) No limitations on foreign ownership of banks by the law, after the twin crises when the Turkish government relaxed entry barriers for foreign investors.[10]
(d) Stronger auditing and regulation compared with previous periods.
(e) Opportunity for foreign investors to take over Turkish banks is easier than in developed countries as Turkish banks are relatively small in size.
(f) Supporting the argument by Kraft (2002): the low level of competition in Turkey among foreign banks could be a reason for increased FDI.
(g) High profitability of some banks in the sector.
(h) Continuous high efficiency of some banks in the sector.

Moreover, the increasing confidence and financial strength indices in the Turkish banking sector can be suggested as another reason augmenting foreign inflows into the country. Table 8.2 shows that the financial strength indices, namely asset quality, profitability, capital adequacy and overall financial strength, have illustrated a continuous upward swing whilst liquidity risk was in a recession during most of the period under focus.

A number of conclusions can be reached on the financial strength of the Turkish banking sector by analysing the indices summarized in Table 8.2. Firstly, the asset quality index suggests an improvement. Secondly, the declining liquidity risk index confirms that the share of liquid assets in total assets decreased with a less than 50 per cent ratio of assets to liabilities with up to three months' maturity. Thus, although the maturity divergence has still been present, a falling movement is observed between 2001 and 2005, except for a slight upward swing in 2004.

During 2005, the liquidity index decelerated, possibly as banks preferred to stay less liquid due to economic improvements and escalating stability in the Turkish economy. In terms of the profitability index, the banking sector suffered a decline during the 1999–2001 period, which increased from 2002. Furthermore, there has been an increase in the capital adequacy index, indicating a sign of improvement in the

Table 8.2 Financial strength indices of the Turkish banking sector, 1999–2009

Period	Asset quality	Liquidity risk	Profitability	Capital adequacy	Financial strength
1999	100.0	100.0	100.0	100.0	100.0
2000	93.3	88.0	93.7	99.4	94.5
2001	73.0	91.6	87.9	111.0	96.9
2002	85.6	74.9	103.9	122.4	101.6
2003	101.0	73.3	105.7	138.7	108.1
2004	109.7	75.0	105.3	142.3	110.8
2005	111.2	69.5	106.7	143.3	110.4
2006	122.6	85.6	106.9	146.3	113.8
2007	121.9	79.3	108.1	146.3	118.5
2008	122.0	86.2	106.3	142.3	118.5
2009	120.8	85.9	108.9	144.3	118.6

Source: Central Bank of Turkey and author's calculations.

capital structure of the Turkish banking sector. Finally, the overall financial strength index reached its highest levels in 2005 as a result of the improvements in the asset quality, successful profitability performance and stronger capital structure of the banking sector.

Identifying the factors that attracted foreign investors, another interesting question comes to mind, namely, why did foreign banks particularly invest in Turkey's domestic banks? The following reasons can be suggested:

(i) Finansbank, Tekfenbank and Garanti Bankası are technologically stronger and more modern than their foreign partners, which can be attractive for foreign investors.

(ii) Alpha Bank mentioned the technical superiority of Alternatif Bank to its counterparts in Romania and Bulgaria.

(iii) Finansbank attracted the National Bank of Greece (NBG) with its high-quality retail products, such as car loans, consumer loans, insurance and so on. Furthermore, NBG aims to make investments in the tourism, industry and navigation sectors, thus its merger with Finansbank provides it with a base in Turkey.

(iv) Fortis is the only foreign bank stating that their reason for investing in Turkey is the existence of relatively few numbers of foreign competitors in the sector.

(v) Dexia Bank invested in Denizbank as there was the potential of increasing its customer base by reaching around 1.4 million retail customers in Turkey.

(vi) Citigroup reported the same objective as Dexia Bank in purchasing 20 per cent shares in Akbank.
(vii) BNP Paribas bought 50 per cent of TEB shares as TEB has been the fastest bank responding to changes in the banking sector among its counterparts in the Mediterranean region.

In my opinion, the granting EU membership would make Turkey even more attractive for FDI in the future. This is due to the fact that Turkey has a highly skilled and adaptable labour force, a large domestic market and the advantage of geographic closeness to the European, the Middle Eastern, Northern African and Central Asian markets. If Turkey becomes part of the EU, it will certainly benefit from increasing FDI as the EU helps in transferring to Turkey financial resources, fixed assets, technology and know-how as well as in creating new jobs and international market access.

FDI in Turkey vs Central and Eastern European countries

Examining the presence of foreign participation in Turkish banking will not be complete without a comparison with Turkey's EU competitors. It can be observed that the total deposits to GDP ratio in Turkey is significantly lower than with all EU members except Poland, Romania, Lithuania and Hungary. Similarly, the loans to deposits ratio, which has been an important indicator of the transformation of savings into investments in an economy, is low compared with the EU-27 average and most of the individual EU countries. This can be attributed to the deceleration in volume of credits in Turkey following the 2001 crisis. The loans to GDP ratio is also lower than that of the EU-27, which may be due to the increase in investment costs resulting from chronic inflation since 1990s, and the high borrowing needs of the government caused by the high public deficit (see Table 8.3).

The level of foreign ownership in the Turkish banking sector ranks as one of the lowest compared with other emerging countries. The 28.7 per cent average share of foreign participation in the EU-27 countries as well as Bulgaria (93 per cent) and Romania (94 per cent) is above the level of the presence of foreign participation in the Turkish banking sector (24.8 per cent). This is supportive of the argument by Steinherr and colleagues (2004) who suggest that Eastern European countries did not have a history of commercial banking activity when they opened up their markets and that the most efficient option of quickly transforming their banking system was to invite foreign banks to be strategic investors. In contrast, the Turkish banking sector has been long established with domestic banks and provides the foreign banks

Table 8.3 Balance sheet items and foreign participation: Turkey and selected EU countries, 2007

Countries	Deposits to GDP (per cent)	Loans to GDP (per cent)	Loans to Deposits (per cent)	Foreign Participation (per cent)
Primary EU members				
Germany	119	130	109	11.1
Austria	111	140	126	26.9
France	83	114	137	12.9
UK	290	288	99	53.4
Italy	73	112	154	17.4
Portugal	118	158	134	23.0
Spain	144	177	123	11.6
New EU members since 2004				
Czech Republic	73	53	72	91.5
Latvia	72	104	145	58.0
Lithuania	42	63	152	83.7
Hungary	51	65	128	57.4
Poland	48	43	91	70.5
Bulgaria	69	67	97	81.6
Romania	32	35	109	82.1
EU-27 average	136	157	116	28.7
Turkey	**42**	**35**	**83**	**24.8**

Source: Author's calculations from Bank Association of Turkey, Financial Stability Report (2007).

with one representative office in order to help manage their activities. Additionally, legal uncertainties, family ownership of private banks and relationship lending practices in Turkey could also raise concerns among foreign investors.

Despite the relatively small asset size and low degree of intermediation of the Turkish financial system, Turkey's potential and its regional situation make it an attractive market. The entry of foreign banks into Turkey's financial markets is expected to enhance competition in the financial sector and improve the quality of banking services and financial products.

Turkey's membership negotiations

The EU went through a massive enlargement process in 2004, followed by the inclusion of Romania and Bulgaria in 2007 (details discussed in Chapter 3). Turkey attached particular importance to the EU's recent enlargement process for two main reasons. Firstly, having played an active role in the ex-Soviet bloc as a trade partner, it was expected that Turkey would aspire for inclusion in the new European architecture. Second, as described below, the association between Turkey and the EU guarantees it full EU membership. This is why, over a very long period of time, Turkey has still continued to insist on inclusion in the EU.

Progress since the Ankara Agreement

Turkey was one of the first candidate countries to apply to join the European Economic Community (EEC), in July 1959, shortly after its creation in 1958. The response from the EEC was the suggestion of establishing an association between the Republic of Turkey and the EEC until circumstances in Turkey permited its accession. However, the Ankara Agreement, which created this association, could not be signed until 12 September 1963 and only came into force on 1 December 1964.[11] The Ankara Agreement aimed at securing Turkey's full membership in the EEC through the establishment of a customs union in economic and trade mattters in three phases, which still constitutes the legal basis of the association.

After pursuing inward-oriented development strategies throughout the 1960s and 1970s, Turkey switched to a more outward-oriented policy stance in 1980. The opening up of the economy followed, with the aim of integrating the country into the EU. Turkey applied for full membership in 1987, but received a response in 1990 stating that accession negotiations could not be undertaken at the time as the EU was engaged in major internal changes (adoption of the single market), and developments in Eastern Europe and the Soviet Union. However, the EU was prepared to extend and deepen economic relations with Turkey without rejecting the possibility of full membership at a future date.

In principle, Turkey's application for accession has been based on the relevant provisions of the Ankara Agreement and the Treaty of Rome. The Council forwarded Turkey's application to the Commission for an Opinion, which was completed on 18 December 1989 and approved by the Council on 5 February 1990. The Commission underlined Turkey's eligibility for membership, but postponed its application until the emergence of a more favourable environment. The reason for this response was that the Commission was exceptionally busy with the urgent procedures of the single market, avoiding its further enlargement. However, the Commission underpinned the need for a comprehensive cooperation programme to facilitate the integration of the two sides as well as finalizing the customs union.

Following this, it was agreed at an Association Council meeting in Brussels (6 March 1995) that a customs union would be created between Turkey and the EU as of 1 January 1996 – to be fully phased in by 2001 – where Turkey would impose no quotas or tariffs on imports of industrial goods from the EU. However, the major exception to free trade is agriculture, for which the average tariff rate is 21.4 per cent. Moreover, agricultural trade is also subject to tariff quotas and price regulation in order to protect domestic producers both in the EU and Turkey. Thus, in terms of further liberalization of merchandise trade, accession will primarily have an effect on agriculture.

At the Association Council of 29 April 1997, the EU reconfirmed Turkey's eligibility for membership and asked the Commission to prepare recommendations to deepen Turkey–EU relations, while claiming that the development of this relationship depends on a number of issues relating to Greece, Cyprus and human rights. The Commission, however, excluded Turkey from the enlargement process in its report entitled "Agenda 2000" disclosed on 16 July 1997. The report granted that the customs union was functioning satisfactorily and that it had demonstrated Turkey's ability to adapt to EU norms in many areas, whilst a number of recommendations, ranging from liberalization of trade in services to consumer protection, and a number of political issues as preconditions for moving the relations forward were proposed.

On 10–11 December 1999, the European Council meeting held in Helsinki produced a breakthrough in Turkey–EU relations. At Helsinki, Turkey was officially recognized as a candidate country for accession. The result was the creation of an Accession Partnership with the EU, indicating that the EU is working together with Turkey to enable it to adopt the *acquis communautaire*. But, in contrast to other candidate countries (EU-10, Bulgaria and Romania), Turkey did not receive a timetable for accession. The 1999 European Council decisions corroborated that Turkey is a candidate for membership but stated that improvement is essential regarding civil liberties, human rights and enhanced civilian control of the military. Following this, a Department for EU Affairs was set up in 2000 to coordinate all Turkey's policies related to the pre-accession process and, as a result, a series of constitutional and legislative changes were adopted by Turkey during 2001–2004.

After the approval of the Accession Partnership by the Council and the adoption of the Framework Regulation on 26 February 2001, the Turkish government announced, on 19 March 2001, its own National Programme for the adoption of the *acquis communautaire*. Since then, progress towards accession has continued along the path set by the National Programme. In December 2002, the Copenhagen European Council concluded that "if the European Council in December 2004, on the basis of a report and a recommendation from the Commission, decides that Turkey fulfils the Copenhagen political criteria, the European Union will open accession negotiations with Turkey without delay". At the December 2004 Council meeting, it was decided to launch negotiations with Turkey and establish a timetable for accession (European Commission, 2004b). Although the process has now been launched, great uncertainties continue to prevail about whether Turkey will be able to achieve its goal of accession to the EU.

Some of these issues have a political grounding, such as the realization of the EU political and human rights criteria formalized by the European Council in Copenhagen in 1993, and acceptance of restrictions on immigration post-accession. On the other hand, the greatest uncertainty might be whether EU governments and societies are willing to accept a large but nonetheless Muslim country as part of the EU. Time will reveal the ultimate outcome. What matters in the short to medium term is the impact that continued progress towards achieving the conditions for membership will have on Turkey.

The EU decided at the highest political level in December 2004 that accession negotiations with Turkey should be opened on 3 October 2005, provided Turkey brings into force six pieces of legislation on political reforms: Law on Associations, Penal Code, Law on Intermediate Courts of Appeal, Code of Criminal Procedure, legislation establishing the judicial police and law on execution of punishments.

Turkey took a number of important steps towards this end such as a major review of the constitution. Thirty-four Articles of the Turkish Constitution have recently been amended. The package of constitutional amendments covers a wide range of issues, such as improving human rights, strengthening the rule of law and restructuring democratic institutions. These form only a part of the deep political reform process that Turkey has initiated, followed by legislative and administrative measures to ensure their implementation. In addition, numerous reform measures have been adopted in the economic framework in line with the National Programme.

Basel II

According to an EU screening report (2007), overall, Turkey's legislation is satisfactorily aligned to the financial services acquis, though there are areas yet to be improved. In the area of banking, a framework for the supplementary supervision of financial conglomerates is still missing. Moreover, legislation concerning the supervision of electronic money institutions is non-existent and has to be developed. Regarding the deposit insurance scheme, Turkey has already established a deposit guarantee scheme under the SDIF, which (at the time of writing) guaranteed up to EUR 31,000. The scheme is partially in line with EU acquis. Although the directive requires credit institutions to join an officially recognized deposit guarantee scheme, the minimum limit of protection is set to be EUR 20,000 per depositor. The protection scheme in Turkey is well above this benchmark.

One of the most important items in the acquis on financial institutions is the harmonization of capital adequacy regulations. The latest EU directive that sets out the capital adequacy framework is the Capital Adequacy Directive 3 (CAD 3). CAD 3, which took effect in 2007 and applies to all credit institutions in the EU, simply translates Basel II into EU legislation. The adaptation of a Basel II type regulatory framework for financial institutions by the EU facilitated Turkey's efforts to comply with this section of the acquis, as Turkish authorities had already opted to implement Basel II provisions fully as of January 2008 for capital adequacy requirements. In fact, capital adequacy requirements in Turkey were already established in line with Basel I (adopted in 1989) and market risk was incorporated in the calculation of capital adequacy ratio in 2002. The Banking Law in Turkey requires banks to maintain a minimum capital adequacy ratio of 8 per cent.

Turkey moves towards EU accession

The big prize for those countries that are immediate neighbours to the EU has been the chance of accession. Even though Turkey was not listed in the most recent enlargement, it is in this category and an ongoing process is supposed to lead eventually to EU membership. Figure 8.5 compares the real GDP growth rates of Turkey and the EU average over the 1980–2014 period, with forecasted figures.

Given the fact that the population of Turkey is about the same size as the EU-10 countries as a whole, and approximately the same size as Poland in economic terms, Turkey can be accepted as another enlargement. And, in political terms, it is easier for the EU-27 to absorb one country instead of many. In addition, the population of Turkey will match that of Germany and will have an impact on the EU's political dynamics. Table 8.4 presents population figures for Turkey and a selection of EU countries.

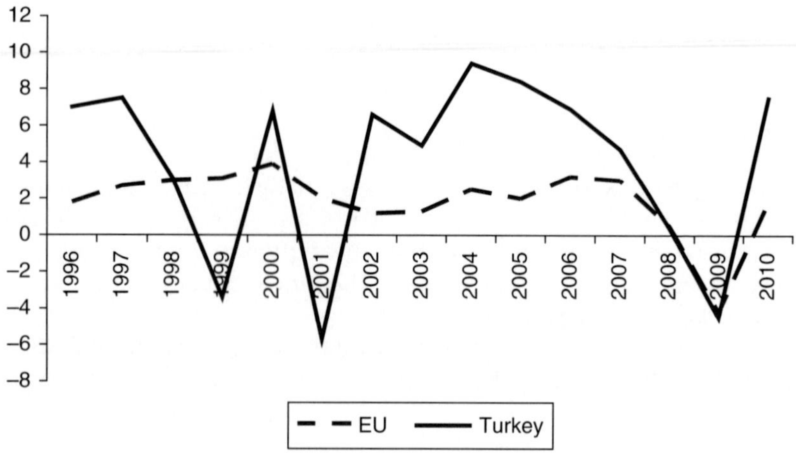

Figure 8.5 Annual percentage change of real GDP growth: Turkey and the EU, 1996–2010
Source: Created by the author from Eurostat.

In terms of population, Turkey would be the second largest EU country after Germany, whilst population projections indicate that it will probably be the largest by 2025, if not earlier. Although Turkey's almost 70 million population is very close to that of the ten NMS at 75 million, it is poorer. The NMS account for 16 per cent of the EU-25 population and 4.6 per cent of EU GDP, while Turkey's GDP in 2002 is only 1.9 per cent of that of the EU-25. In fact, the Turkish economy is roughly the size of that of Poland.

From the economic perspective, the most important fact about Turkey is its low per capita income, which will create economic consequences for the EU as, in the current EU, its largest members – Germany, France, Italy and the UK – also have the largest economies. Political and economic dominance go together. This is not the case for Turkey. A snapshot of main macroeconomic indicators comparing Turkey with the EU averages over the 1996–2006 period is given in Table 8.5. The Purchasing Power Parity (PPP) adjusted per capita income figures for Turkey is almost equal to those of Bulgaria and Romania but more complicated. This is due to the fact that income disparities across Turkey are enormous, in particular comparing the south-east to the west or rural and urban regions.

From the perspective of Turkey, the EU accession will grant numerous benefits. Nor would Turkey have to wait very long to start

Table 8.4 Population and population projections for Turkey and the EU, 2003–2050

Countries	2003	2015	2025	2050
Austria	8,116	8,058	7,979	7,376
Belgium	10,318	10,470	10,516	10,221
Bulgaria	7,897	7,167	6,609	5,255
Czech Republic	10,236	10,076	9,806	8,553
Denmark	5,364	5,447	5,469	5,273
Finland	5,207	5,284	5,289	4,941
France	60,144	62,841	64,165	64,230
Germany	82,476	82,497	81,959	79,145
Greece	10,976	10,944	10,707	9,814
Hungary	9,877	9,324	8,865	7,589
Italy	57,423	55,507	52,939	44,875
Netherlands	16,149	16,791	17,123	16,954
Poland	38,587	38,173	37,337	33,004
Portugal	10,062	10,030	9,834	9,027
Romania	22,334	21,649	20,806	18,063
Slovakia	5,402	5,441	5,397	4,948
Spain	41,060	41,167	40,369	37,336
Sweden	8,876	8,983	9,055	8,700
UK	59,251	61,275	63,287	66,166
Turkey	71,325	82,150	88,995	97,759
Total EU-25	454,187	456,876	454,422	431,241
Total EU-27	484,418	485,692	481,837	454,559
Total EU-28 (inc. Turkey)	555,743	567,842	570,832	552,318
Turkey as % of EU-28	**12.8**	**14.4**	**15.5**	**17.7**

Source: Adapted by the author from UN population forecasts.

reaping the benefits of an eventual EU accession. With the opening of EU accession negotiations in October 2005, Turkey is likely to attract larger sums of FDI in the near future, something which has already been experienced in the banking sector since 2005. The opening of EU negotiations acts as a strong signal that Turkey will eventually become a full member of the EU and will assure foreign investors that the Turkish economy will follow a stable growth path for the foreseeable future and that the legal and judicial environment will improve across all relevant areas of the common acquis.

Turkey will, on accession, be the same size as Germany, meaning that together they will account for almost 30 per cent of the EU's population. The EU will then have five large countries – Germany, France, Italy, the UK and Turkey – and seven "larger" countries, including Poland and Spain. Turkey will certainly impact strongly on the political dynamics

Table 8.5 Macroeconomic indicators: Turkey and the EU, 1996–2006

	1996	1997	1998	1999	2000	2001	2002	2003	2004	2005	2006
Annual employment growth (per cent)											
EU-27	0.5	0.6	1.4	1.0	1.6	0.9	–0.3	0.4	0.7	0.9	1.6
Euro area	0.5	0.9	1.9	2.0	2.4	1.5	0.6	0.4	0.9	0.8	1.4
Turkey	2.1	–2.5	2.8	2.1	–0.4	–1.0	–1.8	–1.0	3.0	1.4	1.2
Employment rate (per cent)											
EU-27	n.a	60.7	61.2	61.8	62.2	62.5	62.3	62.5	62.9	63.4	64.4
Euro area	58.1	58.5	59.3	60.5	61.5	62.2	62.4	62.6	63.0	63.7	64.6
Turkey	n.a	n.a	n.a	n.a	48.8	47.8	46.9	45.8	46.1	46.0	45.9
GDP at current market prices (EUR billion)											
EU-27	7,353	7,759	8,130	8,545	9,160	9,536	9,893	10,057	10,555	10,991	11,583
Euro area	5,762	5,891	6,119	6,400	6,733	7,026	7,271	7,485	7,787	8,054	8,433
Turkey	143	168	178	173	217	162	193	212	242	291	319
GDP per capita at current market prices (PPS, EU-27 = 100)											
EU-27	n.a	100	100	100	100	100	100	100	100	100	100
Euro area	n.a	115	115	114	114	114	113	112	111	111	110
Turkey	n.a	32	32	29	30	26	27	27	28	29	29

Inflation rate per cent change compared with previous year											
EU	n/a	1.7	1.3	1.2	1.9	2.2	2.1	2.0	2.0	2.2	2.2
Euro area	n/a	1.6	1.1	1.1	2.1	2.3	2.2	2.1	2.1	2.2	2.2
Turkey	n/a	85.6	82.1	61.4	53.2	56.8	47.0	25.3	10.1	8.1	9.3
Total population (at 1 January, million)											
EU-27	478.1	480.4	481.1	482.2	483.0	484.5	486.5	488.6	490.9	493.0	495.1
Euro area	302.2	304.5	305.2	306.2	307.5	309.0	310.9	312.9	314.9	316.7	318.4
Turkey	63.5	64.6	65.8	66.9	67.9	68.8	69.8	70.7	71.6	72.5	73.4
Unemployment rate (per cent)											
EU-27	n/a	n/a	n/a	n/a	8.7	8.5	8.9	9.0	9.1	8.9	8.2
Euro area	10.7	10.6	10.0	9.1	8.2	7.8	8.3	8.8	8.9	8.9	8.3
Turkey	n/a	n/a	n/a	n/a	5.2	6.8	8.9	9.3	9.0	8.8	8.4

Source: Adapted by the author from ECB (2007b).

Table 8.6 Voting weights and number of seats in the European Parliament: EU-25, EU-27, EU-28

Countries	Share in EU-25, 2004		Share in EU-27, 2007		Share in EU-28, 2015	
	V. W.	**Seats**	**V. W.**	**Seats**	**V. W.**	**Seats**
Germany	18.1	99	16.9	98	14.5	82
France	13.2	78	12.9	78	11	64
Italy	12.6	78	11.4	78	9.7	64
UK	13	78	12.6	78	10.7	64
Spain	9	54	8.4	54	7.2	44
Poland	8.4	54	7.8	54	6.7	44
Turkey	–	–	–	–	14.4	82

Source: Adapted by the author from UN World Population Division, World Population Prospects (2002).

both among the larger member states and within the EU as a whole. These political dynamics are discussed further below. Here, we look at the likely direct impact on the three main institutions of Council, Commission and European Parliament. Table 8.6 sets out voting weights by population share in an EU-25, EU-27 and EU-28.

Assuming that the EU agrees the proposal in the Constitution for a "double-majority" system of voting, EU decisions will need a majority of both countries and population (50 per cent and 60 per cent, respectively). In the EU-28, no proposal could be passed without the support of at least 15 member countries. In such a system, no single state can dominate; where population size has more power is through the ability to block decisions. If the threshold is set at 60 per cent, then in the EU-25 Germany, together with the UK and France, can block decisions (with 44.3 per cent of total population, or with Italy instead of the UK making 43.9 per cent), though they cannot achieve this in the EU-28 (where they would have 36.2 per cent of population) unless the population majority is set to 65 per cent (Hughes, 2004).

In the case of the EU-28, both Turkey and Germany will have around 14.5 per cent of the vote. Even though they will be strong players, they cannot block proposals together, but would need a third large country to do so. The largest five countries in the EU-28 will account for 60.3 per cent of the vote by population. This is only 3.4 per cent higher than the share of the "big 4" countries in the EU-25 (where they have 56.9 per cent of the vote). So, Turkey will be a powerful player and will add to the already complex set of alliances and blocking combinations that are possible. But in the EU-28, despite its size, Turkey does not add strongly to the dominance of the larger countries. As the debate on voting power in the Constitution shows, questions of power and votes are highly politically sensitive and negotiations for Turkey's accession will not be simple.

Moreover, given its size, Turkey will have a large impact on the European Parliament. Table 8.6 compares the distribution of seats in the European Parliament in the EU-25 and EU-28. Assuming the EU decides to keep a limit of 732 seats in the Parliament, then each country's allocations will have to be reduced to avoid the accession of Turkey, Romania and Bulgaria adding 149 seats (99 [same as Germany], 33 and 17, respectively). If there was a simple proportionate reduction across all countries on the allocation of seats, Germany and Turkey would have 82 seats and an 11.2 per cent share of the vote each (down from 13.5 per cent); France, Italy and the UK would have 64 seats, representing 8.7 per cent of the vote each (down from 10.6 per cent) and Spain and Poland would have 44 seats and 6.0 per cent of the vote (down from 7.3 per cent).

Table 8.7 illustrates that, according to the 2007 figures, Turkey's biggest problems in terms of macroeconomic indicators are its high unemployment and inflation rates and its current account deficit. But we should emphasize its high GDP growth and GDP per capita growth rates, which can be accepted as indicators of good performance and as a promise of development in the near future.

Moreover, according to the report published by the Netherlands Bureau for Economic Policy Analysis, the immediate impact of Turkey joining the EU is estimated as a 34 per cent increase in bilateral trade. Following this, they have used a more comprehensive model to simulate the economic effects in 2025 of a Turkish accession in 2010 on Turkey. Ignoring the potential impact of economies of scale, technology spillovers, FDI or the effects of EU budget transfers, their results indicated a 0.8 per cent increase in Turkey's GDP, a 1.4 per cent increase in its consumption and an 8.1 per cent increase in its exports. The biggest impact is identified in the textiles and clothing sectors. On the other hand, the impact of Turkey's accession on the EU is estimated to be much smaller, given the small overall size of the Turkish economy. Their findings illustrated a EUR 3.8 billion welfare gain, a 0.2 per cent increase in exports and a 0.1 per cent increase in consumption for the EU-15. In the case of EU-10, a 0.3 per cent increase in exports and a 0.2 per cent increase in consumption are predicted.

Table 8.7 Key macroeconomic indicators: Turkey and selected countries, 2007

Indicators	Euro area	EU-27	US	Japan	China	Turkey
Population (millions)	320	406	302	128	1329	69
Share of world GDP (per cent at PPP)	16.4	22.5	21.6	6.7	10.9	1.35
GDP growth (per cent)	2.6	2.9	2	2.1	11.9	4.7
GDP per capita growth (per cent)	2.1	2.5	1	2.1	11.2	4.2
Unemployment (per cent of labour force)	7.4	7.1	4.6	3.9	4	10
Inflation (per cent)	2.1	2.4	2.8	0.1	4.8	8.8
Share of world trade (per cent)	16.3	21.1	11.2	7.1	11.9	1.4
Current account balances (per cent of GDP)	0	−0.9	−5.1	4.8	10.8	−5.8

Source: Adapted by the author from Eurostat (2007).

From the EU's perspective the most probable economic objections to Turkey's full membership can be listed as:

1. Turkey will receive a significant part of the EC's structural funds and will impose an additional burden on countries that are major contributors to the Community budget;
2. The Turkish economy is not mature enough for the single market, and the Turkish industry is not competitive with that of the EU.
3. The free movement of the Turkish labour force could lead to an overly large increase of Turkish immigrants into the EU countries, particularly Germany.

Conclusion

The evidence presented throughout this chapter shows that there is strong agreement that a sound financial system is the lifeblood of an economy, and that proper regulatory and supervisory strategies are among the most important prerequisites for achieving such a system. It is also highlighted that, as well as bank-specific factors, there might be different indicators and causes of financial crises, including those of a political and institutional nature, that may be relevant for a particular country at a particular moment in time.

Financial fragility appears to have played an important role in the Turkish financial crises of 1994 and 2000–2001. In fact, the 1994 crisis' fundamental variables were deteriorating, and large fiscal deficit with high and variable inflation and increasing public sector deficit led to a growing external deficit and an increasing demand for foreign exchange. During the crises years of 2000–2001, factors such as a weak macroeconomic environment – slow GDP growth and a large government, trade, current account and budget deficit, as well as excessively high inflation and real interest rates – and weaknesses in the financial sector, such as moral hazards and the asymmetric information problem, can explain Turkey's vulnerability to financial crises. Recorded FDI inflows to Turkey, despite increasing since 2005 and their beneficial effects, have been exceptionally low compared with those of the CEEC. The main FDI challenges facing Turkey are determining why FDI inflows have remained so low and how Turkey can increase the inflows to desirable levels.

With accession to the EU, Turkey will complete the harmonization of its regulations, liberalize entry and exit into various sectors of its economy, impose hard budget constraints on all its public and private enterprises, liberalize its trade with the EU in services (based on the customs union) and finally join the European single market. Furthermore, joining the EU will require Turkey to adopt and implement the whole body of EU legislation and standards, the *acquis communautaire*. According to EU membership criteria, new members must be able to demonstrate the "ability to take on the obligations of membership including adherence to the aims of political, economic and monetary union". Thus, Turkey is expected to adopt the euro when it is ready to do so, although not immediately upon accession.

From the economic perspective, it can be suggested that Turkey's accession to the EU should be related to its size, per capita income and dependence on agriculture. For the EU, these three factors combine to create a huge immigration potential if migration is freed from most restrictions. Moreover, these factors indicate that Turkey may become the largest recipient of transfers from the EU budget due to its large population, at least under present rules and policies. As a result of these issues, Turkey is expected to face further challenges from the current EU member countries. Given the fact that its population is almost as large as that of the NMS, Turkey as a single country will have strong voting rights in the European Council. There is therefore a big question mark in the EU's mind as to whether or not to allow Turkey's accession.

9
Concluding Remarks

The unifying aim of this book has been to present an overview of the history and the macroeconomic and structural changes, as well as enlargement and development, of the European banking sector, with the major emphasis being on the effects of the introduction of the single currency, regulatory changes and the recent global financial crisis. In addition, its intention was to examine the financial structure and performance of the European banking industry and to look at its future by examining recent developments in relation to the probable candidate countries. Overall, the book contributes to the European banking sector's past, present and future. Specifically, it is one of few works that have examined and brought together various sources in one place; it can be viewed as an extended version of the work *Efficiency in European Banking* by Molyneux and colleagues (1996). The major findings can be summarized as follows.

First, a new institutional setting and a single monetary policy framework designed to achieve price stability were established with the creation of the Economic and Monetary Union (EMU). At the centre of this framework is the European Central Bank (ECB), whose primary objective is price stability. The euro system has provided regular advice and input to the development of the legal, regulatory and supervisory framework for financial services, especially at EU level. However, as the euro-area's integration makes further progress, policies defined at the national level must give greater consideration to the requirements of the Community. Regarding market infrastructure generally, the euro system has successfully contributed to ensuring the safe and efficient flow of money, securities and other financial instruments through payment and settlement systems. Moreover, the introduction of the euro on 1 January 1999 into euro-area countries was a historic event involving years of careful planning and preparation; now more than 320 million people in 16 EU countries share the euro as their currency.

Second, the first ten years of the euro coincided with an unprecedented enlargement of the EU, increasing the number of member countries from 15 to 27. This enlargement was, in many respects, the largest and most comprehensive in the history of the EU. Even though the accession countries have been members of the EU since 2004, the ongoing changes mean that it will take more time before these countries fully complete the restructuring process. Recently, three countries, Croatia, Turkey and the FYROM, have been going through accession negotiations with the EU, as well as five more in the Western Balkans – Albania, Kosovo, Serbia, Bosnia and Herzegovina, and Montenegro – who have candidate country status for potential EU membership. Due mainly to geographic proximity and traditional economic linkages, which are in turn based on large relative comparative advantages, the EU and, in particular, the euro area, represents the most important trading partner of the Western Balkans.

Third, despite the political and economic convergence in the EU, the financial structures of individual member countries remain diverse. We have highlighted two key features of the EU-27 financial sector: the ongoing structural changes in relation to regulatory developments and the application of technological advances both at EU-27 and individual country levels. In addition, internationalization strategies, which in the past were frequently driven by competitive pressures in domestic markets, have been revised in the course of bank reorientation towards traditional banking activities. Branches remained at the core of bank distribution strategies, but their role changed as specific tasks became increasingly automated. The number of bank employees has continued to be reduced and alternative distribution channels have gained pace. Some regions, such as Austria, Ireland, Italy, Portugal and Spain, placed a relatively strong emphasis on electronic banking, while others, such as Greece and the Netherlands, have focused more on expanding the services provided through ATMs.

Fourth, looking at the detailed analysis presented throughout this book, we reached the conclusion that, on average, EU-15 economies are richer than NMS counterparts. However, due to the convergence process, NMS economies have grown faster than EU-15 economies in recent years. The gap between the two groups has slightly reduced over the period of examination, although a longer period of time is required for a coherent convergence among EU-15 and NMS countries. Moreover, it was suggested that the most striking changes were a result of the rapid development in IT and the recent wave of M&As. In particular, a significant financial regulation process spread throughout Europe during recent years. The major changes that occurred due to the application of advanced technologies caused cost reductions, increased speed and created more efficient and effective operation of the financial sector. Furthermore, it is likely that European banks will continue to operate in an increasingly competitive environment as a result of regulatory changes. Therefore, we can suggest that European banks will be under pressure to increase their income and, at the same time, control their costs.

Fifth, analysing the balance sheet structures of European banks not only with respect to the EU-27 average but also with respect to the group each country belongs to, for instance, EU-15, NMS or the euro area, gave us the chance to better understand the homogeneity and developments among such countries over time. The findings of the detailed accounting analysis illustrated that the impact of the financial crisis on the European financial integration process has not been homogeneous. Those segments that had experienced the highest degree of integration over the last decade have been heavily hit by the crisis, and in many cases have seen a sharp reversal in their positive trend over the period 2007–2008. This is especially the case for unsecured money markets, government bond markets and equity markets. However, there is not enough evidence at this stage to assess whether these recent trends can be interpreted as a symptom of increasing long-term market segmentation or if they are linked to a temporary entrenchment by market actors within domestic borders.

In terms of efficiency, the EU-27 had a higher average ROE than the EU-15 over the 2006–2008 period. At the country level, the EU-15 average was drawn down by high losses in the Belgian, German, Dutch, Danish and British financial sectors. In terms of ROA, EU-15 commercial banks experienced higher levels than the others except in 2005, during which euro-area commercial banks achieved the highest level. It is revealed that, apart from in 2005, ROA ratios for EU-27 countries were the lowest among all groups. This can be attributed to the financial help (for a successful financial integration process when they became EU members in 2004) that NMS have received from the EU. On the other hand, the high ROA ratios identified in these countries just before the crisis attracted new competition, which forced a reduction in net interest margins and bank profits, while all groups of EU commercial banks maintained high net interest margins over the 2008 and 2009 period.

A general worsening was observed in the cost-to-income ratios, in that the average CTI increased to approximately 67 per cent in the EU-27 and 70 per cent in the EU-15 in 2008, and has been even higher in the euro-area countries. In terms of liquidity, the euro-area commercial banks presented the highest liquidity ratios during 2007 and 2008, whilst the highest decline was experienced in the EU-15. This is attributable to the fact that big countries such as Germany, the UK, Italy and Spain witnessed severe liquidity problems in their financial sectors. In addition, the asset quality of EU commercial banks also deteriorated in 2008, although developments in non-performing loans to total loans ratio differ significantly across countries.

Sixthly, focusing on the impact of the recent global financial crisis, we suggest that the current European recession is showing signs of bottoming out. After gathering pace through early 2009, the contraction appears to have ended at mid-2009 with the recovering confidence in the financial sector. However, the downturn is easing more slowly in countries that have experienced steep declines in capital inflows. In fact, the crisis has hit Europe particularly hard, perhaps harder than other regions of the world, mainly as a result of the collapse in global trade, the extent of exposure to toxic assets, its reliance on securitization and its dependence on world markets. In this respect, several countries such as Greece, Italy, Hungary and the Balkans have been left vulnerable; the former two because of concerns about their fiscal sustainability, and the latter two due to concerns about their large current account deficits.

Last but not least, the financial crisis has underscored the growing interdependence between financial centres and has tested the ability of EU members to cooperate in developing an EU-wide response. The financial interdependence between the US and the EU means that they share common concerns over the global impact of the financial crisis and the economic downturn. It also means that they both support and hope to benefit from efforts by national governments to stimulate their economies. Such stimulus measures, however, could become a source of friction if some of the larger economies are viewed as not carrying their share of the burden for a global recovery by providing stimulus measures that are commensurate with the size of their economy.

Moreover, the financial crisis has revealed extensive interdependency across financial market segments both within many of the advanced national financial markets and across national borders. As a result, the US and EU members have a shared mutual interest in solving both the financial crisis and the economic recession, because the two crises have become negatively reinforcing events. The evidence presented throughout this book reveals that there is strong agreement that a sound financial system is the lifeblood of an economy, and that proper regulatory and supervisory strategies are among the most important prerequisites for achieving this. Also highlighted is the fact that, as well as bank-specific factors, there might be different indicators and causes of financial crises, including those of a political and institutional nature, which may be relevant for a particular country at a particular moment in time.

Finally, we looked at the long-standing negotiations between Turkey and the EU, and discussed the probable political and economic impact of Turkey's EU membership. With accession to the EU, Turkey will complete the harmonization of its regulations, liberalize entry and exit into various sectors of its economy, impose hard budget constraints on all its public and private enterprises, liberalize its trade with the EU in services (based on the customs union) and join the European single market. Furthermore, joining the EU will require Turkey to adopt and implement the whole body of EU legislation and standards, the *acquis communautaire*. According to EU membership criteria, new members must be able to demonstrate the "ability to take on the obligations of membership including adherence to the aims of political, economic and monetary union". Thus, Turkey is expected to adopt the euro when it is ready to do so, although not immediately upon accession.

From the economic perspective, it can be suggested that Turkey's accession to the EU should be related to its size, per capita income and dependence on agriculture. The most probable economic objections by the European countries to Turkey's full membership can be listed as: (i) Turkey will receive a significant part of the EC's structural funds and will impose an additional burden on countries that are major contributors to the Community budget; (ii) the Turkish economy is not mature enough for the single market, and the Turkish industry is not competitive with that of the EU, and (iii) the problem of the free movement of labour: Turkey's accession could lead to a huge arrival of Turkish immigrants into the EU countries, particularly Germany.

From Turkey's perspective, the EU accession will grant numerous benefits. Turkey is likely to attract larger sums of FDI in the near future, which can be seen as a strong signal that Turkey will eventually become a full EU member and may assure foreign investors that the Turkish economy will follow a stable growth path for the foreseeable future.

Notes

2 Creating a Functioning European Union

1. Economic and political integration among EU member countries means that these countries have to take joint decisions on many matters. So they have developed common policies in a very wide range of fields such as agriculture, consumer affairs, competition, environment and energy issues, transport, trade and so on.
2. See http://www.fxpedia.com/European_Central_Bank#Treaty_of_Paris_-_1951
3. http://europa.eu/legislation_summaries/economic_and_monetary_affairs/institutional_and_economic_framework/treaties_maastricht_en.htm
4. http://europa.eu/legislation_summaries/institutional_affairs/treaties/treaties_singleact_en.htm
5. http://eur-lex.europa.eu/en/treaties/dat/11997D/htm/11997D.html
6. http://eur-lex.europa.eu/en/treaties/dat/12001C/htm/12001C.html
7. Details of Turkey's membership negotiations are discussed in Chapter 8 of this book.
8. The legal personality of the ECB is explained under Article 107(2) of the EC Treaty.
9. A detailed description of the ECB's monetary policy, including theoretical foundations and practical implementation, can be found in *The Monetary Policy of the ECB*, published by the ECB in January 2004.
10. Around 7.8 billion euro notes and 40.4 billion euro coins have been put into general circulation by the central banks of the 12 participating countries of the euro zone. Therefore, it is obvious that the European Banking industry has experienced radical changes since the introduction of the euro.
11. EMU membership application of Greece was accepted in 2000.
12. Under the 1992 Maastricht Treaty, the UK secured an "opt-out", allowing it to determine at a later stage whether it would seek to join the euro.
13. On 14 September 2003, Sweden held a referendum on whether or not to introduce the euro as its currency. The result was 55.9 per cent voting "No".
14. Denmark negotiated a number of opt-out clauses under the Maastricht Treaty. The euro was rejected by the public in two referendums.
15. The context of economic restructuring in transition countries is emphasized by Dornbusch and Reynoso (1989), Hetzel (1990), Sundarajan (1992), Szego (1993), Sachs (1997), Popov (1999), Hermes and Lensik (2000), and Scholtens (2000).
16. European regulations were harmonized in terms of minimum standards to provide a level playing field. These include solvency ratios, the definition of own funds, large exposures and others; however, many countries adopted more stringent regulations than those proposed by the European legislation.

17. On becoming a member of the euro zone, the same provisions that will come into force for the 12 member states on 1 January 1999 will become applicable to other members concerned; these are Articles 104(9) and (11) on sanctions with respect to the excessive deficit procedure; Articles 105(1), (2), (3) and (5) on monetary policy; Article 105a on issuing notes and coins; Article 108a on instruments for the conduct of monetary policy; Article 109 on exchange rate agreements with non-EU currencies and Article 109a(2)(b) on nomination of the Executive Board of the ECB.
18. The legal framework for the use of the euro is laid down in two Council regulations: (i) Council regulation on the introduction of the euro, and (ii) Council regulation (EC) No 1103/97 of 17 June 1997 on certain provisions relating to the introduction of the euro. These regulations are to a large extent based on the conclusions of the European Council in Madrid in December 1995 and on the "reference scenario", which was adopted by the heads of state and government.

3 Enlargement of the European Union

1. The term "PHARE" – Poland and Hungary Assistance for the Restructuring of the Economy – was initially described as an international effort to provide economic support to the emerging Polish and Hungarian democracies. It is the EU's main financial instrument to help with the accession of the Central and Eastern European countries. Created to assist Poland and Hungary in 1989, today the Phare programme encompasses the ten candidate countries of Central and Eastern Europe, Bulgaria, the Czech Republic, Estonia, Hungary, Latvia, Lithuania, Poland, Slovakia, Slovenia and Romania, helping them through a period of massive economic restructuring and political change. The other three candidates, Cyprus, Malta and Turkey, benefit from separate pre-accession funding. Until 2000, the countries of the Western Balkans (Albania, Bosnia and Herzegovina, and the Former Yugoslav Republic of Macedonia) were also beneficiaries of Phare. However, as of 2001, the CARDS programme (Community Assistance to Reconstruction, Development and Stability in the Balkans) has provided financial assistance to the Western Balkans. Following the 1993 Copenhagen Council's invitation to Central European countries to apply for membership, Phare support was reoriented to include a marked expansion in support to infrastructure investment.
2. Schengen area is the borderless zone created by the Schengen agreements between 25 European countries and operates as a single state for international travel purposes. Schengen countries cover: Austria, Belgium, the Czech Republic, Germany, Estonia, Finland, France, Denmark, Greece, Hungary, Iceland, Italy, Latvia, Lithuania, Luxembyrg, Malta, the Netherlands, Norway, Poland, Portugal, Slovakia, Slovenia, Spain, Sweden and Switzerland.

4 Macroeconomic Structure of the European Union

1. Detailed discussions on the recent global financial crisis are introduced in Chapter 7 of this book.
2. See European Economy (No. 3/4, March/April 2001) for a detailed review.

5 Recent Structure of European Banking

1. HHI is the sum of the squared market shares of individual banks.
2. The US department of commerce pronounced Poland's banking system to be the most developed in Central and Eastern Europe.
3. According to 1997 figures, the share of banknotes and coins in circulation ranges from around 2 per cent of GDP in Finland to close to 11 per cent in Spain (ECB, 1999n).

6 Performance of European Banks

1. Additionally, international integration and the entry of new types of competitors boosted competition (Bikker, 1999). See Matutes and Vives (1992) and Vives (2000) for more details.
2. Dietsch and Lozano-Vivas (2000) also confirmed banking structural changes as well as regulation conditions to show differences in France and Spain.
3. The Czech Republic was identified as the largest and Latvia as the smallest country in the NMS.
4. The low level of bank lending in transition countries can be explained by the sharp economic downturn, which resulted in GDP falling to between 15–20 per cent in the first period of economic transformation. Severe recessions led to a massive bad debt problem in the corporate sector, which was dominated at this time by former state enterprises. These bad debts led to widespread defaults and a substantial reduction of banks' loan portfolios.

7 Global Financial Crisis and European Banking

1. An earlier version of this chapter was written by Canan Karatas as an MBA graduation project at the CASE, Koc University.

8 Turkey as an Accession Country

1. According to the Banking Law of 1985, coverage limits were not covering the deposits of banks' major shareholders and managers, inter-bank deposits and deposits at branches abroad.
2. See Bocutoglu and colleagues (2000) for more detailed information on the effects of Russian economic crisis on the Turkish economy.
3. See Akyüz and Boratav (2003).
4. See Ozkan (2005).
5. Interest rates on the Treasury bill were around 95 per cent at the end of November 1999. However, after the adoption of the IMF base stabilization programme on 9 December 1999, they dropped to around 38 per cent by mid-February 2000. For more detail, see the *Financial Times* (12 June 2000), article on the early success of the stabilization programme (Ozkan, 2005).
6. See Yilmaz (2003) for a similar problem in Turkey.
7. A detailed discussion on the FDI flow into Turkey is presented in further sections of this chapter.

8. See Claessens and colleagues (2001), Buch (2000b), and Lensink and Hermes (2005).
9. Several factors leading to an increased FDI have been emphasized in the literature. For instance, Aysan and Ceyhan (2008) see financial crises as the main motivation for foreign banks' entry into developed countries, whilst a low level of competition, deregulation and open access to foreign banks is the draw in developing countries. Furthermore, deregulation is identified as the main factor attracting foreign entry by Coppel and Davies (2003), Weller (2001) and Berger and colleagues (2000). Claessens and Laeven (2004) confirm that greater foreign bank presence and fewer activity restrictions in the banking sector can lead to more competition in banking systems.
10. This kind of behaviour has also been observed in Asian countries after crises (Montgomery, 2003; Domanski, 2005).
11. See www.mfa.gov.tr/agreement-establishing-an-association-between-the-european-economic-community-and-turkey-_signed-at-ankara_-september-1_-1963_.en.mfa

Bibliography

Akyüz, Y. and Boratav, K. (2003), "The Making of the Turkish Financial Crisis", *World Development*, 31(9): 1549–1566.

Allen, F., Bartiloro, L. and Kowalewski, O. (2005), "The Financial System of the EU 25"; available at SSRN: http://ssrn.com/abstract=871454.

Alper, C.E. and Onis, Z. (2001), "Financial Globalization, the Democratic Deficit and Recurrent Crises in Emerging Markets: The Turkish Experience in the Aftermath of Capital Account Liberalization", Department of Economics Working Papers, ISS/EC 01-14; Bogazici University, available at: http://papers.ssrn.com/sol3/papers.cfm?abstract_id=288367.

Altinkemer, M. (2003), "Recent Experiences with Capital Controls: Is There A Lesson for Turkey?", The Central Bank of The Republic of Turkey, Research Department Discussion Paper, June 2003.

Altunbas, Y. and Chakravarty, S.P. (1998), "Efficiency Measures and the Banking Structure in Europe", *Economics Letters*, 60(2): 205–208.

Altunbas, Y., Gardener, E.P.M. and Molyneux, P. (1996), "Economies of Scale, Cost Subadditivity and X-efficiencies in European Banking", University College of North Wales, Bangor.

Altunbas, Y., Kara, A. and Olgu, O. (2009), *Banking Under Political Instability and Chronic High Inflation*. Palgrave Macmillan, Studies in Banking and Financial Institutions, England.

Arslan, H.B. (2007), "Cross-border Bank Acquisitions: Financial and Managerial Analysis of BNP paribas–TEB deal", *International Research Journal of Finance and Economics*, (9): 38–49.

Aysan, A.F. and Ceyhan, S.P. (2006), "Why Do Foreign Banks Invest in Turkey?", MPRA Paper No. 5491; available at: http://mpra.ub.uni-muenchen.de/5491.

Aysan, A.F. and Ceyhan, S.P. (2008), "Structural Change and the Efficiency of Banking in Turkey: Does Ownership Matter?", MPRA Paper 17849, Germany, University Library of Munich; available at: http://ideas.repec.org/p/pra/mprapa/17849.html.

Bailliu, J.N. (2000), "Private Capital Flows, Financial Development, and Economic Growth in Developing Countries", Bank of Canada, Working Paper, 15, July.

Banking Regulation and Supervision Agency (BRSA) (2007), "2007 BASEL-2 Ikinci Sayisal Etki Calismasi (QIS-TR2) Degerlendirme Raporu"; available at: www.bddk.org.tr.

Banks Association of Turkey (1995–2007), "Banks in Turkey 1995–2007 Reports"; available at: http://www.tbb.org.tr/english/v12/2003.asp.

Banks Association of Turkey (2003), *World Economic Outlook*, 2003.

Banks Association of Turkey (2007), "Banks, Branches and Employees, December 2007"; available at: http://www.tbb.org.tr/net/donemsel/default.aspx?dil=EN.

Bartzokas, A. (2001), "Policy Relevance and Theory Development in Innovation Studies", *Enterprise and Innovation Management Studies*, 2(1): 1–18.

Berger, A.N., Deyoung, R., Genay, H. and Udell, G.F. (2000), "Globalization of Financial Institutions: Evidence from Cross-Border Banking Performance", Brookings-Wharton Papers on Financial Services, 23–120.

Bikker, J.A. (1999), "Efficiency in the European Banking Industry: An Explanatory Analysis to Rank Countries", Section Banking and Supervisory Strategies, Directorate Supervision, De Netherlandsche Bank.

Bocutoglu, E. and Çelik, K. (2000), "The Effects of Russian Economic Crisis on Turkish Economy: a Brief Assessment", *Journal of Qafqaz University*, III(I): 123–132.

Boratav, K. and Akyüz, Y. (2003), "The Making of the Turkish Financial Crisis", *World Development*, 31(9): 1549–1566.

Brookings Institute Report (2009), *Tracking Economic Recession and Recovery in America's 100 Largest Metropolitan Areas*, June.

Brynjolfsson, E. (1993), "The Productivity Paradox of Information Technology: Review and Assessment", *Communications of the ACM*, 36: 67–77.

BRSA (2006), "Bankacilik Sectoru Basel II Gelisim Raporu"; available at: http://www.bddk.org.tr/turkce/BaselII/1266ilerleme_raporu_degerlendirmesi_19062006.pdf.

Buch, C.M. (2000a), "Financial Market Integration in the US: Lessons for Europe?", Kiel Institute of World Economics, Kiel, Germany.

Buch, C.M. (2000b), "Is Foreign Control a Panacea? – On Governance and Restructuring of Commercial Banks in Transition Economies," Kiel Institute of World Economics, Kiel, Germany.

Central Bank of Turkey (CBT) (2005), "Financial Stability Report 2005", Volume 1; available at: http://www.tcmb.gov.tr/yeni/evds/yayin/finist/fulltext.pdf.

CBT (2006), "Financial Stability Report 2006", Volume 3; available at: http://www.tcmb.gov.tr/yeni/evds/yayin/finist/finistv3eng.html.

CBT (2007), "Financial Stability Report 2007", Volume 5; available at: http://www.tcmb.gov.tr/yeni/evds/yayin/finist/finistv5eng.php.

Claessens, S., Demirguc-Kunt, A. and Huizinga, H. (2001), "How does Foreign Entry Affect Domestic Banking Markets?", *Journal of Banking and Finance*, 25: 891–911.

Claessens, S. and Laeven, L. (2004), "What Drives Bank Competition? Some International Evidence", *Journal of Money, Credit and Banking*, 36(3): 563–583.

Clarke, G., Cull, R., Martinez, P., Soledad M. and Sanchez, S.M. (2001), "Foreign Bank Entry – Experience, Implications for Developing Countries, and Agenda for Further Research", *Policy Research Working Paper Series 2698*, The World Bank.

Clarke, G., Cull, R., Peria, M.S.M. and Sánchez, S.M. (2002), "Bank Lending to Small Businesses in Latin America: Does Bank Origin Matter?", *Journal of Money, Credit, and Banking*, 37(1), 83–119.

Completing the Internal Market: White Paper from the Commission to the European Council (Milan, 28–29 June 1985).

Coppel, J. and Davies, M. (2003), "Foreign Participation in East Asia's Banking Sector", International Department Reserve Bank of Australia, BIS.

Delors Report (1989), *Report on European and Monetary Union in the EC*, Committee for the Study of European and Monetary Union, Brussels, 12 April.

Dietsch, M. and Lozano-Vivas, A. (2000), "How the Environment Determines Banking Efficiency: a Comparison Between French and Spanish Industries", *Journal of Banking and Finance*, 24(6): 985–1004.

Domanski, D. (2005), "Foreign Banks in Emerging Market Economies: Changing Players, Changing Issues", *BIS Quarterly Review*, December 2005: 69–81.

Dornbusch, R. and Reynoso, A. (1989), "Financial Factors in Economic Development", *American Economic Review*, 79(2): 204–209.

EU Screening Report (2007), "Chapter 9: Financial Services"; available at: http://ec.europa.eu/enlargement/pdf/turkey/screening_reports/screening_report_09_tr_internet_en.pdf.

European Central Bank (ECB) (1999a), "Possible Effects of EMU on the EU Banking Systems in the Medium to Long Term", European Central Bank, Frankfurt, February.

ECB (1999b), "The Effect of Technology on the EU Banking Systems", European Central Bank, Frankfurt, July.

European Commission (2008), "Amendments to the Capital Requirements Directive", October.

ECB (1999c), *Annual Report 1998*, April 1999.

ECB (1999d), "Banking in the Euro Area: Structural Features and Trends", *Monthly Bulletin*, April.

ECB (1999e), "Legal Instruments of the European Central Bank", *Monthly Bulletin*, November.

ECB (1999f), *Possible Effects of EMU on the EU Banking Systems in the Medium to Long Term*, February.

ECB (1999g), "Target and Payments in Euro", *Monthly Bulletin*, November.

ECB (1999h), "The Balance Sheets of the Monetary Financial Institutions of the Euro Area in Early 1999", *Monthly Bulletin*, August.

ECB (1999i), "The Euro Area at the Start of Stage Three", *Monthly Bulletin*, January.

ECB (1999j), "The Euro System and the European System of Central Banks (ESCB)", *Monthly Bulletin*, January.

ECB (1999k), "The Implementation of the Stability and Growth Pact", *Monthly Bulletin*, May.

ECB (1999l), "The Institutional Framework of the European System of Central Banks", *Monthly Bulletin*, July.

ECB (1999m), "The Stability-oriented Monetary Policy Strategy of the Euro System", *Monthly Bulletin*, January.

ECB (1999n), *Payment Systems in the EU*, January.

ECB (2000a), *Annual Report 1999*, April.

ECB (2000b), *Convergence Report 2000*, May.

ECB (2000c), "EMU and Banking Supervision", *Monthly Bulletin*, April.

ECB (2000d), "Foreign Exchange Reserves and Operations of the Euro System", *Monthly Bulletin*, January.

ECB (2000e), *Statistical Information Collected and Compiled by the ESCB*, May.

ECB (2000f), "The Euro Area One Year After the Introduction of the Euro: Key Characteristics and Changes in the Financial Structure", *Monthly Bulletin*, January.

ECB (2000g), "The External Trade of the Euro Area Economy: Stylised Facts and Recent Trends", *Monthly Bulletin*, August.

ECB (2000h), "EMU and Banking Supervision", *Monthly Bulletin*, April, 49–64.

ECB (2000i), *Mergers and Acquisitions Involving the EU Banking Industry: Facts and Implications*, Frankfurt, December.
ECB (2001a), *Annual Report 2000*, May.
ECB (2001b), *Blue Book, Payment and Securities Settlement Systems in the European Union*, June.
ECB (2001c), "Characteristics of Corporate Finance in the Euro Area", *Monthly Bulletin*, February.
ECB (2001d), "Euro System Staff Macroeconomic Projection Exercises for the Euro Area", *Monthly Bulletin*, June.
ECB (2001e), "Financing and Financial Investment of the Non-financial Sectors in the Euro Area", *Monthly Bulletin*, May.
ECB (2001f), "The Economic Policy Framework in EMU", *Monthly Bulletin*, November.
ECB (2001g), "The Euro Area After the Entry of Greece", *Monthly Bulletin*, January.
ECB (2001h), *Why Price Stability*? June.
ECB (2001i), "Consolidation in Central Counterparty Clearing in the Euro Area", *Monthly Bulletin*, August.
ECB (2001j), The Changing Relationship between Banks and their Corporate Customers, May (n.p.).
ECB (2001k), *The Euro Money Market*, July.
ECB (2002a), *Annual Report 2001*, April.
ECB (2002b), *Blue Book, Payment and Securities Settlement Systems in the European Union*, August.
ECB (2002c), *Compendium: Collection of Legal Instruments, June 1998–December 2001*, March.
ECB (2002d), *Convergence Report 2002*, May.
ECB (2002e), "Euro Banknote Preparations: from Cash Changeover to Post-launch Activities", *Monthly Bulletin*, January.
ECB (2002f), *Evaluation of the 2002 Cash Changeover*, April.
ECB (2002g), "Implications of the Euro Cash Changeover on the Development of Banknotes and Coins in Circulation", *Monthly Bulletin*, May.
ECB (2002h), *Report on Financial Structures*, October 2002.
ECB (2002i), "Saving, Financing and Investment in the Euro Area", *Monthly Bulletin*, August.
ECB (2002j), *The European Central Bank* (Public Information Brochure).
ECB (2002k), "The Liquidity Management of the ECB", *Monthly Bulletin*, May.
ECB (2002l), "The Role of the Euro System in Payment and Clearing Systems", *Monthly Bulletin*, April.
ECB (2002m), *Developments in Banks' Liquidity Profile and Management*, May.
ECB (2002n), *Financial Sectors in EU Accession Countries*, July.
ECB (2002o), *Report on Financial Structures*, October.
ECB (2002p), "The Eurosystem's Dialogue with Accession Countries", *Monthly Bulletin*, July.
ECB (2003a), *Annual Report 2002*, April.
ECB (2003b), "Changes to the Euro system's Operational Framework for Monetary Policy", *Monthly Bulletin*, August.
ECB (2003c), *ECB Statistics: A Brief Overview*, August.
ECB (2003d), *EU Banking Sector Stability*, February.

ECB (2003e), TARGET: The Trans-European Automated Real-time Gross Settlement Express Transfer System – Update 2003 (Public Information Brochure), November.
ECB (2003f), "The Adjustment of Voting Modalities in the Governing Council", *Monthly Bulletin*, May.
ECB (2003g), "The Demand for Currency in the Euro Area and the Impact of the Euro Cash Changeover", *Monthly Bulletin*, January.
ECB (2003h), "The Relationship Between Monetary Policy and Fiscal Policies in the Euro Area", *Monthly Bulletin*, February.
ECB (2003i), *Structural Analysis of the EU Banking Sector: Year 2002*. November.
ECB (2004a), *Annual Report 2003*, April.
ECB (2004b), *Financial Stability Review*, December.
ECB (2004c), *Report on EU Banking Structure*, November.
ECB (2004d), *The Implementation of Monetary Policy in the Euro Area: General Documentation on Euro System Monetary Policy Instruments and Procedures*, February.
ECB (2004e), *The Monetary Policy of the ECB (2nd edn)*, European Central Bank, Frankfurt, January.
ECB (2005a), *Annual Report 2004*, April.
ECB (2005b), *Financial Stability Review*, December.
ECB (2005c), *EU Banking Sector Stability Report*, October.
ECB (2006a), *Annual Report 2005*, April.
ECB (2006b), *Financial Stability Review*, December.
ECB (2006c), *EU Banking Sector Stability Report*, November.
ECB (2006d), *EU Banking Structures Report October 2006*. European Central Bank, Frankfurt.
ECB (2007a), *Blue Book, Payment and Securities Settlement Systems in the European Union*, August.
ECB (2007b), *Financial Stability Review*, December.
ECB (2007c), *EU Banking Sector Stability Report*, November.
ECB (2008a), *Financial Stability Review*, December.
ECB (2008b), *Blue Book, Payment and Securities Settlement Systems in the European Union*, August.
ECB (2008c), *EU Banking Sector Stability Report*, October.
ECB (2008d), *EU Banking Structures*, October.
ECB (2009a), *Financial Stability Review*, December.
ECB (2009b), *Monthly Bulletin*, July.
ECB (2009c), *EU Banking Sector Stability Report*, August.
ECB (2010), *Statistics, Pocket Book*, February.
European Commission (1985), "Completing the Internal Market: White Paper from the Commission to the Council", COM (85) 310 final, Office for Official Publications of the EC, Luxembourg.
European Commission (1995a), "Green Paper on the Practical Arrangements for the Introduction of the Single Currency", COM (95) 333, May, Office for Official Publications of the EC, Luxembourg.
European Commission (1995b), "Green Paper on the Practical Arrangements for the Introduction of the Single Currency", COM (95) 333 final, Luxembourg, 31 May 1995.

European Commission (1996), *The Impact and Effectiveness of the Single Market, Communication to the European Parliament and Council*, October.

European Commission (1997a), *Credit Institutions and Banking, The Single Market Review, Subseries II: Impact on Services*, 3, Kogan Page-Earthscan, London.

European Commission (1997b), *The European Union: Key Figures*, Eurostat, Brussels.

European Commission (1997c), *The Single Market Review: Impact on Services – Credit Institutions and Banking*, Office for Official Publication of the European Communities, Luxembourg.

European Commission (2001a), *Exchange Rate Aspects of Enlargement*. European Economy, Supplement C, Economic Reform Monitor, Brussels, February.

European Commission (2001b), *Commission Decisions Establishing the European Securities Committee and the Committee of the European Securities Regulators – Frequently Asked Questions*, June.

European Commission (2001c), *Commission Welcomes Council's Political Agreement on Cross-Border Payments Proposal*, November.

European Commission (2001d), *Financial Services: Commission Launches Out-of-Court Complaints Network to Improve Consumer Confidence*, February.

European Commission (2001e), *Financial Services: Commission Proposes Directive on Prudential Supervision of Financial Conglomerates*, April.

European Commission (2001f), *Financial Services: Commission Proposes Simplified EU Legal Framework for Collateral*, March.

European Commission (2001g), *Financial Services: Commission Urges Member States and the European Parliament to Deliver on Time*, December.

European Commission (2001h), *Financial Services: Europe Must Deliver on Time*, 5th Report, November.

European Commission (2002a), *Report on Macroeconomic and Financial Sector Stability Developments in Candidate Countries*, European Economy – Enlargement Papers, 8 April 2002.

European Commission (2002b), *Update of the Report on Macroeconomic and Financial Sector Stability Developments in Candidate Countries*, European Economy – Enlargement Papers, 11 November 2002.

European Commission (2002c), *A Modern Regulatory Framework for Company Law in Europe: A Consultative Document of the High Level Group of Company Law Experts*, April.

European Commission (2003a), *Enlargement of the European Union – Guide to the Negotiations Chapter by Chapter*, Directorate General-Enlargement, Brussels.

European Commission (2003b), *Progress towards Meeting Economic Criteria for Accession: The Assessment from the 2003 Comprehensive Monitoring Reports and Regular Report*, Enlargement Papers, 19 November 2003.

European Commission (2003c), *Communication from the Commission to the Council and the European Parliament: Access to Finance of Small and Medium-Sized Enterprises*, Brussels, December 2003, Com (2003), 713 final.

European Commission (2005a), *Working Together for Growth and Jobs: A New Start for the Lisbon Strategy*, Communication to the Spring European Council, Brussels, February.

European Commission (2005b), *Cross-Border Consolidation in the EU Financial Sector*. SEC (2005) 1398. European Commission, Brussels.

European Commission (2007), *Integrated Guidelines for Growth and Jobs 2008–2010*, Communication from the Commission to the Spring European Council, Brussels, December.
European Commission (2009a), *Aging Report*, Economic and Budgetary Projections for the EU-27 Member States (2008–2060), EC Directorate General for Economic and Financial Affairs, Brussels.
European Commission (2009b), "The EU's Response to Support the Real Economy during the Economic Crisis: An Overview of Member States' Recovery Measures", European Economy, Occasional Papers 51, European Commission, Brussels.
European Commission (2009c), *Quarterly Report on the Euro Area*, 8(2).
European Economic Community (EEC) (1977), *First Banking Directive*, First Council Directive.
EEC (1988), *Second Banking Directive*, Second Council Directive.
European Economy (1988), *Creation of A European Financial Area*, Commission of the European Communities, 36, May, Brussels.
European Monetary Institute (EMI) (1995a), *Annual Report 1994*, April.
EMI (1995b), *The Changeover to the Single Currency*, Frankfurt, November.
EMI (1995c), *Progress Towards Convergence*, Frankfurt, November.
EMI (1996a), *Annual Report 1995*, April.
EMI (1996b), *Role and Functions of the European Monetary Institute*, February.
EMI (1997a), *Annual Report 1996*, April.
EMI (1997b), *The Single Monetary Policy in Stage Three: Specification of the Operational Framework*, January.
EMI (1998a), *Annual Report 1997*, May.
EMI (1998b), *Convergence Report: Report Required by Article 109j of the Treaty Establishing the European Community*, March.
European Securitization Forum (2009), "ESF Data Report, Q2, 2009"; available at: http://www.europeansecuritisation.com/Communications/Archive/Current/2009Q2-ESF-DataReport.pdf.
European Union (2009), "European Central Bank", *ECB Monthly Bulletin*, 345–356.
Eurostat (1999), *Banking in Europe*, EC, Brussels.
Eurostat, *Statistical Books*, European Economic Statistics (2005–2009).
Eurostat Yearbook (2008), Europe in Figures.
Federation of European Stock Exchanges (FESE) (2009), "European Equity Market Report 2009"; available at: http://www.fese.eu/_lib/files/FESE_EEMR_Year_2009_December_figures_updated_dark_pools_V03.xls.
Gallego F., Hernández L. and Schmidt-Hebbel, K. (2002), "Capital controls in Chile: were they effective". In: L. Hernández and K. Schmidt-Hebbel (eds), *Banking, Financial Integration, and International Crises*. Central Bank of Chile, Santiago, Chile.
Gelos, R.G. and Roldos, J. (2004), "Consolidation and Market Structure in Emerging Market Banking Systems", *Emerging Markets Review*, 5(1): 39–59, March.
Girardone, C. (2000), "Banking Efficiency of Italian Banks", PhD thesis, University of Bangor, Bangor.
Hermes, N. and Lensink, R. (2000), "Capital Flight and the Uncertainty of Government Policies", University of Groningen, Netherlands, unpublished manuscript.

Hermes, N. and Lensink, R. (2005), "Does Financial Liberalization Influence Saving, Investment and Economic Growth? Evidence from 25 Emerging Market Economies, 1973–1996", Working Papers RP2005/69, World Institute for Development Economic Research (UNU-WIDER).

Hetzel, R.L. (1990), "Free Enterprise and Central Banking in Formerly Communist Countries", Economic Review, Federal Reserve Bank of Richmond, 76, May–June, 1–19.

Horton, M., Kumar, M. and Mauro, P. (2009), "The State of Public Finances: A Cross- Country Fiscal Monitor," IMF Staff Position Note 09/21, International Monetary Fund, Washington.

Hughes, K. (2004), "Turkey and the European Union: Just Another Enlargement? Exploring the Impacts of Turkish Accession. Les amis de l'Europe". Retrieved 30 April 2010 at: http://www.cdu.de/en/doc/Friends_of_Europe_Turkey.pdf.

Hunter, L.W., Bernhardt, K., Hughes, L. and Skuratowicz, E. (2000), "It's Not Just the ATMs: Firm Strategies, Work Restructuring and Workers Earnings in Retail Banking", Wharton School, Mimeo.

International Monetary Fund (IMF) (2005a), "Global Financial Stability Report 2005"; available at: http://www.imf.org/external/pubs/ft/GFSR/2005/02/index.htm.

IMF (2005b), "Turkey: Request for Stand-By Arrangement and Extension of Repurchase Expectations", Country Report No. 05/412, 2005; available at: http://www.imf.org/external/pubs/cat/longres.cfm?sk=18713.0.

IMF (2006), "Turkey: Third and Fourth Reviews under the Stand-By Arrangement and Request for Waiver of Performance Criteria", Country Report No. 06/402, 2006; available at: http://www.imf.org/external/pubs/cat/longres.cfm?sk=20099.0.

IMF (2007), "Turkey: Sixth Review and Inflation Consultation under the Stand-By Arrangement and Request for Waiver of Nonobservance and Applicability of Performance Criteria", Country Report No. 07/363, 2007; available at: http://www.imf.org/external/pubs/cat/longres.cfm?sk=21454.0.

IMF (2008), *Regional Economic Outlook: Europe*, Washington, October.

IMF (2009a), *Euro Area Policies: 2009 Article IV Consultation*, IMF Country Report No. 09/223, International Monetary Fund, Washington.

IMF (2009b), *Euro Area Policies: 2009 Selected Issues Paper*, IMF Country Report No. 09/224, International Monetary Fund, Washington.

IMF (2009c), *Global Financial Stability Report*, Washington, October.

IMF (2009d), *Regional Economic Outlook: Europe*, Washington, May.

IMF (2009e), *World Economic Outlook*, Washington, October.

IMF (2009f), *World Economic and Financial Surveys*, Regional Economic Outlook, Europe Securing Recovery, October.

IMF (2009g), "World Economic Outlook, Sustaining the Economic Recovery", October; available at: http://www.imf.org/external/pubs/ft/weo/2009/02/pdf/text.pdf.

IMF (2009h), *World Economic and Financial Surveys World Economic Outlook Database*, October.

Inzerillo, U., Morelli, P. and Pittaluga, G.B. (2000), "Deregulation and Changes in European Banking Industry". In: G. Galli and J. Pelkmans (eds), *Regulatory Reform and Competitiveness in Europe*, II, Cheltenham, 262–328.

Jackson, James K. (2009), *The Financial Crisis: Impact on and Response by The European Union*, Congress Research Service, 24 June.

Jaffe, D.M. and Levonian, M. (2000), "The Structure of Banking Systems in Developed and Transition Economies", *European Financial Management*, 7(2), 161–181 (June 2001).

Kibritcioglu, B., Kose, B. and Ugur, B. (1998), "A Leading Indicator Approach to the Predictability of Currency Crisis: The Case of Turkey", Hazine Dergisi, Working Paper 12.

Kraft, E. (2002), "Foreign Banks in Croatia: Another Look", Croatian National Bank Working Paper W-10. Croatian National Bank, Zagreb.

Marques I.D. and Molyneux, P. (2001), "Integration of European Banking and Financial Markets", EIFC – Technology and Finance Working Papers 14, United Nations University, Institute for New Technologies.

Matutes, C. and Vives, X. (1992), "Competition for Deposits, Risk of Failure and Regulation in Banking", Paper presented at the EEA Conference, Dublin.

Matutes C. and Vives, X. (2000), "Imperfect Competition, Risk Taking and Regulation in Banking", *European Economic Review*, 44(1): 1–34.

McKinnon, R.I. (1991), "Financial Control in the Transition From Classical Socialism to a Market Economy", *Journal of Economic Perspectives*, 5(4): 107–122.

Molyneux, P. (2003), "Determinants of Cross-border Mergers in European Banking". In: H. Herrmann and R. Lipsey (eds), *Foreign Direct Investment in the Real and Financial Sector of Industrial Countries*. Springer, Heidelberg and New York.

Molyneux, P., Altunbas, Y. and Gardener, E.P.M. (1996), *Efficiency in European Banking*. John Wiley and Sons, London.

Montgomery, H. (2003), "The Role of Foreign Banks in Post-Crisis Asia: The Importance of Method of Entry", Research Paper Series No: 51, ADB Institute.

Organisation for Economic Co-operation and Development (OECD) (2004), The OECD Jobs Study, Paris.

OECD (2006), "Cyclically-Adjusted Budget Balances: A Methodological Note", available via the Internet: http://www.oecd.org/dataoecd/0/61/36336878.pdf.

OECD (2008), *Economic Outlook No. 83*, Paris, June.

OECD (2009), *Economic Outlook*, Organization for Economic Cooperation and Development, June.

OECD (1999–2009), *Economic Surveys: Euro Area*.

Öniş, Z. and Aysan, A.F. (1999), "Neoliberal Globalisation, the Nation-state and Financial Crises in the Semi-periphery: a Comparative Analysis", *Third World Quarterly*, 21(1): 119–139.

Ozkan, F.G. (2005), "Currency and Financial Crises in Turkey, 2000–2001: Bad Fundamentals or Bad Luck?", *The World Economy*, 28(4): 541–572.

Özkan-Günay, E.N. and ve Tektaş, A. (2006), "Efficiency Analysis of the Turkish Banking Sector in Pre-crisis and Crisis Period: a DEA Approach", *Contemporary Economics Policy*, 24(3), 418–431.

Popov, V. (1999), "Reform Strategies and Economic Performance of Russia's Regions", Queens University, Kingston, Ontario, Mimeo.

Saarinen, J. (2001), *Information Technology and Development in the Banking Sector*.

Sachs, J. (1997), "An Overview of Stabilization Issues Facing Economies in Transition". In: W. Woo, S. Parker, and S.D. Sachs (eds), *Economies in Transition: Comparing Asia and Eastern Europe*. The MIT Press, Cambridge, Mass.

Scholtens, B. (2000), "Competition, Growth, and Performance in the Banking Industry", Centre for Financial Institutions, Working Papers 00-18, Wharton School Centre for Financial Institutions, University of Pennsylvania.

Schure, P. and Wagenwoort, R. (1999), "Who are Europe's Efficient Bankers?", Cahiers BEI-EIB Papers, 4(1), 105–126.

Secretariat General for EU Affairs (2007), "Programme for Alignment with the Acquis"; available at: http://www.abgs.gov.tr/files/Muktesebat_Uyum_Programi/En/Chapter_32.pdf.

Shaw, E. (1973), *Financial Deepening in Economic Development*. Oxford University Press, New York.

Steinherr, A.T. and Ucer, M. (2004), "The Turkish Banking Sector: Challenges and Outlook in Transition to EU Membership", EU-Turkey Working Paper Series No: 4.

Sundarajan, S. (1992), "Effects of Monetary and Import Price Changes on the Dynamics of Inflation in Six Asian Countries", *Economia Internazionale*, XLV(3–4): 351–363.

SwissRe (2009), "Financial Review"; available at: http://media.swissre.com/documents/2009_ar_financial_review.pdf.

Szego, G. (1993), "Introduction", *Journal of Banking and Finance*, 17(5): 773–783 (Elsevier).

Vives, X. (1991a), "Regulatory Reform in European Banking", *European Economic Review*, 35: 505–515.

Vives, X. (1991b), "Banking Competition and European Integration". In: A. Giovanni and C. Mayer (eds), *European Financial Integration*. Cambridge University Press, Cambridge, pp. 9–31.

Vives, X. (2000), "Corporate Governance: Does it Matter". In: X. Vives (ed.), *Corporate Governance: Theoretical and Empirical Perspectives*. Cambridge University Press, Cambridge.

Weller, C. (2001), "The Supply of Credit by Multinational Banks in Developing and Transition Economies: Determinants and Effects", DESA Discussion paper of the United Nations Department of Economic and Social Affairs, No. 16, United Nations, March.

World Federation of Exchanges (2009a), "Market Highlights"; available at: http://www.world-exchanges.org/files/file/2009%20Market%20Highlights.doc.

World Federation of Exchanges (2009b), "10 Years in Review, 2000–2009"; available at: http://www.worldexchanges.org/files/file/10%20Year%20Review.doc.

Yilmaz, R. (2003), "Bank Runs and Deposit Insurance in Developing Countries: The Case of Turkey", PhD Thesis, American University, Washington.

Index